W9-AZR-871

Becoming Dad

Becoming Dad

BLACK MEN AND THE
JOURNEY TO FATHERHOOD

LEONARD PITTS JR.

LONGSTREET
Atlanta, Georgia

Published by
LONGSTREET, INC.
A subsidiary of Cox Newspapers
A subsidiary of Cox Enterprises, Inc.
2140 Newmarket Parkway
Suite 122
Marietta, GA 30067

Printed in the United States of America

1st printing 1999

Library of Congress Catalog Card Number: 99-60103

ISBN: 1-56352-501-1

Jacket and book design by Burtch Bennett Hunter

DEDICATION

Bear, this is for you.

ACKNOWLEDGMENTS

Allow me to gratefully acknowledge some very large debts.

In the first place, I thank God.

Beyond that, a project like this doesn't come together without the support and help of a lot of people whose names don't show up on the dust cover.

My editors at the *Miami Herald* have, over the years, been picky, demanding, and difficult to please, and have made me a better writer because of it.

My agent, Janell Walden-Agyeman of Marie Brown and Associates, guided this project from inception to fruition with soft-spoken persistence and unflagging faith.

My family and friends, along with dozens of complete strangers, were gracious enough to open their lives and hearts to the scrutiny of my readers and me.

My wife, Marilyn, has been down with me and up with me for twenty-something years now: my best friend and spiritual advisor, my editor and advocate, my love and my life.

My children, Markise, Monique, Marlon, Bryan, and Onjél, and my grandson, Eric, have taught me that Dad is the finest thing a man can ever hope to become.

Becoming Dad

PART ONE:
Masks and Armor

Papa is a man who can understand
How a man has to do whatever he can.

— James Brown

ONE

"I'm writing a book about black men and fatherhood."

A pause. A dry laugh. And then: "What does the one have to do with the other?"

The man on the other end of the long-distance connection was himself a black father, an old friend of mine.

Take his response as a warning sign of what a thorny patch one wanders into in any effort to untangle the complexities of black fatherhood. We don't seem to think much of black dads. Theirs is the face we have chosen as an emblem for the failure of fathers, for absence and abuse and a general inability to come to terms with the obligations of paternity.

It is a portrait supported to some degree by grim statistics and, perhaps to a greater degree, by myth and misconception. Not that the exact proportion matters much in the end. The *perception* of black men as failed fathers is real and abiding, and so must be dealt with.

But there is another reality, one that often goes undocumented by statisticians, reporters, and academics. It is of those black men, scarred by their own upbringings, who, by force of persistence and will, make decent and honorable fathers of themselves. This is the story that gets missed.

So I tried again with my friend. "A book about black men and fatherhood," I repeated. "And about how those of us who had hard times with our own fathers go about trying to become good fathers ourselves."

No jokes this time. No laughter. This was a story he could relate to.

Not that he's the only one. Indeed, for me it is, by definition, a very personal tale. I am a father of five. And my father was, well . . . it wasn't *The Cosby Show*, let's put it like that.

The first time he held us at gunpoint, I was nine years old. The second time, I must have been about fifteen. I don't remember what triggered it, either time. I just remember his livid eyes and the length of the rifle barrel separating us—his wife and his four children—from him. The first time it happened, I was so afraid. The second time, we had been fighting and I don't remember feeling any fear at all. Just rage.

Which pretty well sums up my childhood journey with Leonard Pitts Sr. From fear to rage.

Even now, he sits in memory like a boulder in a river so that everything that I know, feel, or ever dreamt about fatherhood must flow around him. He is never gone, even when I believe him to be, even when I haven't thought of him in a very long time. He is always there.

I was a disappointment to my father. That much must be said first. He didn't like me.

My father had wanted his firstborn child, his son and namesake, to be brawny, strong, and athletic. I was skinny, shy, and smart. He wanted a kid who spent his afternoons outside in the fresh air chasing baseballs. I preferred to spend mine curled up on my bed absorbed in Marvel comics and Beverly Cleary novels. I have a clear memory of lying in the top bunk reading a *Fantastic Four* comic book one afternoon and eating Chee-tos while a rainstorm pounded overhead and thinking to myself that life doesn't get much better than this.

Which was not the sort of thinking that would endear me to my father. He wanted something other than the bookish little boy he got in me. And so he tried to change me, by force and by persuasion. One Christmas, he bought me a baseball pitching machine. I don't remember ever using it.

I was not gifted physically. In the schoolyard at recess, we used to play a game called sockball—similar to baseball, except that there was no pitcher and when the offensive player came to the plate, he or she was to knock a volleyball as deep into the outfield as possible. I'd make it a point to pick a spot in the field where I thought the ball was unlikely to be hit and stand out there praying to God that it would not find me.

I remember one time God ignored that prayer. I heard fist meet ball, looked up, and to my horror saw the thing lofting right toward me. Instinct took over. I closed my eyes, thrust my arms out before me, stiff as Frankenstein's monster. When I opened my eyes again, I was holding the ball. The other kids were cheering. No one was more surprised than I.

You'd think I would have taken from that episode the lesson that if you give it your best, there's no telling what you can do. Here's the moral I took: Next time, find a better place to stand.

Not that I was completely inert. When I was home with my sisters and brother, we played freeze tag and hide-and-seek and a bunch of strange games of our own devising. But still, I spent most of my time in solitary pursuits. Preferred it that way. Part of me still does.

I remember being fascinated by ants. Spent afternoons in the yard digging up their nests, flooding them with water, and watching the workers scurry to safety, white larvae in their mandibles. Or I'd go to the library and check out every single book they had on ants; once I even lugged home a college-level entomological text. Spent weeks trying to decipher that thing.

I was a nerd. More to the point, I was not the kid my father wanted. Wasn't a kid a farmer's son with seven years of education could easily relate to.

He wanted a boy he could roughhouse with. When I was real young, he'd pin me to the floor so I couldn't move, then laugh and tell me to get free. I'd try for a minute, then start crying instead. He couldn't stand that. He'd pull away looking disgusted and fix my mother with an accusing glare. "You're making a punk out of the boy," he'd say.

In black lexicon of that day and this one, "punk" was about the worst thing you could call a man. Means someone who is weak, a sissy, unmanly. I didn't quite understand that then, which I count as a blessing, because my father used that term to describe me all the time. Said it to anyone who would listen. It was the word that spoke his great conviction that I was coming up to be not quite a man.

Unlike Keith, who was born four years after me. By the time my brother was a toddler, my father had pretty much given up on me. He shifted his efforts to Keith instead, declaring that whatever mistakes my mother had made with me would not be repeated. Daddy decided to personally oversee this new child's upbringing. Keith would be a man.

The defining day came when Keith began preschool. He got home and told of having fallen, somehow ending up on the ground with a view up some little girl's dress. It didn't mean anything, but Daddy chose to see it as an act of knowing trickery, a ruse to get a peek at the forbidden regions of budding womanhood. And it made him proud, confirmed everything he'd said about Keith being the real man among his two sons.

Keith quickly picked up on the way this hound-in-training behavior pleased our father, and it wasn't long before he was playing Pop like Lotto. A ritual developed: Every day when he came home from preschool, he'd have a report for the old man on the color or condition of some little girl's panties. Once or twice, even the teacher's. Each day, his reports were more detailed.

"I don't like her," he said one day, wrinkling his nose in disdain as he talked about some little girl. "Her panties are too raggedy."

That one brought down the house. Daddy repeated it endlessly for his drinking buddies, the men who gathered on our porch to slug down cheap wine and whiskey. "He can't tell you nothin' about what he learned in school," said my father proudly, "but he know all about the little girls' panties." Daddy beamed like a headlight.

And afterward he would tell my mother. "I'm raising a *man* here. That ain't nothing but a punk you got there."

It's a miracle to me that my brother and I never hated each other, indeed, grew to laugh about it as we got older. And the laughter is loudest when we speculate on how our father might have reacted had he lived long enough to see that Keith did, indeed, grow up to be a man, albeit a gay one.

It's probably a mercy that my father died when he did.

We moved all the time, all over central and south-central Los Angeles. I went to six different elementary schools. The rent would go up or my father would get into a fight with the landlord and next thing you knew, there was some rickety old truck backing up to the front door and all our belongings were loaded onto it.

The hell of it is that my father was a World War II veteran; if he had used his GI benefits, he could have *bought* a house with no down payment. But he was never interested in that. My mother, on the other hand, always dreamt of having a home of her own. It was the one thing she wanted. One day, a real estate man even picked us up in his car and took us around to see some houses. They were freshly painted and impossibly roomy. Mama seemed positively giddy that day and the four of us children picked up on her excitement. "Is this where we're going to live?" we asked. "Is this our new house?"

My father swiftly ended the speculation. I remember exactly what he told my mother when we got back home. "I ain't buying no house for you and your man to lie up in after I'm gone."

In my father's mind, this was logic. So it wasn't very long before a moving truck pulled in where the real estate man had parked his car.

One gray morning not too very long ago, I got into a rented car and took myself on a tour of some of the places where we lived. All of them reeked of my father. All of them made me remember.

The first stop was on Via La Reina in the Aliso Village housing project. It's an ugly block building in a maze of the same, all of them orange and dirty beige. It must have been 1962 or 1963 when we moved there; I would have been five or six, but I remember that day so clearly.

My cousin Al and I were running in and out, exploring the place while my father and the other men were trying to manhandle our things through the door. The projects seemed so huge to me, so filled with lovely possibility.

Aliso has changed a lot since then. It was largely black at the time, but it seems that everyone there speaks Spanish now. On the wall across from our old front door, I saw that someone had painted the Statue of Liberty. People are seen streaming toward her. They are brown and tiny, indistinguishable as ants.

Standing at our old front door, you can almost but not quite see the off-ramp from the freeway. I remember the day someone came running to tell Mama that a policeman had collared my father there for driving drunk. She raced off to where the officer had him handcuffed and she begged the man to let him go, told him my father was just a few feet from home, close enough to walk. But the officer took him to jail anyway.

I couldn't tell you how many drunk driving arrests my father racked up in the '60s. He got in so much trouble in the seamy nightspots around Central Avenue that a judge once made staying off Central a condition of his release from jail. Daddy worked only sporadically, usually as a janitor. He'd keep a job for a few weeks, and then drink himself out of it. Wouldn't work again for months. And my mother—sick from a heart condition and hypertension—couldn't work. So we were raised on welfare.

I walked around the side of the building to the spot where we were having a party for my sister Linda's sixth birthday in 1965 when my father got a call that his brother-in-law had been killed in a car accident in Chicago. Daddy stood there in front of all those little kids in their party hats and Sunday dresses and cursed my mother like a dog until she gave him what he wanted—the money from the welfare check.

"All I got to do is tap the phone and my sisters will send me money!" That's what he used to boast all the time. He said it so much that I grew up thinking Chicago some glorious city in the sky where my aunts lived in palaces of plenty. But apparently his sisters didn't send anything that day. My father took everything we had in the house and used it to go to the funeral. Mama had to beg money from her family and friends in order for us to eat the rest of the month.

Aliso is also where we were living when my youngest sister was born in 1964. Rachelle was a premature baby, so tiny she almost didn't survive her own birth. My mother's condition was also precarious after Rachelle's birth and they spent a long time in the hospital together. It was while they were there that I woke up one morning and stumbled downstairs into the living room. I found myself staring into the harsh light of an unshaded bulb. A woman I didn't know was there, cutting my father's hair. I realize now that she must have spent the night.

For reasons I've never understood—was he that stupid, careless or cruel?—my father didn't exactly struggle to hide his affair with this woman. Layla was her name, though I'm not sure of the spelling. He used to take my sister Linda and me to her house. Once, he took me with them to an amusement park in Long Beach. She bought me a bag of malted milk balls, which I took home and showed to my mother as she was making dinner. "Look what Auntie Layla gave me," I said.

Mama became angry and threw the candy away. I didn't understand.

Didn't understand, either, something that happened after she put him out of the house and he came to the door pleading for another chance. When she refused to open the door, he knelt down to the mail slot, begging me to ask Mama to change her mind. Tears were rushing down his face and that made me cry too, so I beseeched her on his behalf, but Mama stood firm and sent him away.

She and I sat there on the couch in front of the window to watch him go. My father got as far as the car at the curb. Then, it was as if something possessed him and he wheeled around and hurled himself at that window.

I was younger and quicker than my mother, so I managed to dive from the couch just in time. When he kicked the window in, she caught most of the glass herself. Then he turned and ran.

It wasn't long afterward that she let him come back home.

Those were the days when hope and fury rolled across the land in twin waves—one a cooling breeze, the other a tongue of fire, and the only question was, which one would get you first. Watts burned in those days. John Kennedy went to Dallas in those days. Malcolm X went to the Audubon Ballroom in those days. And Martin Luther King, still gloriously alive and in the fullness of his power, used those days to dream.

My father was about forty. I wish I could know what it all meant to him. Wish I could know if he felt the waves moving toward him, if he braced himself for the impact of one or the other. Or if he was already too far gone.

For a couple of years in the middle '60s, we lived at Sixty-ninth and Hoover, third building back from the street down a long driveway. It was in that house that I blurted out for the first time something I had felt for quite a while: that he didn't love me. Mama made him come and assure me that he did. He seemed awkward and uncomfortable as he stood over me and did as she said.

She was always doing that, now that I think of it—always looking for ways to knit the two of us together. I took her a drawing once and she admired it and then passed it over to him. "Look how talented our son is," she said. He gave the drawing a glance and a grunt of approval. He didn't seem very interested.

Maybe he loved me. He probably did. But he wasn't very good at showing it.

One time, he snatched away my books—he hated to see me reading—and ordered me to go outside and play. In response, I snatched up a packet of toilet paper or a tube of toothpaste or something and read the label loudly, defiantly. I would prove that he couldn't make me what he wanted me to be, couldn't stop me from doing what I loved.

His shoulders seemed to droop as he watched me. I went away feeling as if I'd won something.

We were in that house one night when the lady who lived next door came pounding on our door. My father opened it and there was her husband behind her with a butcher knife. I'll never forget what happened next. Mama held the woman and my old man stepped out to confront her husband. Talked him down from his raving, soothed him with honeyed words that drew the heat from his eyes and made him lower his knife. Years later, after they had moved away, we heard that the woman's husband had shot her and their two children in the head one day; she survived, but the children did not. I wonder, sometimes, whatever became of her.

It still amazes me that on a night when this woman shivered just inside our door while her husband stood there with his big knife raised, *my* father, of all people, was the peacemaker.

I had never known him to make peace before.

It took me a while to find the place where we lived in the late '60s. The area has changed and I don't navigate those streets as surely as I once did. For a moment, I thought the old house on Eighteenth Street had been torn down, but on a second pass I saw it, sitting there nestled behind trees and flowers, a two-story duplex.

God, how Mama hated that house. Hated it most of all the places we ever lived, I think. It was in an industrial district; we used to hear trucks coming and going at all hours.

The night we arrived to inquire about the place, she made it clear that this wasn't where she wanted to live, but unfortunately, the landlord loved to drink as much as my father did. They got to sharing a bottle and swapping lies and the next thing we knew, it was a done deal. My father never even asked my mother what she thought.

He was so drunk on the way back that the car kept drifting across the lanes. Mama was angry at what he had done—you could see it in the set of her jaw—but she didn't say a thing. Didn't want to start an argument and have him kill us in a crash. I sat in the front seat between the two of them, silent and scared, talking to God.

We were living in that house the day we got home from church to find squad cars parked at angles before our front door, lights splashing the building with streaks of urgent red. Turned out that while we were gone, my father had gotten into an argument with one of our neighbors, Mr. Ware, and had taken a shot at his house. Didn't hit anyone, thank goodness.

The police took him away and he might have spent a little time in jail, but he didn't change. My father used to pull out that shotgun all the time to settle his arguments. My late cousin Nathaniel, whose tastes in liquor ran to costlier and more sophisticated drinks than the quarter-a-bottle white port my father favored, remembered a time when he was staying with us and came home from work to find half a gallon of his bourbon gone. It didn't take a lot of guesswork to figure that my father was the culprit. "We got into it," Nate told me. "So he went and got the shotgun, said he was going to blow my brains out. I told him, 'Go ahead and do it.' And your Mama stepped in between."

My father kept the gun loaded under the bed. He drew bravado from that thing. Terrified us just knowing it was there. After my father died, Mama asked Nate to get it, unload it and take it away.

The last house I visited that day was the one we were living in when my father died. The man who lives there now was kind enough to let me inside. I was eager. And I was scared.

It's not the house I used to know, of course. The current owner has painted it, torn out the pantry where Keith used to hide under the table during my father's rampages. My parents' old bedroom is now a den; mine and Keith's is a storage room. And yet, I knew this house intimately. The side door that never opened, the mantle where Mama had her Martin Luther King commemorative plate, the back porch where the pipes burst in the 1971 earthquake.

Being in there for the first time in almost twenty years was like being on the set of a TV sitcom—a place you know well, or think you do, until you walk in and discover it to be small, about three-quarters the size of real life.

There was an unreality to the place, an echo of events long gone. Each room speaking to me. None louder than the tiny kitchen that once seemed so huge, where he used to come in and slap my mother around. And the two doors side by side just off the kitchen, through which Linda and I would come running.

My father made our lives hell.

And yet, for all of that, he was one thing many other fathers were not: He was there. Present and accounted for every day. Emotionally absent, mind you. But there, at least, in body. I know so many men, so many black men, who cannot say the same. So many men for whom the absence of father is a wound that never scabbed over.

The truth is, mine was not the worst father who ever lived. There were times he was fun to be around, times you felt good just being in his presence. Times you locked up in memory's storehouse of the things that make you smile.

Like the morning Mama was sick and he got up to fix breakfast for us. My father was a good cook when he put his mind to it—he had learned in the military—but he couldn't bake worth a damn. So breakfast was these hockey pucks that looked like biscuits. Linda and I were still trying to down our first helping when Keith went back into the kitchen for seconds. Still gulping it down when he returned for thirds. Each time, Daddy slathered those awful biscuits with pure butter and crowed with manly pride.

"See, that's why the kids won't eat your cooking," he yelled to my mother. "You don't know what you doing. You need to learn to cook like me. Keith been back for three helpings so far!"

As Daddy was boasting, Keith stopped by the table where Linda and I were still struggling. "You guys don't like 'em?" he whispered. "You don't have to eat 'em. Do what I do."

Mystified, we followed our five-year-old brother to the back door. He opened it and there was our dog, Trina, tail wagging eagerly. It turned out Keith had been feeding her his breakfast all along. Still playing Daddy like Lotto. When my father found out what was going on, the poor man was flummoxed. Bad enough he'd been had, but he'd been had by his favorite child, which was worse. Unforgivable. He lived another eight years and never baked again.

Nobody ever told that story better than the old man did, by the way. He was a born raconteur. Granted, he never let truth get in the way of a good tale, but even his lies were entertaining and sincere. Nobody ever spun bigger fibs with a straighter face. He could make you laugh so hard you couldn't breathe.

I loved him so much on days like that. On days when he had us doubled over and helpless, days when he was sweet and ribald and funny. Days when he put on his Old Spice and his stingy brim hats and seemed to me the handsomest, most self-possessed man in all the world.

It was at night that I feared him. At night that I lay awake in bed, ears straining, reaching into the darkness for sounds from the living room. I heard Mama watching television. Heard the vacuum cleaner running.

And always, eventually, I heard the sound I was waiting for and dreading, the one that made my stomach clench. The rasp of metal on metal. His key in the lock.

I willed my breathing to stop. Listening. *Listening.*

The first few moments always told the tale. If drinking had taken the edges off his aimless day, I could relax. Maybe he would call for dinner as he collapsed into a chair. Maybe he'd yell for one of his "bulls"—meaning us kids—to come take off his shoes and socks and put them neatly by the side of the chair. Soon he would be dozing and the night would pass in peace.

But there were so many other nights, nights when drinking left him abusive and mean. You could hear it in his voice from the moment he hit the door, even before he called Mama "bitch" for the first time.

How many nights did I lie there, hearing that word, and hoping against faithless hope that it would end there? More nights than I can remember.

Hoping against hope.

But it always happened the same way, those nights. Voices rose. The language turned bitter and abusive. Then he was on her, fists raised. And suddenly we were on the run, Linda and I, sprinting across the kitchen from our rooms to hurl ourselves between them. Night after night, my sister and I stood face to face in the hot space between our parents, pushing and crying and begging for peace.

Night after night. Night after night.

And sometimes, days.

One of my aunts sent money once to buy shoes for her nieces and nephews. Mama took us to Sears. Daddy warned her beforehand she better not spend all "his" money, that she better leave him something to drink with. But even that wasn't enough. He followed her from rack to rack in the shoe department, cursing her. He was loud and abusive, forgetting where he was. Or not giving a damn.

People were trying not to see, struggling not to hear. They turned away, embarrassed for us. And my mother bore it all with a composure I will never understand. She compared sizes and prices and if you had seen only her face, you might never have known that he stood over her, hands curled into fists, calling her a bitch. Over and over again . . . "bitch."

The word grates me to this day.

I didn't want shoes. I wanted to disappear. Wanted to slink into the shadows and die. I wanted that afternoon to end. But it never did. It never has.

Days like that are why I didn't bring friends home from school with me when I was young. Never. Not once. Didn't even want the other kids to know where I lived.

Because you never knew which father you might find: the charming funny one, or the abusive one who walked around the house in his underwear calling everyone names.

I thought I was the only one who had a father like that at home. More than "thought," I *knew*. No one else was going through anything like this.

I was wrong, of course. Found that out one day on a visit to a friend's house. Walter was a chubby kid and, like me, not really popular. He invited me over one Saturday afternoon to see his comic book collection. We were back in his bedroom, where I was ogling *Tales of Suspense*, when there came a loud cursing and yelling. His father. I looked up at Walt and there was such shame in his eyes. Such humiliation and hurt.

I wanted to say: *Hey, man, don't worry about it. I hear this stuff all the time.*

But I was only thirteen, so instead I just looked back down at the comic book and pretended I didn't hear.

I wonder sometimes whatever became of Walter. If, like me, he reached a point where he'd had enough, where he couldn't take any more. Where he began to fight back. As I became taller and stronger, I refused to passively absorb my father's abuse or see my mother suffer under his fists. As I became bigger, I began to return his blows.

He came into the dining room one day yelling at Linda. Raised a beer can as if to throw it at her. I leapt from the other side of the room, grabbing him by the legs and taking him down. We wrestled on the floor until somebody pulled us apart. Mama took me out of the house, made me go into the backyard. Held me there when all I could think of was how much I wanted to get at him.

We fought all the time in those days. There was a rage in me.

A few years ago, I visited my mother's best friend, Isabel Gordon, in Mississippi and she recounted for me the letters Mama sent in those years when my father and I were always coming to blows. "She had to talk to you nightly because she was scared you were going to do something to him," she said. "And I told her then, 'I hope he stops doing whatever he's doing so that child won't have to stain his hands with his daddy's blood.'"

Her words jolted me. To the best of my recollection, I never thought about killing my father. But on the other hand, I did think about seeing him dead.

He used to like the Bill Withers song, "Lean On Me." "Now that's a good record," he'd growl. "Rest of that shit you listen to ain't nothin'."

"If you like that one," I'd say, "maybe you'll like this one too." And I'd turn the record over. As it happens, the flip side of Withers's original Sussex Records single is a song called "Better Off Dead" that describes a life with which I was painfully familiar. The drums percolate and then up comes Withers's laconic voice:

She couldn't stand me anymore, so she just took the kids and went.
You see, I've got a drinking problem. All the money that we had, I spent.
Now I'm'a die by my own hand 'cause I'm not man enough to live alone
She's better off without me and I'm better off dead now that she's gone.

It ends in a burst of drum beats meant to simulate gunfire. My mother heard me playing it for him one day and made me stop. I don't think my father ever understood.

Recently, I listened to that record for the first time since my father died. The words made me collapse into a chair. I had forgotten how much anger was in me.

And yet I never stopped seeking his approval, never stopped searching for a way to make him like me. As I got older, he did seem to find a backwards pride in some of the things I did. He began to trot me out as he did Keith, for the entertainment of the drunks on our front porch.

I'd recite poetry for them, give them the adolescent rhymes about loneliness and love that filled my notebooks in those days. One of my father's friends was a pompous know-it-all named Lloyd, a black dead ringer for the mailman on *Cheers*. Daddy loved to egg him into intellectual confrontations with me. Lloyd would challenge me about current events or history, and I would throw out some combination of twenty-five-dollar words. It was never long before Lloyd would back off, palms raised in defeat.

The men would laugh, Daddy loud among them. It was satisfying, but never quite as much as I'd thought it would be. It never made me feel as if he loved me or even really knew me. I was just doing tricks for his friends.

Leaving the circle of men, I'd pass Keith, going out there to do his own tricks. He had this routine where he'd pretend to be Daddy. He'd mash one of the old man's hats down on his head, throw a rumpled jacket across his shoulders, wrap a bottle in a crushed brown bag and stumble around yelling, slurring his words.

Everybody howled at this imitation of my drunken father. Amazingly, nobody laughed louder than Daddy himself.

We didn't know the word "alcoholic" then. Didn't know the language of drinking as disease. Didn't realize that this was why he couldn't hold a job, reign his rage, love us as fathers do.

I don't know if it matters. I don't know if it would have made a bit of difference. Maybe. Maybe those times he promised to change, those days when he said he was going to be a better man, maybe they would have meant something then. Something besides another damned disappointment.

He said it about once a year: I'm going to stop drinking, going to change. Once a year, he seemed to step outside the moment and be shamed by what he saw.

One time in particular I'll always remember. Daddy and I were driving on Central Avenue in south L.A. when the car died and we had to get out and walk. We must have been thirty or more blocks from home, but that didn't matter. Daddy loved to walk and I did, too.

After a few minutes, we stopped in a park to take a break and found a table in the shadow of some trees. My father seemed anxious, seemed to have something on his mind, but it took him a while to speak it. When he did, he uttered the last words I ever expected to hear.

He said he was sorry. Said he had not been the father he should have been. Said he was going to change.

His face was close to mine. There was need in his eyes. It mattered to him that I understood. That I believed.

And I did.

I've never known where that moment came from, never understood what brought it on. All I know is that he did what he said. He changed. For about two weeks, he changed. Stopped drinking, stopped being abusive. There was laughter and peace in our home.

It was like living on the skin of a bubble—a thing of beauty and yet, I feared to breathe.

Not that it mattered. Two weeks was all he could do. Two weeks and he picked up the bottle once more.

Maybe if I had known the language of alcoholism as disease, I would have realized how much it took for him to achieve even that. But I didn't, so all I knew was the betrayal.

It wasn't the first time it had happened. But it was the first time I had looked into his eyes and seen the need, the first time I had truly dared to think the dangerous word *maybe.*

The first time I really believed.

And the last. I never believed anything he said again.

TWO

So I wake up one morning and I'm in my middle thirties and fairly successful, and that's when it hits me: Because of him, I am missing many things. Little pieces of myself I ought to have.

I can tell you the exact moment. I'm rushing to a crucial out-of-town job interview. Actually, a continuation of one. My prospective employer has asked me to return for a second day—which is fine and even flattering, except that I packed only one tie on this trip, the one I wore the day before. The one that was pre-knotted for me as usual by my wife.

I don't like ties, don't wear them very often, and when I do, she prepares them for me. But now I'm stuck. Don't want to wear the same tie I wore yesterday, so here I am running late for the big interview upstairs, standing in a corporate bathroom fuming and struggling and getting nowhere with a tie I bought not ten minutes ago.

I want to laugh. I want to curse. The man in the mirror stops for a moment, takes a deep breath.

Missing pieces. See, I can't knot this tie because my father never taught me how. Now I'm grimacing in the mirror, looping the thing over and under and in and out and hoping that when I'm done, it'll look presentable. Making it up as I go along and praying no one will notice.

Which strikes me as an apt metaphor for what we do, we black men raised in the absence of our fathers. Because we are missing so many pieces.

And maybe there's something pathetic about it—halfway through life, and still tallying up the hurts and slights of childhood. Except that the missing pieces have this way of intruding on present days, of catching you when you least expect. When all you want to do is tie the damn tie and get on to the interview, missing pieces stop and remind you of what you didn't have. You feel like a fraud, like you're making it up. Like someone trying to do advanced calculus without ever having learned the multiplication table.

So here you are, big man going for the big interview . . . and you can't even knot your own tie? Who you trying to kid?

Who, indeed?

The guy in the mirror gives up. Pulls off the tie and slips it into his pocket. Leaves the bathroom open-collared. Just trying to get by. Missing so much.

Didn't have that someone who teaches you "man" things and makes you want so badly to learn, so desperately to please him—as if his approving nod might validate your entire life. Didn't have that man who makes things right by the force of his presence, like having Jordan on your team in the last minutes of a crucial game.

Missing so many things. It's a common refrain among African-American men.

For some of us, Dad died. For others, he just never came around. For still others, he never noticed we were there. And for some, he was an abuser who spoke with his fists and left the house in everlasting uproar every night. Children wailing, mother bruised and weeping, father cursing them like he would strangers in a bar.

I am missing so many things. Memories of peace. Nights of calm.

So why be surprised—any of us—that at some point the things you're missing catch up with you? Maybe it comes when you're struggling with the tie. Maybe when the jailhouse doors clang shut behind you. Maybe when the bullet embeds itself in your yielding flesh.

Maybe when your baby cries for the very first time.

Every day, black boys and black men become black fathers with no one to show them how fatherhood is supposed to go. And then what? Where do you go to learn this trick, to make yourself this thing you've never seen? This father. This dad.

And who still has faith in your ability to learn?

The last census found that 64 percent of all African-American children are growing up in one-parent households. The overwhelming majority of the time, that parent is not the father. The Census Bureau also reports that nearly half of all black families are headed by a single mother. So the vast majority of black kids wake up every day without Daddy at home.

Though the problem is more acute in the black community, fatherlessness is, of course, a growing problem that slices across demographic boundaries. More white children, too, are growing up without a father's guiding hand.

Surprisingly, there is not a great body of literature concerning the effects of fatherlessness on children. And even less than that on the subject of fatherlessness among *African-American* children. It's a topic that has, for the most part, gone unexplored by social scientists, who have tended to concentrate their efforts on the study of children raised without mothers. But what information does exist is profoundly troubling in its implications. A 1996 University of California, Santa Barbara study found that boys raised without their fathers are more than twice as likely to engage in delinquent behavior and that girls in the same situation are more than twice as likely to become teenaged mothers. The National Center on Fathers and Families, which is affiliated with the graduate school of the University of Pennsylvania, reports that children raised without their fathers tend to do more poorly in school, engage in earlier sexual activity, feel less certain of their own worth, and be raised in poverty. A 1998 study by researchers at Princeton University and the University of Pennsylvania says that young men are twice as likely to be jailed if raised without a father.

These are not just statistics. We are losing our children. And, again, the problem is more acute—problems *always* seem to be more acute—in the black community.

We can talk about race and crime and the cheap, addictive drug that hit African-American neighborhoods like a bomb in the 1980s. We can talk about education and unemployment and the selective persecution of the justice system so that in some places, "driving while black" might as well be part of the criminal code.

Yet even granting each of these concerns its individual space, who can deny that the most immediate threat facing black children is the simple fact that black fathers are not at home? And that we are being changed by this in ways that ought to alarm us all.

Fathers are becoming obsolete. A luxury appointment.

A black friend of mine, Mary Ann Wilson-Woods, remembers how, as she was preparing to leave the hospital after giving birth to her first child, the nurses held an exit interview in her room. When one of the women saw the new mother's marital status, she said in surprise, "Wow, you're *married?* That's really odd."

"Odd," she said. Which is, well . . . an odd thing to say. But then, many of the women served by the hospital are young and black, and marriage has become something of a rarity among that group. Seventy-eight percent of black families were headed by married couples in 1948. By the time the '90s dawned, that number slipped to 48 percent.

Another friend, Leonard Foster, remembers a Mother's Day when he was in church and the preacher looked out over a sea of brown faces, and asked that all single mothers approach the altar. One by one they came, rising from the pews with babies on hips and toddlers in tow. From all over the church, they made their way forward. Until there were almost no women left sitting.

Is anyone surprised?

You could hear this coming in the dichotomy of song lyrics we've been singing for years: "Mama, loving you is like food to my soul" versus "Papa was a rolling stone"; "Don't you know we love you, place no one above you" versus "Daddy could swear, I declare."

In the middle of "I'll Always Love My Mama," a '70s Philly soul anthem, there comes a spoken section where the singers start talking about their fathers. Where mother has been depicted as a fount of wisdom, love, and discipline, "Pop" is described as staggering home drunk, clothes wrinkled, trailing balls of lint. The recollection is followed by raucous laughter that somehow sounds desperate, strained, and not quite touched by mirth. There's an ambivalence toward Pop that the singers don't even try to hide.

It resonates. I remember the afternoon I told one of my father's sisters that I was on the way to the cemetery "to visit my mother." Bad choice of words, because as it happens, my parents are buried together. "Visit your *mother?*" said Aunt Mildred, indignantly. "Well, what about your father?"

I made an excuse, told her that Mom's death was fresher, having come more recently. But it wasn't the truth. Not nearly.

Fact is, that man took my childhood. He abused my siblings and me. He abused my *mother* when I could do little more than watch. He taught me anger and fear at an age when I was too young to handle either.

"What about your father?" she asks me, and I don't know how to answer. I try to love him, I try to hate him, only to find that both emotions hang off me like an ill-fitting garment. There is no resolution. I can't make it work in my mind.

What *about* him? I want to say. What about him?

I see boys having good times with their fathers—I see my own children having a good time with *me*—and I get jealous, feel deprived. So, yeah, what about my father?

Because of him, I am missing so many things.

Including the most vital: The knowledge that the most important man in my life noticed me, valued me. The simple assurance that he loved me.

Fathers and sons alike, we pretend it doesn't hurt. We are charlatans wearing masks, pretending we know what we're doing, pretending that we are tougher than pain. Lying to those around us and to ourselves.

A cool pose. That's what Janet Mancini Billson and Richard Majors called it in their 1992 book, *Cool Pose: The Dilemmas of Black Manhood in America*. And, though Billson and Majors wrote specifically about younger men, much of what they had to say rings true to lesser degrees of older men as well.

A cool pose is an air of unflappability. A swagger of impenetrable cool. A way of seeming in control, said the authors, of exerting dignity and worth in a world that denies those things to black men.

Everyone knows the statistics. Throughout the '90s, they became distressingly familiar, these bloodless quantifiers of black male misery:

- About one in three young black men are under control of the justice system, either in prison, on probation, or on parole.

- The leading cause of death for young black men is homicide.

- Unemployment for black men is more than twice that of whites; roughly *three times* that of white men twenty and over.

- Black men in Harlem were found by a study in the *New England Journal of Medicine* to have less chance of living to age forty than men in Bangladesh. Bangladesh is a poor and mostly rural country in South Asia.

A cool pose, then, begins to make a certain amount of sense. A way of fighting back by opting out. Why enter the game if it's rigged against you? I can't lose if I refuse to play. You can't hurt me if you can't reach me. We make our faces fortresses, our eyes guarded windows.

To be a black man in America is to wear masks and armor. This is the lesson a black boy quickly learns.

I used to play a game with my middle son in which I asked him to tell me the difference between a woman and a man. He was little then, far too young to know anything about sexual organs or chromosomes. So he could never point to a defining characteristic I couldn't counter.

Women have breasts, he'd say, and then I'd point out some fat guy who did, too. Women wear dresses, he'd say, and I'd remind him that women also wear pants. Women have long hair, he'd say, and I'd show him some woman who didn't or some man who did.

It always frustrated Marlon. He *knew* there were differences—he could see them—but he could never quite put them into words.

That was then. Now he's a gangly teenager, all arms and legs with a dusting of hair on his upper lip tracing the outlines of the mustache he'll someday have. And his notion of what makes a man have been filtered through the thug rap imagery he sees on the video channel. He has come to understand manhood—particularly black manhood—as a certain style of shirt, a particular posture, a specific look in the eyes, and, most of all, an attitude of can't-be-touched and don't-you-try. Masks and armor.

They call it being "hard." It is the litmus test for young black men.

The actress Jada Pinkett Smith was on a talk show once, extolling the way her then-fiancé, rapper and actor Will Smith, romanced her. The picture she painted was a charming one—surprise flowers and other acts of sweet thoughtfulness—and the audience was appropriately enchanted. But Smith, sitting next to her, felt the need—albeit in jest—to lower his voice to a comical baritone and assure the men watching that he was still "hard."

It struck me that if the need to be hard is felt even by an affable actor beloved by the white mainstream, if it is felt even by my son who has spent his entire life in the cocoon of a nuclear family, then what hope is there, really, for a young man coming of age without his father on the streets of some urban hell? What else can he define himself by? I mean, at the end of the day, Smith has his box office receipts and Pinkett, my son has his mother and me. What does that black kid have, except the ability to be hard?

He grows up hiding in that ability. From himself and from the world.

I met a man named Grailyn who told me it took having his heart "cracked" by two women he loved for him to realize, "I'm not that rough and tough individual I project to be."

So why put forward that image?

"Everyone has an image to project," he said. "The 'hood I grew up in, you couldn't be no soft guy. You had to get respect. You had to fight, you had to do certain things."

As black men, we often find ourselves doing those things, living a "caricature" of masculinity. That's the telling term favored by Dr. James H. Cones III, a clinical psychologist and assistant director of the counseling center at the University of California, Irvine, who, with coauthor Joseph White, has written about the psychology of black men in a book called *Black Man Emerging: Facing the Past and Seizing a Future in America.*

Even black men, he feels, have difficulty forming a fully rounded image of black manhood. "So they have to go on what basically is a stereotype, or what they read or what they see." The problem, he said, is that so many black boys are not raised around black men, and so they form their impressions from media and other unreliable sources. Television's nightly parade of black thugs, athletes, and dancing fools becomes a self-fulfilling prophecy.

He was not surprised when I told him I knew many black men who held low opinions of other black men. Many of them, he argued, have doubtless had limited close interactions with black men. "But the lived experience, those people who've actually had contact with black men, get a richer experience of what black men are like, and many of those are very positive.

"If you look at many of the boys involved in gang behavior, one of the ways of understanding it is that these are often boys who don't have experiences with black men—a father, father figures, and that type of thing. If you grow up in a family where men are numerically scarce—you're a minority as far as gender is concerned—then you're going to have an increased need to know what being a man is about. At the same time, you're going to have this void in your life because you don't have someone to teach you or show you what being a man is about. So sometimes, boys will use each other and join an organization or a gang and really celebrate their manhood with each other in that way. When you don't know the full person, you tend to exaggerate what a man is. You look at some of these gangs; they tend to be sort of exaggerated masculinity. Hypermasculine."

One of Marlon's friends is a young man whose smile I've seldom seen. Every time he comes by, he's scowling like he's got a stomachache. Even Marlon is fiercely adherent to and protective of his manhood rituals—ferociously intolerant of perceived slights, obsessive about getting his "respect." He was searching through my closet for something to wear to church one Sunday and flinched backward as if struck when I unthinkingly made the mistake of offering him a pink dress shirt.

My son takes his cue from the gangsters of rap who were so immensely popular in the middle '90s. Gangsters don't wear pink dress shirts.

Of course, gangsters—real ones, at least—also don't live in suburban colonials with minivans in the driveway. One rainy night, I took Marlon and his younger brother, Bryan, out in that minivan for a drive through an impoverished section of town. Stopped on a commercial strip. Across the street, some shadowy male figures were loitering under an awning. I invited my boys to get out and take a walk with me. Both energetically and emphatically refused, even when I repeated the offer. Instead, they urged me to get the car moving again.

My boys tried to hide it, but they were scared of that place. I was amused and gladdened. And a little guilty, too. Because I knew that for those young men across the street, this neighborhood wasn't an object lesson. It was home.

Nevertheless, I wanted my sons to understand the difference, to know that the urban rituals and styles they have been fed by media are actually the stuff of someone else's life. And for that someone else, it's more than style. It's masks and armor they can't take off—a barrier standing between them and a good job, between them and education, between them and a loving relationship with a good woman.

Indeed, in 1996 a young black woman told the *New Yorker* magazine that the idea of a man and woman in a loving, lifelong relationship was a "fantasy." She added, "I've never met many people like that, have you?"

Small wonder. Manhood, in the definition embraced by young black men, is often a one-dimensional cartoon of sexual conquest. Seems like every kid with a beeper and a group of "boys" to impress fancies himself a "player" these days. The white man who said black men were a bunch of unfeeling players would find himself the object of incandescent outrage. Yet black men say the same thing themselves every day in this exaggerated parody of manhood so many embrace. A player plays as many women as his bankroll, stamina, and smooth talk can sustain, but never truly swears himself to any. White men may talk about their fear of commitment, but black men raise it to a badge of honor.

As Cones sees it, many young black men seek to prove themselves men through exaggerated sexual adventure. "One becomes a man by how many women he's had sex with or had children with. And that has very little to do with becoming a man in real life."

Even less to do with becoming a viable father.

"We as black folks were never taught how to be fathers to our kids," a black father named Clyde of Yonkers, New York, told me. "The father image was never there. See, that's what I never wanted to do to my kids. I wanted to teach them what it is to be a father. Because I was never taught to be a father. You can give 'em money and this and that, but it's not like being around, being a father."

"I think black men find it so easy to walk away because it's not a foreign concept to them," says Timothy, a black stepfather who lives in Modesto, California. "Quite a few of us have been raised by women. So it's not as though they're subjecting this child to something they haven't already dealt with themselves. It's self-perpetuating, because this generation we find ourselves in now, it's more normal [to see] a single-parent household than it is to see two of them together."

Timothy's father walked away from the family when he was ten. Andrew, who lives in Los Angeles, was in diapers when his parents split up. He sees in black men a chronic "lack of responsibility."

"Meaning we want to have sex, we enjoy sex, but don't want to assume the responsibilities for having sex. We want to have children, but don't want to assume the responsibility for taking care of the children, training the children, that kind of thing. We want the prize without running the race. That's the problem. We're looking for the pot of gold all the time, but we don't want to have to walk, we don't want to have to look for it. We just want it to drop in our laps."

And there it is again, that sense of black men being awfully hard on black men.

"If the men you're interviewing are saying that men are not doing what they're supposed to be doing," said Dr. Brenda Stevenson, a history professor at UCLA who is married to James Cones, "then I suppose it's an indictment of the way in which African-American men are socialized—largely by women in our society. And I also think it has a lot to do with the ways in which we define black manhood. What I mean by that is, do black men define themselves as fathers? Is black manhood now defined in such a way that fatherhood is not part of that definition? And if not, then we have to ask the question, why isn't it?"

The question is heartbreaking and crucial. Because now, when families, communities, and country need black men to stand and be fathers to our children, some of us falter like someone just asked us to build a spaceship and fly it to Pluto. We wonder how you do this thing and how you know you're doing it right.

I have two stepchildren and three biological children, all from the same wife. I fancy myself a decent father to them. But the fact is, there's never a day that passes when I'm not wondering whether I am doing it all wrong. Every temper tantrum they throw, every teenage phase I grapple with, brings home to me a reminder that I'm just tap-dancing here. Like trying to knot that tie in the bathroom mirror, just making it up as I go along.

I wondered if I was the only one. Wondered if it was just me who wrestled with these fears and inadequacies, who felt like a faker courting exposure, pretending something he doesn't truly understand.

I wondered, so I started asking around. Started searching out black fathers who'd had difficult relationships with their own fathers. Went to friends and neighbors and family members, and groups that specialize in helping men to become better fathers. The idea was to construct a conversation with my peers on the ways in which we, as black men, succeed or fail at making ourselves fathers.

Or better yet, dads. Because any man with a decent sperm count and a willing partner can become a father. But a dad, a man who has earned the respect and love that syllable implies . . . that's the goal, isn't it? That's the place we seek to reach.

I didn't expect much, to tell you the truth. Thought there would be reticence and reluctance and an unwillingness to take off the mask and remove the armor. Thought the topic so intimate that no one would want to explore it.

I was wrong. In dozens of interviews, the thing that repeatedly impressed me was that where fatherhood is concerned, black men had an eagerness—a need—to unburden themselves of heretofore unspoken feelings and fears. At first, I thought maybe it was just because we live in an age of confession when everyone's dirty laundry waves in living color from a talk-show set.

But it wasn't that. The nation has developed a habit of talking about black men as if they aren't in the room, dissecting their failures without inviting them to participate in the discussion. These men were simply saying to me things they had been wanting to say, dying to say—answering questions they had waited to be asked for a very long time. Over and over, I had the sense of having stumbled into some man's interior monologue, his most private thoughts about himself and his role.

And I kept seeing myself there. My own father and me.

I spoke to drug dealers and businessmen, counselors and coaches, executives, students, playboys, and a preacher or two—asking fathers about their fathers and sons about their sons. Almost to a man, they were remarkably generous to me, allowing me to probe well past the level where I'd have expected to be turned back. Men who, in my estimation and theirs, had failed to become good fathers were amazingly candid in discussing why. And those who had succeeded in that quest against all reasonable expectations were just as willing to talk about how.

The process awakened in me thoughts I'd not dared think for years. Took me back to the father I'd have sworn I left irrevocably behind me.

It's a funny thing. I had buried him so deep in my mind that I'd almost forgotten him. My sisters and brother and I, we didn't talk about him after his death. It was as though an unspoken understanding had raised a wall between us: We had gone through hell together and would pretend the trip never happened.

When I unburied him, when I put him back together, I expected a rush of pain—and found it. But there was also something I had scarcely dared to hope . . . some small bit of understanding. Old pieces suddenly fit, old mysteries began to knit themselves together. Into a new picture—not pretty, not simple, but new—of my father, my family, and me. It helped me to know myself better, to understand my own passages.

I still remember the day I got married, the day I took an instant family and how it abruptly occurred to me that I didn't have the slightest idea how to do this thing that was expected of me. Didn't know what a father was supposed to be.

Because I was missing so much. And it wasn't until I unburied my father, put him back together in my own mind, retraced the steps through hell, compared my journey with that of other men, that I realized I'd also been blessed. Many of us go through hell, but some never get out.

A small thing, perhaps.

But then, we are missing so much. We make do with what we have.

THREE

The question, then, is simply this: What happens to a man? What is the turn a black man takes, the mistake he makes that steals from him both the opportunity and the ability to be a good father? Which is the first false step on the journey? Does it happen after life beats him down and closes off avenues of advancement and achievement? Does it happen when the child is born and thus goes abruptly from being abstract theory to concrete reality? Or does it happen at the very beginning, when a woman first goes to the doctor or the drugstore to get confirmation of her nagging suspicion?

Does it happen then, right in the middle of what's supposed to be a moment of hope?

If so, what can a man say? Who can he tell his misgivings to? Certainly not the woman. She comes to you with the news, says, "I'm pregnant" or "We're going to have a baby," and your heart is supposed to break free of its moorings and go floating inside your chest.

You are supposed to be thrilled, lost in a time of great joy. But maybe for some men it is just as much, or even more, a time of fear. Maybe the fear comes instantly, or maybe a few hours or days later. Either way, it steals in on cat's paws, a silent shadow abusing hope, whispering a litany of "what ifs."

What if I'm not ready? What if I can't afford it? What if I can't save enough for college?

And the big one: What if I fail?

You try to dismiss it, perhaps, as a bad case of the jitters that are part and

Mark and his girlfriend, Nichelle

parcel of any crossing into a new phase of life. And maybe you're right. Maybe you get away with it.

Unless, that is, you're a young black man with no firsthand idea of what and how a father is supposed to be and no one to confide this emptiness in. And maybe, if that's what you are, the question broods over you like clouds, a possibility too real and too near to be easily vanished.

That's how it was for Mark, a young man I met in Washington. And, tellingly, how it *wasn't* for Jermaine, who lives in Compton, California.

They are alike in many ways. Both black, both male, both eighteen when I met them. And both fathers-to-be with pregnant girlfriends. I find it useful to think of them as opposite sides of the same coin, each a doppelganger for the other, a look at the ways life might have been different, if only. . . .

And the "if only" tells the tale because, though they have a lot in common, Mark and Jermaine are nothing alike.

Mark was a tenth-grade dropout hoping to get into a job training program, Jermaine a student at the University of Southern California.

Mark's father died when Mark was "four or five" years old. Jermaine has a close relationship with his dad.

Mark described himself as scared of fatherhood, apprehensive about what he was getting himself into. And Jermaine? Sitting at the dining room table of his family's home, I asked him if he, too, was scared.

Jermaine

"Nah, I'm not scared," he said with the offhand confidence of a young man yet to be seriously bruised by life. "I believe I'm ready. I think a lot has to do with me being raised in the church: I look at it as a blessing. There are a lot of people out there who will never have the opportunity to be in the situation I am. I figure since I've been blessed with it that I'm going to make the most out of it and turn it into something positive.

"I think I'm going to be a good father," he continued. "Like I said, it has a lot to do with home training and the way I was brought up. That's a very solid foundation. It gives me a reference, things I can look back to and get things from. Not saying that what worked for me as a child is going to work for my child, but [it does] sort of set a foundation and give me an idea of what to expect."

He was a square, solidly built young man, speaking softly, his eyes averted in evident shyness. His father sat by his side gauging his answers, nodding approval. On impulse, I lobbed him a softball question, knowing what the answer would be, but wanting to hear it just the same. Who's your role model? I asked. Who do you look to in figuring out what kind of dad you're going to be?

"My father," he said, right on cue. "I was blessed to always have a father in the home. I have a lot of friends who don't have a father. Right off the bat, the difference is obvious, as far as home training—things they would do in public, or the way they would treat certain people, or things they would say to certain people. The difference is so obvious."

As obvious, perhaps, as that between him and Mark.

Not that the distinction is immediately apparent. Like Jermaine, Mark has a bashful demeanor and if he didn't tell you, you might never know about the beatings or the drugs. His girlfriend, twelve years his senior, was a receptionist in the Washington, D.C., branch of the Institute for Responsible Fatherhood and Family Revitalization, a national organization that counsels wayward fathers. We met in one of their offices.

Mark told me he came to the United States with his mother and three siblings at the age of two. His father remained behind in their native Guyana, dying of diabetes a few years later. Mark's parents were never married.

I asked him about not having a father around.

"Sometimes I wonder what it's like," he admitted. "If I did have my father around, would I have saved a lot of stuff that I went through? Instead of wanting to be out hanging with my friends, if my father was there, I probably would have been able to spend more time with him than getting in trouble.

"I went through a thing when I was stealing from my mother when I was little. I remember one time I took her money at Christmas. We didn't get anything that Christmas."

How much did you take? I asked.

"Hundreds."

How old were you at the time?

"About seven. Took all her money. I hid it in the McDonald's. Came back the next day, it was gone."

Why would you do that?

"I don't know. I was just like that."

Then Mark started describing another misadventure, this one several years later. "I went over on that bridge right there," he said, indicating an overpass about two blocks away. "We was just walkin' and my friend picked up a big ol' paint bucket and said, 'Watch. I bet you I can smack somebody right in they windshield with this big ol' paint bucket.' He was holding it, he was timing it, and he just threw it. Then I was like, 'Watch me hit it with this bottle.' And then everybody just start throwin'. Everybody just joined in and start throwin'. Then the police came. I got locked up for that. That same day or the next day, I got out."

I had driven to the interview that day under the very same overpass. People die like that, I told him. Mark's soft demeanor never changed.

"I know," he said. "That was right around the time some [other] boys threw some rocks and hit a lady's car and she died from it. I ain't even knowed it was that big like that. They had me going to court and stuff."

Court wasn't much of a deterrence. "I was still gettin' into trouble," said Mark. "I was stealing cars, I was going to stores stealing. I was beating up people, assaulting people, getting all types of charges. Then they told me that if I didn't want all my charges to be on my record, [I could go to] a job corps [for] court-committed kids that got issues they want to deal with.

"They was saying my mother was neglecting me," he continued, his voice skeptical. "So they didn't feel like my mother's house was a fit place for me. I had went to the job corps. They kicked me out of one and sent me to another one. So I end up doing four years instead of two. I had just came home not too long ago."

You say you had "issues," I said. What were they?

"I had anger problems."

Who were you angry at?

A sly look. "I don't know. I was just a bad boy."

I pressed it. If you're angry, you've got to be angry at somebody, I said. Even if it's only yourself.

"I guess I was. I don't know what I was angry at. I was angry at something, though. I used to be beating people up a lot. And I had an issue with female authority. I didn't like females having authority over me. They said I was, like, depressed and I was isolating myself. They put me on this drug, they said it was going to help my mood swings."

I asked him to tell me more about his mother.

"She used to whip me real bad," he said. "All of us used to get whipped real bad. She used to hit us with sticks, iron cords—anything she could grab her hand onto, she'll hit you with it. One time, she broke my leg. This is when I was young. She broke my leg and they took me from her and put me in a foster home."

You're about to be a father, I said. Do you really think you're ready for that?

"I don't know. I'm trying to be prepared for it."

But could "trying to be prepared" be enough? So many men come up the hard way and say they would never do to their children what was done to them. Then they turn around and do it anyway. We become what we have seen. It takes more than a notion not to.

What if I fail?

"I don't want to be like that," repeated Mark. "Me and my sister used to say the same thing: We weren't going to treat our kids like our mother treated us. But I see my sister treating her daughter like my mother used to treat us. Then I think like, dag, I might turn out to be just like that. About all I can do is make the best of it."

In a perfect world, of course, no eighteen-year-old has to worry about what sort of father he's going to be, because no eighteen-year-old is making babies. Men that age, by and large, haven't the maturity—emotional or financial—necessary to successfully raise a child. So such a child almost always begins life with a deficit, a disadvantage to be surmounted.

Yet is it too simplistic to suggest that the hole will be less deep, the odds not quite as long, for Jermaine's child than for Mark's? Or that the primary reason for the disparity is obvious? In a word, Dad.

Asked if his oldest son is prepared for fatherhood, Jermaine's father, Jerry, was unequivocal. "No, I don't think he's ready," he said. But in the next breath, he added, "I see he's making changes in his behavior; he never was a kid who ran the street.

"I sat down with him and said, 'Because you have a child coming into this world, life priority is going to change. Don't look for your girlfriend to raise the child by herself. I mean, from the time the child is born, you're going to have to spend some nights . . . go get the baby and you get up at night, change the diapers."

Jerry, who is in his mid-forties, was born in Shreveport, Louisiana, and raised in Los Angeles, where his mother moved him and his six siblings when he was still young. She had divorced his father, of whom he said, "The only thing I really remember is that he was an alcoholic and when he did come around, it was like a disturbance."

Jerry remembered himself as a quiet child, conscious of not wanting to cause pain for a mother who already had more than enough. "I kind of realized that she was going to work every morning, trying to support seven kids.

I have one brother who's older than me, he was the one who had lots of problems. Not physical problems, behavior problems. My mom spent more time with him. I guess I just didn't want to be like that. I just took the other route. More independent, you know? I guess I was a pretty good child."

He spoke with quiet pride of the family—a daughter and two sons—he and his wife Winona have raised in their neat corner of Compton, California. The only shadow to cross that pride came when he talked about the day he learned that Jermaine had a child on the way. And even that was only fleeting.

"I wasn't happy," he conceded. "But I also knew . . . no sense in crying over spilled milk. So I sat down with both of them and told them the circumstances, the situation. It didn't make any sense to go into the dialogue of, how did this happen? We *know* how it happened. We had that discussion before this thing ever happened. The fact of the matter is, it's happened now. I just presented to him the facts: Your priorities are going to change now. When you make a decision in your life, it's going to impact the child forever. If you get in another relationship with someone else, you're going to have your child to consider, too."

Maybe no one is ever prepared to be a father for the first time, no one ever quite braced for the onslaught of new responsibilities and emotions that comes. It's difficult to imagine, though, that anyone might be *less* prepared than an eighteen-year-old man who has arrived at this life change unexpectedly.

But Jermaine, at least, has seen fatherhood up close, knows the contours and the smell of it. From his perch in the midst of middle-class comforts, he has seen his father go to work, take the family to church, check the doors at night. As Jerry puts it, "When your dad's in the house, you can sleep better at night."

Mark can only imagine what that contentment might be like. Can only strive to create it out of intuition and want. He stressed that he was struggling to prepare himself for the difficult task ahead.

"[I'm] trying to get stable. Get me a steady job where I go to work, be able to have that finance to take my kids and have them and spend time with them. I don't want to be mean to my child. I mean, a baby only gon' know what you teach 'em. A baby brain is like, blank. And everything a baby learn come from how you treat 'em.

"I don't want my child to be in no ghettoish neighborhood so he can pick up some bad habits. I want to put him in a nice neighborhood where it's nice kids around, kids that don't curse and got respect for people. Them the type of kids I want my child to hang around. And I don't want to be a mean father to my child. I want to be a loving parent, talk to my child. And I don't *never* want to whip 'em."

Hope was bursting out of him in a sudden spurt like water through a dam. But fear was close on its heels.

"That's what I *want*," he emphasized, his voice becoming a near whisper. "I don't know how it's gon' turn out. I be scared."

Really? I asked. What are you scared of?

"That I ain't gon' raise 'em right. That they gon' be messed up. I can't say that, 'cause I can't predict the future. But I do be scared, because I ain't never raised no baby before. I know what I want to raise him like, how I want it to be. But things don't always work out."

Have you told anybody you were scared?

"I told my baby's mother. I don't think she listened. I think it just go in one ear and come out the other."

He straightened a little, raised his eyes to mine. "But I can't get scared now," he said, and it seemed as much for his assurance as for mine. "I know with my baby coming, I got to be a different person. I can't be gettin' high, drinkin', cussin', all like that. Letting my baby see my mood swings. If the baby see something like that, he gon' think it's all right. I've got to change my ways."

But there it was again, fear stalking hope. His voice dropped once more, became a murmur of confession. "I don't know what kind of father I'm going to be," he said.

FOUR

There are many ways for fathers to fail. None is more devastating than spousal abuse. And if you don't believe it, consider the picture.

Father beating on mother. Pushing her down. Closing his hand on her throat. Hammering her with his fist.

While you *watch*. Watch and cry, because there's nothing else you can do. You're too frightened, too ineffectual, too *small* to make him stop. To even make him notice you. Your parents don't hear your cries over the sounds of their own carnage.

It is like being trapped inside a nightmare from which there is no wakening. It is hell. Indeed, perhaps the worst injury a man can inflict on a son is to beat his mother.

Not just because it shatters the peace, nor because it brings physical injury. But also because it diminishes a boy, saddles him with a sense of obligation he's not equipped to handle. He feels that there ought to be something he can do about this. And of course there isn't.

No one ever idolizes a woman as a boy does his mother. It's wrenching for him to watch a man mistreat her, beat her, make her cry, frustrating to see this when there's no way you can help, nothing you can do but swallow your impotence and make solemn, bloody promises to nameless "somedays."

As in, "Someday, I'm going to make him stop." And you never forget. Never.

I had a conversation with a Washington, D.C., man named Ricky about his stepfather. "This man right here," said Ricky, pointing to a picture of the man, "God rest his soul, he put a little bit of know-how into me. He raised me. What little bit of morals I got, I got from him. But they good ones. He was my mother's husband, but he wasn't my father. He was a wife beater."

He said it just like that, one thought leading seamlessly into another. The result was that it hit me from out of nowhere, a left hook I never saw coming. *He taught you morals, but he was a wife beater?*

"Yeah," said Ricky. "That man right there. So I didn't have no guidance as far as a man was concerned, 'cause he was in and out of jail. If he wasn't beatin' on my mother, my mother was trying to get away from him. So we didn't have no man in our life."

How did you feel about him?

"I forgave him for the things he did to my mother, to me and my sisters and brothers. As far as I'm concerned, he was forgiven when he left our household. Just so long as you stay away from my mother."

My skepticism must have shown on my face. "I ain't had no hatred toward that man," insisted Ricky. "He was good, far as I was concerned. I'll tell you what: Ain't a thing a woman can outdo me in, but sewing. She can't out-cook me, she can't out-clean me, she can't outdo nothing. I learned it all from that man. I give all the props to him."

I still couldn't quite buy it. Had the feeling I wasn't hearing the whole truth. Or that Ricky couldn't bring himself to speak it. I understand you've forgiven him, I said carefully, but when it was happening, when you were just a boy, what was going through your head?

Ricky cut me a sidelong glance. "You really want me to say it?" he asked.

I nodded.

"Kick his ass," he said. "Even though I'm just too small to do something. That's all I wanted to do: fuck him up."

Never forget.

Indeed, virtually every man I spoke with whose father or stepfather had beaten his mother had memories that ran along the same line. And most could recall with clarity the moment their father's rage pushed them beyond endurance, pushed them into making a stand.

Me, I was fifteen. It was the same night he pulled the shotgun on us for the second and last time. The sequence is fuzzy in my head, but I remember leaping on my father's back as he brandished a knife against my mother. Kept hitting him with my fist on the side of his head. Almost broke my hand. Didn't care. I had made my decision: It stopped right here.

I didn't know it then, but I wasn't the only one making such a vow or taking physical action to enforce it.

* * *

My neighbor, Mike, grew up with an abusive stepfather. For the first years of his life, Mike had no idea the man wasn't his biological father. Or that his brothers were actually his half brothers. Even now, he doesn't draw the distinction when he talks about them. Chris and Warren are "my brothers." The stepfather is "my dad."

Mike with two of his children, Jarrett and Jessica

"He was a really interesting man," Mike told me one afternoon as we sat in the den of his split-level home in the Maryland suburbs of Washington. "He was a provider. He worked at Bethlehem Steel in Baltimore. I used to idolize him when I was real little because I thought he was a hard worker.

"But he had a real dark side. He would drink a lot of alcohol. And he would abuse my mom. Fight her, beat her up." Nor did he limit his abuse to his wife. Mike remembers sneaking out of the house one night, only to be caught by his stepfather, who whipped him with an extension cord. Left welts all over his body.

"He would stop off and drink," said Mike, "come home and be real belligerent, throw food all over the house, curse everybody out, wake everybody up in the middle of the night. One time he came home and locked my mom in the room and went to sleep. Took the key.

"I remember my mom crying. She called me Tony, my nickname. 'Tony, find the key, find the key. I've got to get out.' I was real little then. I must've been nine or ten. I remember my mom crying on the other side of the door and I'm searching all over the house trying to find the key."

Mike said his two brothers never bore the brunt of his father's mistreatment. "Being that I never knew I wasn't his biological son, I really didn't know why he was so abusive to me and not so much to my brothers," he said.

"Anytime I would do anything, he smacked me around. He would buy my brothers mini-bikes and I'd get a two-wheel bike I got handed down. I'm thinking, 'Why is this guy dogging me like this?' My brothers are riding around on Kawasakis and I'm riding around on a two-wheeler.

"My mom is trying the best she can to maintain equality between my brothers and me. But that made me strong. I never ran back saying, 'Chris and Warren have this and I don't have that.' I just worked. I raked leaves, I washed cars—you name it, I would do it just to have money. It was like a passion to be able to go out and get whatever I wanted and not have to get hand-me-downs from my brothers."

Mike told me that as he grew older, his father was "gone all the time," either working his shift at the steel mill, driving his taxicab on the side or drinking. Just gone. "I was almost like a father to my brothers," said Mike, "because I was watching over them while [Mom] was working a part-time job and then, [my mother] was also going to Morgan State University working on her advanced degree. I had to cook for my brothers, I had to wash for my brothers. This guy's never home."

Finally, said Mike, there came a night when he was seventeen that his father gave him an ultimatum: Pay two hundred dollars a month in rent or find another place to live. Mike moved out, taking a room in a basement not too far away.

"Before I left the house, I told my brothers, 'Don't let Dad beat on Mom. I can't be here to protect you now. Don't let him hurt her.'"

The admonition soon proved prophetic.

"It was a hot summer night," said Mike. "Must have been 1974. I remember the basement was so hot, you could barely even breathe down there. The phone rings and it's like one o'clock in the morning and it's my brother Chris. 'We did what you said. Dad came in, started beating on Mom, so we beat him up.'

"'*What!?*'

"'Yeah, we beat him up. Me and Warren, we beat him up.'

"'Where are you?'"

Mike's brothers had taken refuge in the home of a nearby friend. He told them he was on his way. But before he went to get his brothers, he stopped at his father's house. Found his mother in the kitchen. At the sight of him, she screamed for her son to get away, get away, because his father was raging out of control. But before Mike could leave, his father was there.

"His mouth is bloody. They really did him good," recalled Mike with a mirthless laugh. "I was real proud of them, you know? And he says, 'Your brothers done beat me up. I guess you want to do the same.' I looked at him, I said, 'No, it looks like they did a pretty good job to me.'"

Seeing that his mother seemed to be okay and still screaming for him to leave, Mike turned and walked to his car. His father followed him. "I was very afraid of him because of all the abuse. I had a friend of mine who had given me a little .22—probably would have blown up in my face. He comes to my car and he's beating on my window. 'Get the hell out! I want to talk to you!' So I reach up under the seat and I get my gun. He never notices.

"He beats on my car again, I get out of the car. [He says,] 'You're an asshole and you're a son of a bitch, and I never liked you. I should kick your ass right now!'

"I took my gun out and I put it right to his face and I said, 'I'll blow your fuckin' brains out right now. I swear to God, I'll blow your fuckin' brains out.' And that's the first time that I ever stood up to him, man to man. I'm thinking, 'I don't live with you anymore, you're abusing my mom, you come out here threatening me. Well, this is your shot. This is it.'"

The someday he had promised himself for years had finally arrived.

Mike said his stepfather backed down screaming, "This ain't over. I got a gun too! This ain't over!'"

But it was. Mike's stepfather went to jail the next morning. "About a week after that, my mom was talking to me, she was at her wit's end, she couldn't stay in the house. I ended up helping her move out on her own, getting separated and divorced."

I asked Mike what his relationship with his father is like these days. He said, "Nonexistent, pretty much. I've seen him maybe once in three years. He doesn't call me, I don't call him. But he calls my other brothers all the time. Does it bother me? No. He really wasn't ever there for me. If he gets sick or something, I'll go make a courtesy call or something but other than that, it doesn't really bother me. No matter what, I still remember all the pain. He's never, ever said two things: (a) I'm sorry, or (b) I love you.

"If he ever came to me and said, 'I'm really sorry for the way it was,' that might make it better, but until that happens, I don't care."

* * *

I met a minister in Los Angeles, a man named Charles, who came to a similar breaking point with his own father. Charles and I talked in his large, tastefully appointed office. His father, he told me, was a "functional alcoholic"—able to reign in his drinking enough to hold a job, even though the paycheck often went to buy more booze.

"A very angry man," said the son quietly. "I think it had a lot to do with being gifted, but not necessarily having the opportunities. As well as not being ambitious."

Because of that, "I think there was this frustration and resentment that was just continuous. I think he acted that out toward us by just being angry all the time, extremely mean, verbally abusive, sometimes physically abusive. We grew up with the threat of what he might do from week to week."

Some nights, Charles's father would come home and engage in a sadistic ritual. "He'd be going through the silverware in the kitchen. We all knew he was about to get a knife and come upstairs and then he'd say, 'I'm going to kill your mother' or something like that. And he'd stand over my mother with this knife. Just out of the blue. Just randomly. Nothing triggered it. It wasn't where she did something that made him angry. It was just something that he did.

"We got to a place where my sisters and myself, we were used to it and we wouldn't even move. And my mother would tell us, 'He's not going to hurt me, so just go to sleep. He's just bluffing.' He never used any of those weapons, but the threat of that was always there."

I asked Charles to describe how he'd felt about his father. There was no equivocating. "I hated him," he said. "Up until [I was] a teenager, I hated him. When I was a young kid, I was like the mediator. I would try to negotiate with him sometimes for him to change his behavior. Or I would do things to try to divert his attention."

He hated him and yet. . . . "I loved him, I cared for him as a kid. And I was saddened by how he would behave and that would make me feel really bad, but I didn't want anything bad to happen to him."

There were times, said Charles, when he was able to catch glimpses of another father—a gentler, milder man.

"Once in a blue moon, he would take us someplace. He took us to baseball games. Sometimes in the house, we would box and we used to enjoy that. We could hit him as hard as we wanted to. He was an excellent boxer and everybody in my family knows how to box—all my sisters, my brother.

"The times where I really felt affirmation from him would be when I had been in a fight in the neighborhood and I whipped somebody and then I would go home and tell him. His words would be, 'Did you kick their ass?' And I would say, 'Yeah.' And we would slap five and we'd laugh and that was just like where we really bonded." The memory of it made Charles smile.

I asked him if fighting had been his only source of affirmation.

"No," said Charles. "Christmastime. My father was real big on holidays. Buy a lot of toys and gifts and put those things together and just be real excited about our response. And if you were sick, he was compassionate. Depending on who would come to our house to visit, sometimes he would be extremely nice to everybody. But we kind of felt like that was a show."

It was, said Charles, vital to all concerned to maintain the fiction of the happy home. "We had that thing that black folks have, that our business is our business and you don't talk about your business in the street."

So instead of talking or acting, the oldest son just took it, just absorbed his father's abuse, stacking each violent act inside himself one by one, until there was no more room. There came a final night, said Charles, when his father walked in and hit his mother. "It almost doesn't qualify as a hit. It was more like a gentle push."

But it was one push too many. "I jumped out of my bed and grabbed him and was about to throw him down twenty stairs. My mother was screaming for me to put him down and I just body-slammed him to the floor. I told him, 'If you *ever* put your hands on my mother again, I will not throw you down those steps.' I said, 'You see that back window? I'll throw you out that back window.'

"It never happened again," said Charles. "He never did that again. And even some of the verbal abuse slowed down significantly. Or at least, he wouldn't do it around me.

"I was at a place where I wasn't going to have any more of that. It was like, that's the end of that. That's the last one. And that's what I meant. If I saw anything that even resembled that, then I would engage in an argument where I'd initiate it. And I'd make sure that *he* backed down. So that it transitioned from him being this bully to me being this person who would not be bullied."

Charles's father died a few years later.

I asked the minister if he thought his father ever understood the pain he'd brought his son. Charles said, "No. There were a few times when he said he was sorry to my mother for stuff. But I don't think he made those types of connections."

* * *

So often, the fathers don't seem to understand the pain they bring. But the sons never forget. They pack these things up and carry them into adulthood and into families of their own. The violence they saw and felt as children becomes the mortarboard and brick of their own identities as fathers.

They tell themselves they've grown beyond it, overcome it, controlled it, so that what they went through no longer affects them, will never touch their lives again. They think they can get away.

They are mistaken. I know this for a personal fact.

We once had in our neighborhood a young couple whose marriage was dying loudly, publicly, and physically. Nasty brawls that spilled out of the house, drew the police, and shattered the tranquillity of the night. The carnage of their relationship became the stuff of neighborhood gossip, usually prefaced with a perfunctory lament for their lost privacy and our lost peace.

Mostly, people just wanted it to stop, wanted the husband and wife to either end the unseemly displays or else just take them out of the neighborhood. Me, I wanted one thing more. I wanted to protect her. Understand: I hardly knew either of them, hadn't a clue as to the issues in their conflict, but nevertheless, the urge to defend her was strong. I'd get up in the middle of the night for a glass of water and glance out the window just to make sure everything was okay over there.

"If she needs a place to stay," I told my wife, "tell her she can stay here. Any help we can give her, let's give it." My wife had heard me say it before, has heard me say it since; it's my standard response any time a woman we know is facing physical abuse in a marriage. "We have plenty of space," I'll say. "We can put the boys together in one room. Or we can clear out the playroom and put a bed in there. Tell her she can come here."

I call it my damsel-in-distress reflex. It's no mystery, of course, where this urge to rescue stems from. I grew up wanting to protect and being, for the most part, unable to do it. So now, every woman in trouble is my mother. There's something sad about it, I think. Even something a little pathetic.

But I can't help it—I cannot *stand* men who beat women. Granted, most people would find it difficult to admire such a person, but I'm talking about something deeper, a visceral loathing.

It is, perhaps, the one sin I know I would never be able to forgive myself. Nor would I ask my wife to forgive me.

Never hit a woman. *Never.*

I had no idea when I said it how common a vow that is among the sons of violence. Nor how commonly broken.

* * *

Andrew, who lives in Los Angeles, grew up hating the violence of his abusive stepfather. "There was this one time I was playing on the porch," he said. "My mom had left and it was just him and me in the house. And he

Andrew

said he told me to come inside—I didn't hear him. So he came and grabbed me . . . threw me into the house. I mean, *literally* through the kitchen and into the dining room. Didn't touch the ground. Missed the entire room, actually. Then he proceeded to whip me for being disobedient. I didn't even know what was going on."

Andrew said his stepfather was also violent toward his mother. And as much as he hated it, "to some extent, it seemed normal. That's kind of what husbands did then. When wives and kids step out of line, they'd get beat up. Or yelled at or whatever. It made me very uncomfortable. But it was also kind of accepted . . . like getting a whipping."

Andrew left home at twenty-one and was married about two months later. "Needless to say, it didn't work very well. I knew how it was supposed to be, I just didn't know how to make it happen."

He was married for a little more than a year. He and his wife were actually together for about six months.

Those months were marked by Andrew's violence against his bride. "My father-in-law told me: 'If she gets out of line, kick her butt.' And my mother-in-law told me that, [too]. My mother-in-law told me, 'She's got an attitude and from time to time, you're gonna have to put a foot in her butt. So do what you've got to do. She's gonna get a stiff neck on you, get up in your face and all like that, and you're going to have to put her in her place.'

"I thought it was excellent advice."

He still remembers the first time. His wife had stayed out all night, arriving home just before dawn. He was worried before she got there, angry when she finally did. "I'm like, 'Where have you been?' She's telling me, 'It's none of your business.'

"My concern was that she was having an affair. The reality of the situation was that she had seen me with a lady at work—we worked at the same place—and she didn't like it. Nothing going on, we were just talking. But anyway, she saw us together and she and a friend of hers went to a football game and then she just stayed at her friend's house to piss me off.

"So anyway, she cursed at me. She called me a motherfucker. And I just . . . *pow!* Popped her one. I didn't even know. I just blinked and it was done already. After that, I had to leave. I left, packed all my stuff up and came to Mom's house. We talked it all out and got back together again. And I went back. From that point on, she just didn't trust me in anything. She knew I was going to do it again."

And he did.

"Basically, the same thing happened again. She got to calling me out of my name and all that kind of stuff and I hit her again. This time, though, she hit me back. The first time, she was shocked. I was shocked myself. The second time, there wasn't a blink there. There was intent. I meant to pop her."

Andrew said he bears "full responsibility" for the fact that his marriage ended shortly thereafter. Talking with a counselor might have saved the relationship, he knows, but that's not what he had learned from his stepfather or even his father-in-law. Instead, they had taught him to impose his will on a woman physically. "That's what I understood: If she gets out of line, kick her butt. Needless to say, I know better than that now."

Like Andrew, Lawrence in Washington, D.C., grew up in a home where violence against Mother was common. As a child, he made himself a promise to avoid the sins of his abusive father. As a man, he broke that promise on numerous occasions.

Lawrence has been married three times, twice to the same woman. They parted company for the first time when his oldest daughter was three. By his own description, he'd been a party man, running the streets and spending time with everyone except his family. He wasn't there for her, he said, so one night when he came home from work, she wasn't there for him. The apartment was empty. She had packed up and disappeared.

"I believe that she, as well as her family members, feared that because I had a gun, if she wanted to leave me, I would just go berserk."

Four miserable years later, Lawrence finally found his child and her mother, living in south Florida. "I went to her very apologetically, 'Baby, I'm sorry. It won't happen again, let's get back together.' We got married. Three months later, she was two months pregnant. Called to have the police take me out the house, because I was fighting with her."

He didn't return to that apartment until three weeks after his second daughter was born. His frightened wife wouldn't let him in. He said he wanted to see his baby, so she held the newborn up to the window. That was the first and only time he would see his daughter for ten years. "She was just out there."

Eventually, Lawrence decided to try marriage again, this time to a Cleveland woman who had a child of her own, a daughter. Lawrence's new wife became pregnant. He made a concerted effort to do better this time. "I was there," he said, "for all the prenatal appointments, except for two when I was out of town. When [the baby] was about four months old, I would take her to work with me."

He was working on his promise, willing himself to be a good father. But eventually and, perhaps, inevitably, the propensity toward violence caught up with Lawrence again. He stood up to demonstrate.

"She's about five foot four," he said of his second wife. As he spoke, he made his left hand a claw and held it, arm fully extended against a wall, pinning an imaginary woman there. Then he cocked his right fist. "I would pick her up by her neck and I would hold her against the wall like this and beat up on her," he said.

"One day I had her like this, and I drew my fist back. And her daughter screamed out. 'Daddy, Daddy! Please don't!' And that's the only thing that kept me from hitting her. I just opened my hand and dropped her. And I think about two hours later, [I] forced myself on her sexually. That's the kind of person I would be; I would be violent and then want to become sexually involved."

Lawrence told me his last physical episode with that woman was in October 1990. After that, he sought counseling.

Cleveland, a man who lives in San Diego, traveled a similar route to the same destination. When I met him, he was three months out of jail after serving a six-month sentence for wife beating. Counseling, he said, has helped him control the tendency to hit his wife.

"My stepfather was very abusive," he said. "He would beat me up with his fists. He used to wake me up in the middle of the night, about three in the morning, telling me I didn't break the wood. 'Get out there and break the wood!' It would be raining, I'd be in the backyard breaking wood.

"He pulled a gun out on me and my sister. I was maybe seventeen at the time and we got into it and I fought back. And when I fought back, it was a shock to him. I always covered up and cried or balled up like a knot or whatever. But this time I fought back and then my sister jumped in and hit him in the head with a lamp. Then we ran.

Cleveland

"We was outside crying, wanting to come back in the house. He was in the window with a .22 rifle. He just pointed it at us, talking about, 'Don't come in my yard!' That's when [my mother] sent me to Mississippi. I went to Mississippi for about a summer."

It was, said Cleveland unnecessarily, a "rough" upbringing. Became rougher when he fathered a child at sixteen by a girl two years younger. "It really wasn't a relationship," he said. "It was a young thing. Young love. I wasn't looking at the consequences down the road."

Not long after the baby was born, those consequences became plain. The girl's mother kicked her out of the house. Cleveland woke up one rainy morning to find his girlfriend and their baby huddled in his garage.

"She stayed with me about a year. Then we moved to her father's house, 'cause her mother and father separated. We were living there. But I was gang-banging, I wasn't really being a father to my child, a good man to her. I was beating her up."

In her father's house?

Cleveland nodded. "In her father's house, yes. He pulled a knife out on me, threatened to kill me. I was like, 'Don't get in this relationship. You gon' get yourself hurt, old man.'"

Not surprisingly, the day soon came when his girlfriend had taken enough. "She said she don't want to be in a relationship no more. That's when I went downhill. I mean, that's the worst pain of my life I ever felt. Honest. Right there, when she told me that, that's when I knew I loved her. That pain would not go away for a long, long time."

Cleveland's mother had separated from his stepfather, so he went home to live with her. She kept trying to console him, to tell him things would be okay. "I didn't want to hear that," he told me. "I just started going out and drinking, I started smoking that dope. I just went straight downhill. I couldn't get myself back on my feet.

"It got as far as me really almost killing myself," he said. "It got that bad, where I just didn't care about life, period. I thought that was it. It was over with. I kept trying to ask my ex-girl, say, 'Hey, we can work it out. I know I can do better.' She was like, 'No.' She had another man and she wanted to get on her own."

Cleveland lived on the street for about eight months. Went to prison after that on a parole violation. Left prison and went to a drug rehab center. After rehab, he met a new woman, fell in love and married her a few months later.

He had it then, his chance to walk away into the sunset with a happy ending. Instead, Cleveland began beating his *new* wife. It defies common sense, of course. Beating his girlfriend is what ended the first relationship and tore his heart out. So what would make him do the same thing to his wife?

Cleveland said, "It's got to come either from me being abused or. . . ." His voice trailed into silence. Then he said simply, "That's why I'm trying to find out what's going on with my family, my background. I found out my grandfather was abusive to my grandmother. I have to find out where it's actually coming from so I can try to change it."

* * *

It is not too much to suggest that one man's propensity toward a violent marriage might come from the same place as another man's propensity toward a peaceful one. Comes, in other words, from the behavior we see as children and our reactions to it. You only have two choices, after all: To reflect the things you saw or reject them.

So Lawrence in Washington swore he wouldn't be the sort of man his father was, then went out and became exactly that. I swore I wouldn't be the sort of man *my* father was and became instead a would-be rescuer of women I don't even know.

Reflection and rejection. Dissimilar results from the same impulse. The one thing both have in common is that both are extreme. The one an extreme of violence, of course. But the other an extreme that seeks the salvation of total strangers, an extreme that says to a woman, if I ever so much as lay a hand on you, I will have ruined myself for all time, become a person undeserving of understanding and beyond the reach of redemption.

And if the second extreme has the benefit of keeping peace and safeguarding quiet in a family, it is, nevertheless, an extreme. Born out of the too many nights my father visited violence upon his home.

"We all have our own issues, our own baggage from our past," said the psychologist Cones. "We can react to that where we're aggressive or zealots about a certain issue, or we might repeat the wrongs that were done to us. Whatever it is, it's *our* agenda and can be harmful to the child we're trying to raise."

Often, said Cones, we do what we do as parents in an effort to heal our own wounds without taking into account the unique needs of the child we're supposedly trying to raise. "People often overcompensate for their own wounds," said Cones.

We forget that in the things we do—and don't do—we mark our children. Mark them in their attitudes and behaviors. Shape who they become. The force of it can be as irresistible as gravity itself, though the result is often unpredictable.

Rejection, reflection.

Of course, it is probably never easy between fathers and sons. Maybe it is not supposed to be. The son reaches an age where he has hair in places he never did, feels stronger than he ever was, and begins craving a chance to test his mettle against the father, craving a chance to one day beat him. There's something primal about it: The old lion challenged by the young one and displaced.

Difficult as that passage is, it becomes more so when the relationship is marked by violence. More painful when the son carries into that crucible the weight of promises made to "somedays."

But if the cycle of violence can be broken, then you discover something different about that passage. Something hard but ennobling, painful but proud. Something that links you in a brotherhood of commiseration and legacy with every father who ever saw himself bested by a son.

I remember one afternoon when my son Marlon was angry at me and eager for revenge after some punishment I had given him or some plan I had spoiled. So he asked if I was up to a game of basketball in the driveway. Foolishly I agreed, thinking he had in mind little more than a pleasant few minutes of exercise. But there was nothing pleasant about it. My son's face was taut with concentration. He played me like it was the last minute with a tie score in game seven of the NBA Finals, slapping the ball disdainfully from my hands and going hard to the hole like Michael or Magic on a mission. The kid had dropped in a series of twisting layups and pinpoint jump shots and was on the way to a shutout before I realized what was going on. This was no game. This was a challenge, the young lion going after the old.

I rallied myself, and we played a game for the ages that afternoon. Impatience, speed, and youth versus size, strength, and age. Youth almost carried the day. *Almost.* In the end, though, my last layup bounced through the net and gave me a narrow victory. Bragging rights. Didn't last too long. There came a day, not too long after, when I could no longer handle him on the court.

He taunts me now, trying to get me back out there, and I just wave him on. It's his court now.

So it goes for this rite of passage between fathers and sons, this moment when the son stands before the father, looks him in the eye, and demands to be acknowledged as a man in his own right. I had my moment while clinging to my father's back, hitting him and screaming words I no longer remember. Mike had his while pressing a gun into his father's face, Charles had his while preparing to slam his father down twenty stairs.

And my son found his while lofting long jump shots over my outstretched hands.

The young lion roars. The difference here is that, afterward, he laughs. Through wounded pride, I laugh with him.

It strikes me that this is as it is supposed to be.

FIVE

Consider two songs, both written by the same composers and performed by the same group, the Temptations.

In "Papa Was a Rolling Stone," the hit from 1972, five boys who've never known their father gather around their mother and beg her for information about him, any scrap of knowledge upon which they can base some sense of identity. "I never got a chance to see him," complains one. "Never heard nothin' but bad things about him." But she replies to their questions the same way each time: "Papa was a rolling stone, wherever he laid his hat was his home."

The lesser-known second song, recorded a few years earlier, describes much the same situation. In fact, it is perhaps not too much of a stretch to suggest that the protagonist of "Wherever I Lay My Hat" could be "Papa" himself, a happy-go-lucky rogue forever on the move. In the song, he is heard warning a woman not to expect commitment from him. He tells her forthrightly that he's a heartbreaker who's up to no good. "I'm the type of guy who is always on the road. Wherever I lay my hat, that's my home."

Two songs. Two starkly different images. And if composers could be accused of sending contradictory messages, well, it might also be argued that they are simply summing up the psyche of black America on the subject of its missing men. When it comes to the absence of black fathers, there is a yin and yang, counterbalancing self-images. On the one side, roosters on the strut, players at play. On the other, children left stranded without father's guiding hand.

It has become so commonplace as to be unremarkable, this phenomenon of children and mother on their own and Dad as an infrequent drop-in visitor. We tell ourselves it makes no difference; if you ask a man who was raised without his father about it, he will, likely as not, launch into a song of praise for his mother, lauding the way she took on the roles and responsibilities of both parents—the implication being that while having a father around would have been nice, there's nothing essential about it. Nothing the child missed that still haunts the man.

There is almost a defensive toughness to the assertion, a defiant tone that seems aimed directly at the missing man. A way of telling him that there is nothing he could have contributed that the family couldn't get along just fine without. A way of saying that they didn't need him anyway.

But you don't have to scrape too deep to discover another level of feeling, a layer where hurt pools together and the unanswered—sometimes, unspoken—question is always the same: Why? Why wasn't he there? Why did he leave us behind? To hear that question or simply to see it reflected in the eyes of an adult man in whom the absence has left empty spaces is to lose patience with the tacit cultural sanction of players at play.

Families headed by single mothers are more apt to live in poverty, and the sons of such families more likely to wind up in trouble, on the run, behind bars. So it seems past time to quit pretending that fathers are expendable in the lives of families. Talk to men whose fathers were not there, and one thing becomes plain. Players may play, but this is not a game.

* * *

Randy was eight years old, standing on the train platform at Forty-second Street in New York City with his grandmother. They were waiting for the train to Yonkers, last leg of the journey back from a vacation in his native South Carolina. He was, as he puts it in retrospect, "high" from this trip because he'd been able to spend time with his father, whom he hadn't seen in a long time. The man had taken him around, treated Randy and his sister well, gave them two dollars apiece as they boarded the train back to New York.

So Randy was completely unprepared for what his grandmother told him as they stood there waiting. His father, she said, had asked her to deliver a message: He wasn't really their father. They weren't really his children. He was a dark-skinned man and they were much too light. Their mother must have had another man.

"When she told me that, it shot me to pieces," said a grown Randy ruefully. He was nursing a cup of coffee, sitting at a conference table in a small office in Yonkers.

Were you his biological son? I asked.

"Yes. My mother wouldn't lie to me about that," said Randy emphatically. "And see, I felt it in my heart. When I went by my heart, my heart never led me wrong."

And yet . . .

For all the assurance he felt, he wrestled from that moment forward with a burrowing doubt, a wisp of a "what if" that nagged him for the next nine years. Nagged him until, at seventeen, he returned to the South for an uncle's funeral. There, he was spotted by some of his father's other sons. Randy said they recognized him because he had grown into the mirror image of their father. The brothers wanted to take Randy to see him.

"I didn't want to go with them at first; I resisted. So they threw me in the back of the car and brought me to see him. He looked me over, then he realized that I was his son. But by that time, I was too hurt. '*Now* you want to say that you're my father? What could you do for me now? When I was eight, that could've carried me over till I was seventeen. Because then, I still knew where I came from.'"

The day his father disclaimed him, it became impossible to know that for sure. His aunt had pointed out another man to him, said that might be his true father. But at the same time, his heart and his mother were both pointing to the man he'd thought of as father for the first eight years of his life.

He didn't know. Just didn't know.

"There's an old saying," said Randy, "'Mother's baby, papa's maybe.' A whole lot of African-American men seem to think that way."

I know the expression well. I heard it often from my father's lips, this folk rhyme whereby black men simultaneously acknowledge and protect themselves against the humiliation of being a cuckold. Few things strike more devastatingly at masculine pride, after all, than the notion that the child you thought was yours, the one you raised as a product of your loins and lineage, was actually some other man's baby all along.

Randy said his father rejected him after hearing rumors that his mother was "out there fooling around. If you're out there and you hear rumors, [and] instead of finding out for yourself, you're going to take the rumors [on faith], then that's just stupidity," said Randy contemptuously. "You should find out from the mate you've been dealing with.

"My father must have felt guilty," he added, "because at that same time when he said I wasn't his, he was out there cheating. My half brother is only eleven days younger than I am."

* * *

Clyde, who also lives in Yonkers, was very young when his father left the home. He still remembers the impact it had on him. "Look like the person I had looked up to [for] leadership in my household was gone. My mom was with somebody else; to me, it wasn't the same. There was a man in the house, but it wasn't my father. That bond wasn't there. I can't even put words to it.

"When you've got a father in the house," explained Clyde, "it's like somebody that can tell you things wouldn't no other man tell you. Like, how to react around girls, or how to really be a man. See, I feel like I missed all that. I didn't have nobody to tell me how to be me. I feel my father knew more about how to be *me* because I was a part of him."

Clyde's apartment was in a grim and institutional housing project not far from the Hudson River where he lived with his wife and his youngest children. He moved gingerly about the place, hobbled by rheumatoid arthritis in the knees. On one wall hung a collage of family photos just above a rack of vintage R&B albums and an older computer. On another wall, someone had affixed homemade signs with inspirational aphorisms:

- "Obstacles are what you see once you take your eyes off your goal."
- "One can learn more from life's trials than from life's triumphs."
- "Adversity causes some people to break down and other people to break through."

Clyde told me he wants his children to have things he never did.

He was, he said, about six when his father went to prison for peddling drugs. "Damn near anything illegal, my Pop was involved in at one time or another."

For the son, it was the beginning of a downward spiral. His grades fell. By the time he was twelve, he was dealing drugs himself. By the time he was sixteen, he was a father; the girl was two years younger. And by the time Clyde was seventeen, he was in prison like his father—actually, in prison *with* his father—for dealing drugs.

Clyde wouldn't even have known his father was there, except that prison officials got the two namesakes' mail mixed up. After discovering their error, they allowed father and son "a few minutes" together to talk.

It's a conversation painful to imagine. Even the most disconnected of fathers wants his son's life to be an improvement upon his own. What must it be like, then, to be sitting in jail for drug trafficking and have your long-lost son come before you, having come to the same sorry place for doing the same sorry thing?

"The only thing he said to me [was], 'Son, you're in the wrong place. This ain't the place I want my child to be in. I hope this is your last trip here. *Please* make this your last trip.'"

But part of the reason you were there, I said, was because of him.

"I was there for the mistakes *I* made," countered Clyde.

But he wasn't there to stop you from making those mistakes, I persisted.

Clyde conceded the point. "You're right," he said. "But the only thing I could say to him was, 'Hey, when I get out of this, I'm going to straighten my act up. I won't be coming back through this. This is it for me.'"

It wasn't, though. Clyde did two subsequent stretches in prison, one for drugs and another for armed robbery. He spent seven years in all behind bars, the most recent sentence ending in 1988.

In the meantime, his children—ultimately, he had eight—were coming of age largely without him.

"I was in and out of the house," he said. "I was always coming to visit them. I'd visit them at least once a month. They'd hear from me. I would always try to give them stuff, stay in contact with them."

After his last stint behind bars, Clyde decided he'd had enough of hustling. "You get tired," he said. "That's where I'm at now. It's just like a revolving door. You get tired of doing the same old thing. You know the outcome."

I asked him if he resented the fact that his father was never there.

"I don't hold no anger against all that. If I ever got the opportunity to see him today, I would ask him some questions about how could I correct some of these mistakes with mine. How could I change the way with mine, so we don't have to repeat some of these same things I went through."

Of course, Clyde doesn't know for sure where his father is or even if he's still alive.

"I couldn't exactly tell you. It's been some years. If he was alive, he'd be in his late sixties. Last time I heard, he was back in jail."

* * *

Robert, who lives in Atlanta, is another man who lost his father to the prison system. He was left with an anger he has yet to resolve.

Robert was three when "Josh," as he calls him, went away. It was fifteen years later—Robert was eighteen and on his way to a military induction center—when he saw his father again. They ran into each other on the street. "He was going to try and give me some fatherly advice," said Robert, his voice dripping scorn. "*Then*. At *that* time."

Robert's mother was a domestic and he, his sister, and brother were raised in a housing project. It was a nice place to live at the time. "The idea of what projects are today and what projects were then was totally different."

One thing, however, was the same. "I would say in our projects . . . there was ten families. Out of that ten families, only two husbands and wives."

I asked Robert about his relationship with his own father. "It's really difficult," he said, "because there is no father-and-son relationship. It's just a relationship. I can't even call him Daddy. I really can't. Because I don't feel no 'daddy' for him. None. He's my father, and I acknowledge that. But I just feel nothing for him."

It must be very difficult, I said.

"It really is, man. I look at my brother-in-law; he's got three boys and I look at how they relate to him and how I relate to my father, and it's totally

Robert

different. Night and day. And my father, he's up in his seventies now and he's had major operations and everything." He gave me a direct look. "Were you raised with your father?" he asked.

Well, yes, I said, but he was drinking and abusive.

"Yeah," said Robert, "but he was there, though, right? And if he got sick and had a major operation, you would be there. See, *I* wouldn't be there. I ain't never been there with my dad. I had went to see him in the hospital, but that was just . . . well, he's my dad and I better go and see him.

"One night, I got mad and I told him just how I felt. And he tried to put the blame on my Mama, talkin' about she wasn't this and she wasn't that, and that's why he was this and he was that. And that's kind of hard to hear. It really is. Mama was *there*."

Robert said he and his own son get along very well. But, he added, he's still "learning every day" how to be a father. Robert Jr., he said, knows his grandfather and loves him, but doesn't get along with him. "My father [got] married and [the lady] had three sons and her sons had kids. And my father took more to those kids than to *me*," complained Robert.

He heard what he'd said then and quickly corrected the slip. "I'm not going to say 'me'," he said, "'cause *I'm* grown now . . . but to his own grandson."

Why, I asked, do you think your father didn't maintain contact with you when you were a child?

"I don't know. You can write letters from jail; I didn't receive no letters or anything. Nothing."

Robert saw his father exactly twice in the fifteen years the older man was in prison. "When I was about ten years old and he was in jail in Alabama, he escaped and came to Georgia and came to our house. And when he busted in the house, the police was right there and took him back out. I saw him then. And then his mother died and he was able to come to the funeral."

Other than that, the only father Robert knew was a figure in a uniform in a picture on a shelf at his grandmother's house. "I used to look at that picture and see how much him and I looked alike. There were little underlying feelings that I really wanted to see him, and get to know him. They were there."

Robert had thought he might be able to resolve those feelings, to get to know his father when the older man finally got out of jail and they met as adults. It didn't happen.

"I'd say for about three weeks after he got out of jail and I was at home, we ran together. But when we ran together, it was going to a bar, having a drink, smoking cigarettes, doing some dope and stuff like that. And it hit me: This is not the way a father is supposed to act with his son. He was trying to out-party me."

* * *

Curtis is my stepson's natural father. He also has three other sons and a daughter. I met him at his home in South Gate, a suburb of Los Angeles.

He is a big man, but there's a weight about Curtis that has nothing to do with his girth. You look at him and you get the sense of a man bent under the burden of his own life. His disappointments and doubts are borne like boulders balanced on his shoulders. There's a bruised expression in his eyes. He watches you through curling vines of gray cigarette smoke. Even his sighs are heavy.

Curtis had just finished making a pot of spaghetti for his two youngest boys, Victor and Christopher. It was a Sunday night and in a few minutes, he would have to return them to their mother's apartment. He and I sat at a dinette table to talk as the rambunctious boys sat in the kitchen and dug into the spaghetti. Every few minutes, he would admonish them in a stern

Curtis with Christopher (left) and Victor

voice to keep it down. We hadn't been talking very long when one of the boys piped up with a request for bread.

"Yeah, sure," said Curtis with weary resignation as he got up to attend his son.

When he returned to the table, I asked about his father.

"Don't remember my father at all," he said. "I can remember three or four of the locations we lived growing up, various things from school, this, that, and the other, but no recollection of him. I know he's in Omaha, Nebraska. It's not something I really pursue with my mother. I know that his running buddy, my cousin, he's [said] the reason they separated was that [my father] liked to play around, have a good time . . . wasn't all that responsible."

Curtis was taken to Omaha once when he was seven or eight years old to meet his father. The experience didn't impress him. "You're introduced to him. Here's this guy who's older, slightly bald and he kind of looks like you. Somebody tells you he's Dad and it's kind of like, 'Okay.'"

He didn't see his father again until he was about eighteen years old. Didn't give him much thought either, he said. "Father" was just a guy who was always behind on paying child support, always promising to send bicycles that never actually arrived. Sometimes, on birthdays and holidays, "Father" was a voice on the telephone. The conversations were awkward and seldom lasted more than a few minutes.

"You hear as a child, 'My mom and dad,'" said Curtis. "'Dad' is something I didn't relate to. Mom handled everything. Mom was the provider, Mom did the discipline, Mom handled the business. It was Mom. Dads were this thing that other people had.

"Our grandma—we called her Grandma Hun—my first recollection of her [is of an] evil, stout, stone-faced woman. Always with a frown, wrinkles in her head, dipped snuff, which I thought was the most disgusting thing I've ever seen in my life. She had this turkey leg bone, about a foot [long] easy. Wrapped in plain brown grocery bag paper with a white string crisscrossing it. And that was her 'act-right.' 'Don't let me have to pull out act-right.' This item will make you act right. She had no problem popping you one."

The discipline provided by a tough mother and a no-nonsense grandmother was enough to get Curtis through his teenage years in a rough neighborhood with a minimum of pain. Other boys were running with gangs or getting into trouble. Curtis was a good boy. No gangs, no trouble.

But no father, either. You wouldn't think that lack would nag at a man who, after all, escaped childhood without the scars that so many black men carry. But all these years later, he has an anger for his father that hangs in the air, as palpable as the smoke from his cigarettes.

"I've been telling Mom for years that if I ever see the man and I get close enough to him, I'm going to knock him on his ass."

His mother has tried on a number of occasions to get him to talk with his father. Even tried to trick him into doing it once. "She called me from downtown L.A. and told me her battery was dead. I'm [thinking], All the people she works with, all the employees going in and out of there, why she got to call *me* to come down there? 'Okay, fine. Be there in about a half hour.'

"Got to where she told me the car had stalled and she got out and then the passenger door opened. I didn't think nothing of it at first; I figured one of the employees just came out to sit with her. And there's my father. He came over and offered his hand, I shook it. And then Mom came over and said something about he'd be in town for a minute. . . . 'I didn't think you'd come down any other way, [and] I wanted you to see him.'

"I immediately copped my stance," said Curtis, "that one foot behind the other, and I dropped that right hand. She kind of sidestepped a little bit so she could look over his shoulder and she was shaking her head: don't do it, don't do it. And I'm like. . . ." He pantomimed the act of restraining his blow with great effort.

There have been times, he said, his mother has simply pleaded with him to forgive his father. Curtis can't. "See, *she* was there," he explained. "I'm putting everything on him; my mother could have been a complete and total bitch that just drove him completely out of his mind. I don't know. I don't know that she cooked to his liking, or she went through his money. [But] I know who was there, who was issuing out the discipline, who kept the lights and phones and gas on.

"He was supposed to be *around*," insisted Curtis, his voice sharp.

"I'm a Sparklett's Water man. I'm laboring and carrying everyday. I make fifty thousand dollars a year, but so what? Why isn't it that if he were here, I'm not in a three-piece suit in an office someplace signing a piece of paper everyday? It's not his fault, obviously, that I didn't go further with the education; I got the job three years out of high school. I got married immediately after high school to a girl I was with since seventh grade. I got a job over at Builder's Emporium, I got myself an apartment and I settled down to my family and just dealt with whatever came up within my limited income. One day, my water man said they were hiring.

"So I'm lucky that way. I'm sitting in *my* house, the vehicle outside is paid for, some other toys in the back, paid for."

There was a "but" hanging there unspoken. I voiced it tentatively.

But you feel that with your father's guidance, you could have done more, been more, had something you don't have?

"Absolutely, positively," said Curtis. "Even if it's just a better understanding of how to communicate and deal with my own."

One other thing he doesn't have—and longs for—is the American ideal of the nuclear family. Every time he reaches for that brass ring, he said, he comes up short. His relationship with the woman who is now my wife was a teenage affair that drew to a natural close. His first marriage turned shaky, he said, when his wife got into drugs. It ended when she was murdered. A second relationship, with a much younger woman, ended, he said, when she left him for another man, taking his youngest boys, Christopher and Victor, with her.

Curtis said he's tried to be scrupulous in his obligations toward his sons and their mother. "I see to it that she gets her money for these boys before I pay the house note. I've never once in three years been late. This is a responsibility I feel to them and that's instilled in me by my mother. Kids come first. They are the priority. They did not ask to be here, they did not put in an order to be born. *I* placed the order, *she* did the manufacturing, *we* became parents."

You're not really happy with the idea of being a weekend father, I said, are you?

"Oh, hell no," said Curtis, emphatically. "None of those kids were accidents. The condoms were tossed in the drawer. 'I want a son. By you, from you, with you.' . . . This was a commitment. This was permanent. I already had grown kids; I was willing to start all over with this woman to raise another family.

"Single life sucks. I don't care what nobody says. They can sit up there and talk about the independence of coming and going when they get ready to, coming in at two and three o'clock in the morning and nobody saying nothing to 'em, being able to go this club, that club, smile in this face, that face, and all the rest of this stuff. *No.*"

When you're married, he said, "You have somebody to come home to."

He nodded toward his boys who had finished dinner and were playing loudly. "Every time I think I need to quit, I need to bail out, I need to get a one-way bus ticket to Arizona or something like that, Mom is there in the back of my head. *They* are there. If I bail out, what's going to happen to them? They're going to become some [housing] project rejects, hair not combed, teeth all falling out, don't know how to speak: 'dis, dat, duh.' I just can't see abandoning them.

"And right now, I'm coming up short in my mind."

He's upset, he said, that their mother allows them to eat cold cereal for breakfast instead of fixing them something hot and, in his mind, more nourishing. It makes him unhappy that his boys' behavior is "semi-wild." As if to punctuate the point, one of the boys giggled just then. "This kind of background noise," he said grimly, "I find irritating. My standard response to them is, 'Hold it down. You're not outside, this is not a park. You're in the house.'"

So you have this ideal in your head you've not quite been able to reach in your life? I said.

He nodded. "I think that's why I resent shows like *Cosby* and the Bradys. It's so much bullshit. If it's a half hour show, the first fifteen minutes is screwing up and the last fifteen minutes is getting out of it, with the apologies and the revelations of mistakes they made. No. It's just not that way. It's all so phony. It's not life. The things that they have on *Cosby* and *The Waltons*, where everybody's just so interwoven and everybody's in touch with each other . . . my kids may come to me if they get a scratch and want me to take care of the boo-boo. They'll come to me, the provider, to fix them a meal, give them a snack. Maybe in a burst of silliness on my part, I'll get down and tickle 'em and tumble around for awhile, but I don't feel like it's a natural thing, me playing with my kid. I feel silly. But I know that he is enjoying the hell out of that."

It was something, he said, that he never experienced as a child. His mother worked the graveyard shift. She didn't have time for "silliness." So when he does it with his children, he said, "I feel like I'm going through the motions. I don't feel it inside to reach out and grab him, to give him that hug, to get down on the floor and scrape up my knees, roll around with him and tickle him and stuff. I'm expected to do that, so [I] put my feelings aside and get down there with him."

It was getting closer to the time Curtis would have to drive his boys back across town. He began to yell at them to get dressed. I could sense he dreaded what he was about to do.

"Their mother is not unfit," he explained. "She don't use drugs. But they are solely with her because she wants that damn check from the government. Welfare." He spat the word.

That has to make you mad, I said.

"You're damn right it makes me mad. I don't have to pick their brains. When they come to me Friday evening, I ask them, 'Have you guys eaten yet?' It'll be, 'No.' Well, when did you eat last? 'This morning.' And then some other things they say when they're talking to me . . . as far as they're concerned. . . ."

Curtis stopped. His eyes welled with tears and his voice frayed as he struggled to complete the thought. "As far as they're concerned . . . this is normal," he said bitterly. "Mom lives in one house, Daddy lives in another house. If that was the way you came up, you would think that's the way things are supposed to be. *I* pretty much felt the same way. I didn't know my father. Mom took care of everything and that was just it."

The anger rose in his voice then. "I don't see where today's fathers—thirty and younger—are ever going to get it together," he said, "because they don't have a clue from their childhood. Mom sat on her ass, waited for the check to come. When the check came, the party was on. Eightball, weed, cocaine, whatever they're doing now. Six-, seven-, eight-year-old kids outside till ten o'clock, come in when they get good and damn ready. Mom may have already passed out on the couch. If she's not sleep, she's watching the video [channel] or her and the latest uncle are in the back room some damn place. The kid comes in and is pretty much taking care of himself."

Out of all the things you missed from not having your father at home, I said, which one bothers you most?

"Can't really say," said Curtis, "because I didn't have it to miss it. If I could've had the interaction with the man, my father, I don't know, he might not have been a toss-the-ball-in-the-front-yard kind of guy. He might not have been a 'Let's-go-camping-and-jump-on-some-horses' kind of guy. I could be a mirror image of him, but I don't *know* that."

I asked him to imagine having a conversation about these things with his father. He couldn't.

"I don't have anything for the man. If I got a telegram saying he died . . . oh well. I'm not going to scrape up funds to buy a ticket to Omaha to go to his funeral. I doubt if I would feel anything but sad."

Do you hate him? I asked. Curtis's eyes met mine. For a moment, I thought he might weep again.

"When you asked that question," he said, tapping the center of his chest, "there was a quiver of nervousness right in here. It's like something just turned off. I can't answer that. I just have a . . . a *pressure* where he is concerned. Whether it's something that needs to be cut open so it can explode or something that needs to be buried a little deeper, I can't explain it. It's just a feeling. Leaning more toward hate than good."

* * *

There is no shortage of reasons.

This is what you discover when you ask some men why they spread semen like Johnny Appleseeds of sex, then turn up missing in action when the time comes to make a commitment and deal with the result. Indeed, you can find as many reasons for the failure as there are men to discuss it. Some blame mothers who won't let them see their offspring. Some point to financial concerns. Some attribute their failures to their own inadequacies.

The common denominator is that the fathers tend to see themselves as helpless victims of circumstances they couldn't control. Some habitually refer to their children as "mistakes" they made. And many make multiple "mistakes," apparently learning nothing from any of them.

Go looking for reasons and you find them. But you also find men who seem alarmingly reluctant to take ownership of their own lives.

None of the men will say these things, of course, and most would doubtless object vociferously to that judgment. But I met fathers who had to stop and count on their fingers before they could tell me how many children they had. Fathers who couldn't spell the names of their own sons or daughters. Fathers who didn't know how old or even where their children were.

When love and lust make the blood drum in our temples, we bend rivers and lift mountains to get with the sweet young thing we desire. When somebody challenges our manhood, we court physical danger and take foolish risks to prove we've got what it takes where it counts.

Yet we stand meekly aside when circumstances separate us from our children? Why do we accept the idea that there is nothing we can do?

There's something wrong with that reasoning. Something self-excusing and self-deluding. How can a man *not* be a father to his child? How do you reach the point where you are okay with that?

William would say the questions miss the point. He'd say some things are easier said than achieved. He'd say it's hard for someone who hasn't been there to appreciate the myriad reasons a father can be separated from his children.

William has virtually no relationship with his offspring. In this, he's not much different from his father and namesake, who separated from William's

William

mother when their child was still a baby. The father is remembered by his son as a distant and largely uninvolved figure.

That son, now a thirty-one-year-old telephone company account executive in Atlanta, is one of those men who habitually refers to his children as "mistakes." The first such error was made when he was in his sophomore year in college—Jackson State in Mississippi. "I fooled around with a lot of girls. And then one girl I dated ended up being pregnant. We went through debate about that, about having the child, not having the child. Ended up getting married, because that's what she wanted to do. It was either marry her or she was going to go back to Michigan. We wanted to be together, so I said I'd do the Spike Lee, as I call it—the right thing. I was twenty-one, she was twenty-two. The baby was six months old when we got married.

"That was probably the worst mistake of my life. I mean, your life changes after you do these things. And I see myself making probably the same mistake my father made. Starting too young and having to regret it. Nobody gives you instructions on how to be a father, how to be a husband. You just kind of land into the situation."

The marriage lasted two and one-half years. Of that time, all but a few months were devoted to paperwork on the divorce.

"I was very immature and we argued and fussed and I just . . . I wasn't ready and I was very fearful and wanted to be in control of everything. We got married in Michigan and I was up there in her hometown and didn't have any family or anybody I was familiar with and she was constantly off, gone with her family. I just felt I was marrying her to give the baby a name and so she could have my last name, so her parents wouldn't be ashamed. That's the way it felt to me. She was still doing her own thing; we were two individuals."

It seemed to William like an assault on his very manhood. "I'm thinking, 'I'm the man, I'm supposed to be responsible. We're going back, we're both going to finish college.' We just fought and argued. Next thing I know, the end of the summer, time to go back to school, I'm married now, got a wife and kid, she says she's not going back. It was a mess. And we've been fussing and arguing ever since.

"It's almost a situation where you're damned if you do, you're damned if you don't," said William. "We got back together the following year. It was after my mother's death. I moved here to Atlanta and got a job with the Atlanta Police Department and she came here. Arguing and fighting started all over again. She only stayed a couple of months and then she left, went back to Michigan."

Somewhere in the attempted reconciliation, William and his wife conceived their *second* child. He had, he said, always dreamt of giving his children the things he didn't have—the most important thing being a father in the house.

"Things just don't work out that way," he told me flatly. "You don't control your destiny.

"I sit back and I think now, I would hope to never tell my daughter that I was scared, or didn't want [her]. It wasn't so much I didn't want to be a father, because I didn't know what being a father was about. I didn't want to have a child or children, if that makes any sense."

And yet, he went ahead and had a second child anyway? I couldn't understand and told him so.

"I didn't know we were going to end up conceiving a child," explained William. "She ended up pregnant and that one . . . in a way, I was hoping it would kind of bring us back together."

William's second born was a son named Darion. "She gave birth to him and I think I found out a couple of days later.

"Not long after he was born, we made plans to try a second time to get back together and make it work. She came down and it was just too many variables, too many ifs and things I felt that I wasn't in control of. Almost like she wasn't dependent upon me; she was still dependent upon her parents.

"I felt like I knew the best, or I knew what was right or what had to be done. And she should have listened. I've since changed my views about all that. But I was very hardheaded and stubborn and it didn't help much in that relationship."

William's two children by his ex-wife are in Michigan. He said he's allowed to have them every summer and every other holiday, but he actually sees them only every other year.

So how does a father maintain ties with children he sees so infrequently? "It's difficult," conceded William, adding that he and his ex-wife still don't get along very well. And then there's the matter of money. When the kids come to visit, he said, he has to pay for their transportation to Atlanta, pay for child care, pay, pay, pay.

"How can I say it? True enough, I'm not supposed to look at it as a financial situation, but the amount of support that I pay and just the way that whole thing works out, it's very difficult. And then when I get them, the money that I spend on them and the things that I try to do. . . . And I feel that she's not helping promote a relationship with them."

He's upset that when he calls, the children are not enthusiastic about talking with him. Sometimes, they refuse to come to the phone and his ex-wife, he complains, won't make them do it. And even when the children do pick up the phone, William said, it's difficult to talk with them. "It's almost like they just hold the phone up. I really, really have to pry a conversation out of them.

"The bottom line is, it hurts so much to call them and talk to them and not get the feedback and not be able to cooperate with her, and not be able to work things out financially and other things we need to be working out with the kids. It just makes you say, 'I'm trying and trying and trying and just . . . I'm making the same mistakes [my father's] making. I don't know what to do."

William said his ex-wife has notified him that she wants more money from him. "She wants to get the child support raised to $625 a month.

Right now I'm paying a total of $250 a month. Which isn't that much, okay, but keep in mind that she gets all my tax [refunds for back child support] and in the last couple of years, that's been about ten thousand dollars. It's a situation where I'm damned if I do or damned if I don't. If she doesn't get it on the front end, she's going to get it on the back." William told me he takes home forty-two thousand dollars a year.

"There's a lot of things I'm bitter about," he said. "And unless you're a non-custodial parent, as the courts call it, you wouldn't understand. People can sit here and say, 'But those are your kids. You're supposed to pay this. You're supposed to be responsible for this.'

"People don't understand . . . it's a big picture. And you have to weigh a lot of different things. I didn't have a chance to finish my degree. Therefore, you aren't able to get the job you want and the salary you want. Struggling with that, then having to make ends meet just like anyone else, having to pay off the amount of child support that they set.

"People have to understand that I don't have five hundred dollars or six hundred dollars a month extra that I can put over into a bank account, invest, or give away. I don't have it. I'm living damn near check to check just like everybody else."

And if all that isn't bad enough, William has *other* children for whom he's also paying child support. Two others, to be exact, by two other mothers, both in Atlanta. "Like I said," he explained, "I keep making the same mistakes my father made."

But why? I asked.

The question seemed to catch him off guard. "Why?" he repeated.

Yes. *Why?* If you put your hand in the fire once because you don't know fire is hot, okay, that's an understandable mistake. But what would possess a man to put his hand back into the same flame a second and third time?

"It's easy to say," said William, weakly.

"I'm not out there sleeping around a lot, but what happens is, I'm in a relationship and we're learning about each other and I tell her straightforward that I really don't want any more children. Young woman, she gets pregnant. She expects me to change how I feel about that.

"I would end up taking up two hours explaining what I meant when I said that to her. Honestly, I *do* want more children, but what I should have said is, I don't want to go through another divorce, I don't want to go through another separated household, I want to have children by the woman that I'm going to love and be with forever. Happily ever after."

But happily ever after keeps receding for William, it seems, like the horizon in a bad dream. His third child is a daughter whose name he has trouble spelling. That child's mother took him to court last year for child support: $235 a month.

"Then, [I] made the same mistake a year and a half later. Therron's mother is Melba. Lord, I don't know what happened. Me and Melba dated, but we weren't in a relationship. I told her I didn't want any more kids, but she got pregnant. She said she wasn't hearing that. And she took me to court for child support." That's another $235 a month.

"I know everybody's going to say, 'You should have used protection. You're a ho, you're a dog.'"

How do you feel about that? I asked. What do you say to the idea that you're confirming that stereotype of black men?

"How do I feel? I say that when it comes to being a black man, they don't judge us as individuals. I mean, we are judged by so many different stereotypes and have so many hidden pressures, that people just don't understand.

"Give me any scenario and I'll tell you exactly how a black man has to respond to the situation. I mean, you basically have to appease more people. . . . I'm six foot three . . . they're intimidated by my color, they're intimidated by my size, so when I speak to them, I have to speak more professionally, so they know, 'Okay, he's an educated black man. He's not a threat.'

"You deal with it," said William. "I'm blessed to be black, I'm blessed to have the size I have. But yet and still, you're tired of people looking at you. I mean, I used to be a police officer. And when I was in uniform, white people would speak to you all the time. Little kids come up to you, 'Hi, Mr. Officer.' But when you're out of uniform, whether you're wearing a pair of jeans or a nice pair of slacks, people are clutching purses, people are looking at you like you're the scum of the earth.

"I don't want to be an angry black man," said William almost pleadingly. "I don't want to walk around with an attitude that everybody's out to get me, everybody's out to do me wrong because of the color of my skin. No! But there have been instances where it has been documented.

People don't understand how you feel. Even black women don't understand what you go through."

I understood everything he had said. Recognized that he bled from the same wound all black men do. I also noticed that he had not answered the question.

What kind of relationship do you have with the two kids that are here? I asked.

"I see myself making—and I reiterate, I see *myself* making—the same mistakes, my *individual* mistakes. I'm not a stereotype," said William. "I make my own mistakes," he said. "Bad judgment calls.

"But as far as the relationship I have with them, because of the difficulty I have with their mothers, I've kind of kept a distance. I didn't want to set myself up for the heartache or the heartbreak of not being in the house with them, or being an active role. I said, I'm going to distance myself. I don't want to be a part. If I can't have it all, if I can't be a full part, I don't want any part of it. Didn't tell people that, but that's the approach I took."

Don't you think being distant from them hurts the kids? I asked.

"Very much so."

What are they going to say twenty years down the line if I'm doing the same interview with them and I say, "Tell me about your dad?"

"Darion, he's a character," replied William. "I mean, me and him . . . I play with him and I try to be so strict on him. You want him growing up respecting authority and learning things that my mother and my father did instill in me. My mother more so than my father."

Another question had gone unanswered, so I rephrased it. "I guess what I'm asking," I said, "is, how are they going to remember you?"

William's eyes glistened. "I don't know," he admitted softly. "If they turn out good, they're not going to give me credit for it, if they turn out bad, they're going to blame me for it."

"That's got to hurt."

"Yes," he said. I could barely hear his voice.

* * *

William impressed me as a man who was too willing to justify and rationalize his own failings. But one thing about him struck a chord: One way or another, black fatherhood often comes back to money. Economic issues have always made it difficult for African-American men to remain with nuclear families. Even as far back as the antebellum period, money worked to break up the black nuclear family.

Under slavery, said historian Brenda Stevenson, "African-American women and not men were associated with children. When you look at a slave list and they list families, for the most part, the woman's name would be listed, but not the father's name. People didn't associate men with families for the most part and for a good reason; men were often physically removed from their families. Men were sold much more often than women were and they were sold at an earlier age than women were."

More than 130 years after the end of slavery, money continues to contribute to the breakup of the black nuclear family.

So much of the way men identify and value themselves as fathers has to do with their ability to "bread win," to provide. Yet, with black male unemployment running at better than twice the national average, many black men are unable to find their validation in this traditional role. Race, as always, plays a role; employment discrimination means skilled and qualified men are locked out of jobs and advancement they deserve.

For men without skills and qualifications, the situation is worse. There was a time when a man with limited education could count on finding plentiful physical work. A strong back provided assurance of employability. But the economy has changed, nudging away from unskilled manual labor toward information technologies. And machines have taken many of the remaining physical tasks out of the hands of men.

So it becomes harder for a man to provide. It's a failure that diminishes a man, that emasculates him and leaves him desperate and resentful.

"That's what made me start hustling," said Clyde, who became a father at sixteen, "because I wanted to give my son things.

"I didn't have no summer job. I had missed the little summer job program. So I started making a little money on the side. I bought him Pampers, milk, little clothes. I always looked out for him." He spoke with the pride of a man who had fulfilled his purpose, even though his illegal hustling had cost him seven years of freedom.

"For people who are unemployed or who are underemployed," said

Stevenson, "their inability to provide the amount of income they need to provide for their children, [for] food, clothing, medical attention, is extremely important and it has had a negative impact on our society—particularly as our society has become much more centered on materialism in the latter half of the twentieth century. The inability to participate in a materialistic and capitalistic culture has had an impact on African-American families."

So what do you do if you're a black man who is, or even *fears* he is, unable to legitimately do what society says real men always do? Too often, you find illegitimate means. Or you opt out of even trying. And you make opting out a point of pride.

There's a pattern in African-American culture, a telling trait of the black psyche: We take that which is awful and subvert it, rob it of its power to hurt us, or even make it a badge of honor. Thus did "nigger," the harshest epithet in the white racist lexicon, come to be embraced by some blacks as a word denoting brotherhood. Thus did hog entrails become a delicacy called chitlins, aloofness and disengagement become cool, pain become the blues.

And, thus did men castrated by their inability to do the things that would prove their manhood simply redefine the equation, allowing themselves an attractive alternative to a standard they could not reach. The rogue. The player. The papa who was a rolling stone. And suddenly it comes to seem natural that black children are raised in the absence of their fathers, that epidemic numbers of black young people make children but never marry.

Andrew, who lives in Los Angeles, told me his teenage daughter actually "feels uncomfortable because she has two parents. It makes her feel strange that she's one of two or three kids in her class who have both parents at home."

He said he's tried to explain "that raising a child requires two parents." Yet still, it's not easy for her. She stands out among her friends because of his presence in her life. "When she's in school or she's talking to one of her classmates, she'll say something like, 'My dad said so-and-so.' And they'll look at her like, 'Your dad? Your dad lives with you?' Everybody's looking at her like, What kind of weirdness is that?"

It's a troubling place we have come to. Having a father in your life seems a form of weirdness. Not having one seems natural.

* * *

Ivory had never met his oldest daughter. "*Never* seen her," he said, emphasizing the word.

According to him, he was in California in the navy and his daughter's mother was in Virginia where they had met. "We were engaged," said Ivory. "She was supposed to come out here and we were supposed to raise the family and live the life. But she decided she didn't want to leave home, she didn't want to come out here, so I was out here by myself."

Ivory said that, after his discharge from the navy, he called his girlfriend to arrange to see his daughter for the first time. "She told me if I wasn't going to be there with her and raise the family with her and help her out and be with her, then as far as she was concerned, I didn't have a daughter."

This made you angry? I said.

"Yeah. Exactly. I was like, why should I bow down to your wishes? I've been bowing down to you all this time. I used to do everything I could to keep her happy. I would send her money, I used to buy her things before she was even pregnant. I felt like I was just used."

I asked Ivory why he didn't just go see his daughter anyway. Get a lawyer, if need be. He told me he has few legal options, because the child's mother left his name off the birth certificate. I asked Ivory how old his daughter was. His eyes questioned the ceiling. "Let's see," he said, ". . . she's got to be . . . four?"

We did the math together. She was six.

Ivory has two younger children, a daughter and a son by his estranged wife. "I haven't seen them in the past year," he said, "because me and [their] mother don't get along." He married that woman when she became pregnant, he said, not wanting to repeat what had happened with his first child.

Ivory told me he never really knew his father, who split from his mother soon after she became pregnant. "He didn't want to have me, so she decided she was going to have me anyway."

His father, he said, went on to raise another family in New Jersey while Ivory was growing up with his mother and grandmother in North and South Carolina. "He came down when I was between nine and eleven. He took me on a vacation with his family, my brothers and sisters."

Ivory

As Ivory sees it, his primary problem is that he is helpless before the charms of women. He said that he grew up around older guys and "unintentionally" became a player. He said this with a straight face. "I've loved women ever since I was a kid," he explained.

I asked Ivory if he could envision himself married and settled. "I'd like to think so," he said, unconvincingly, "but I'm not sure. Ever since I could read, basically, I've never, ever had one girlfriend and she was just it. From a little kid, I've always had at least two, three of them. I don't know where it came from, whether it's in my blood. I don't know."

I asked if he thought he had missed anything by not having his father around.

"Not really. I grew up with love, know what I'm saying?"

* * *

By Ivory's assessment, his father's absence wasn't an important factor in his life. Take it as one more sign of the way we have come to diminish the idea of fathers and fatherhood.

Diminished them to the point where one might fairly look at a father and wonder, who needs this guy anyway? After all, haven't we just spent a generation planning around his absence? Tolerating and excusing it? Haven't we spent years making allowances for and reorienting our society around the needs and concerns of single mothers? We have convinced ourselves that fathers are not, strictly speaking, necessary.

"My mother was the man," Ricky told me. "And the woman. Mother and father. That's just the way it was."

One often hears black men say this, intending the ultimate tribute to mother, that "strong black woman" of myth and truth. But there's a price to be paid for that strength, isn't there?

Washington Post columnist Donna Britt once wrote a column which pointedly reminded readers that black women have needs, too. She is, she said, "[sick] of the undying stereotype—and often, undeniable truth—about women of African descent: Whatever comes, we will be strong."

And why shouldn't a woman be sick of having to be strong? A back that is always bent under the weight of two person's burdens must ache something fierce. And the anger towards the missing person kindles into a generalized scorn for him and all his kind that can, in turn, act against the best interests of both mother and child.

As Timothy, a stepfather in Modesto, California, puts it, "More times than not . . . a black woman's pride will come between her child's welfare and what's best for the child. She'll say, 'I'm raising my baby by myself. I don't need no man.' And she'll move on, in spite of the fact that she's about to subject that baby to a single-parent household—latchkey living and day care residency. All that's going to happen just because pride jumped up out of her face and said, 'I don't need no man.'

"That doesn't go on as much in other cultures as it does in ours. You'll find the same situation in a Caucasian culture, where a woman and a man are together and they have that child and that woman [is] going to say, 'You've got a responsibility here. Now, how are *we* going to handle it?' And nine times out of ten, they'll get some kind of arrangement here, *or even get married* for the sake of the child."

In embracing the notion of male and female equality, we have also embraced the less worthy notion of male and female *interchangeability*, the idea that there are no insurmountable differences between the sexes beyond the obvious physical ones. This, despite testimony from experts such as writers Deborah Tannen and John Gray that women and men tend to perceive, communicate, and value themselves in dissimilar ways.

On the social front, this misbegotten notion has led to confusion and uncertainty. In families characterized by strong black women and absent black men, it has given support to the disastrous notion that maybe fathers aren't really that necessary after all.

Of course, if one is defining fathers strictly as breadwinners and pondering a population of males for whom high unemployment is an abiding crisis, then maybe that's a defensible conclusion. As the old expression goes, "I can do poorly all by myself." In other words, who needs a man unless he's in a position to contribute to the financial well-being of the household?

It's something black women often say. And black men often feel.

* * *

"I know I ain't done nothing for these kids," Ricky, a Washington, D.C., father told me sorrowfully. He has six boys by three different women, none of whom lives with him. Ricky made his voice into a woman's scornful screed. "'Your sorry-ass father ain't done nothing for you!'

"If you got any kind of feelings," he said, "it make you feel low as shit. So low it make you want to go out and rob somebody to put something in her hands. Hurt somebody just to get some Pampers, so your baby won't be shitty."

Ricky had no regular employment. He was living with his sister in a modest apartment in a filthy neighborhood and had no idea where at least one of his sons was living. How had he come to this pass in his life?

Ricky told me he didn't have his first son until he was twenty-five, just out of the U.S. Army Reserve. "I came back to this place and my body started making a bum out of me," he said. "I got to gettin' heavy into the girls and I just made a bum out of myself. Making all those babies and didn't have the right job or the right means to support, to be there. Having these relationships, breaking up, leaving kids here and there.

"I go see my boys, I'm around them. I'm active into their lives, but I'm not *there* with them. That's why I feel as though I made a bum out of myself."

Ricky never knew his own father. His stepfather was an abusive drunk who was eventually put out of the home by Ricky's mother. When Ricky's first son was born, he said, "I felt like a father. I felt responsible right then, 'cause I went right out and got me a job."

You hadn't done that before? I asked, incredulous.

"What I'm gon' do that for?" he demanded. "Why would I want to go out and get a job when my father died and left me some Social Security? I ain't had to do nothing. I would work a summer job. Other than that, I would work when I wanted to work. I didn't have no responsibilities. My mother was there for me. Everything I ever needed, my mother got for me."

I asked him to define a father.

"A father is a provider. He oversees everything that goes on in his children's life. If it's something he don't like, he put the stop to it right then and there and the kids don't give up no resistance. That's how I was brought up. I don't know how you was brought up, but if I say do something, that's what I mean do. I'm not gon' tell you do something that's gonna hurt you. I'm telling you something for your own good."

There seemed something wishful in his words. His definition seemed to have been imagined together in his mind but never tested in real life. Where, I wondered inwardly, do you find this father who snaps his fingers and has his way and kids who never resist?

"A father," continued Ricky, "is there when that first pacifier goes in the mouth, that first tooth comes out, the first steps. And basically, when you changing them Pampers, that baby looking up in your face, he's gon' remember your face. Every time you stick that bottle in his mouth, or put a spoon of food in his mouth, he's remembering your face. That's what I've done for all my babies. All of 'em.

"That's how they love their daddy so much. I take 'em their presents. When I've got a job, I'm lookin' out for my kids." Of course, he added ruefully, he hadn't had a job lately.

I asked if he could envision himself married some day.

"Oh yeah," he said cheerfully. "I just came from the court building with a young lady I want to marry. I've got the application in my pocket. But see, I'm not going to rush into that, because when I get married, I want it to be right. I want to be situated where when I leave that temple or whatever, come back home, I want to have that laid for her and them. It's never perfect, but I got to have something before I get married—a job that's gonna pay me enough to give up support and live on my own.

"Money ain't never been no big thing for me. If you got it, you got it, if you don't, you don't. My goal now is to get my [trucker's] license and drive. I done been in the security field, I done been in the labor field, I do a little bit of this, a little bit of that, I wash cars, I cut hair, I put floor tile down, I put drywall up; there's not too much I can't do. But the whole thing about it, I want to drive."

In Ricky's vision of the future, then, he drives his way to material prosperity. Whatever consumer item his boys want, he is there to provide for them in a choice of sizes and colors, no question asked. The ability to do this seemed integral to his vision of successful fatherhood. And by this measure that meant so much to him, Ricky knew that he had not been a very good father to his sons.

"The most important part of the year for me is Christmas," he said. "Christmas is a day, kids look for that. That love and attention. You put the toys together, play with 'em. If you're not there for Christmas, if you don't have nothin' when you come in that door. . . ." He didn't finish the thought. He didn't have to.

Christmas was about five weeks past when we spoke. I asked Ricky if he'd been able to do what was so important to him—bring gifts to his sons and spend time playing with them. He said no. Instead, he got into a dispute with his latest employer and was fired before the holiday. "I been out of work ever since then," he said. "They denied my unemployment and everything.

"I got drunk Christmas Eve night. Drank too many boilermakers and for some reason, me and my sister got in an argument. Or I done something to one of [her] kids' toys and didn't realize what I was doing. I bent the axle, she cussed me out, and I just flicked out on her. Just snatched all the Christmas lights and stuff. She had me locked up.

"Got out Christmas morning, came on home, fixed the house back up, apologized, fixed the toys, kids went on about their business, house is clean and everything is back to normal."

The phrase sticks like a bone wedged sideways in a windpipe. "Back to normal." Father despairing in one place, boys separated from him in three others. *Back to normal.* You want to rebel against the very idea.

But Brenda Stevenson says that if there's one thing it's important to understand about African-American families, it's that they've *never* really conformed to the model that the rest of the country considers "normal"—meaning the nuclear family with one father, one mother, and two and one-half kids. In the black community, she says, the *extended* family has been the more frequently embraced standard. She argues that, while it is true "to a certain extent" that black men are less involved with their families than they once were, the statistic that says most black children are raised without their fathers is deceptive in the sense that it leads people to believe such children grow up without the influence of men. In other words, while an individual child's father might not be in the house, *somebody's* father often is.

"If you look at the relationship of men who are not necessarily the father of all the children, or may be a relative of the mother, you will find that there *are* males who are associated with the family," she said.

The question is, Is that enough? Is that a standard the African-American community ought to be contented with, a norm that satisfies or even addresses the overall problem of fatherlessness that plagues us? It's worth noting that the same University of Pennsylvania/Princeton University study which found fatherless boys twice as likely to wind up behind bars also found that the presence of a stepfather did nothing to better those odds and, in fact, actually tended to make things worse. Boys whose mothers had remarried were *three times* as likely to be incarcerated. It seems to indicate that, though stepfathers, mentors, and other father figures might help alleviate some elements of fatherlessness, they are not a panacea for what ails the abandoned child.

Larry, a Los Angeles man whose father and mother separated when he was only six months old, told me, "I had uncles that were around that took the place of a father figure. I didn't miss my dad a lot until I [was] starting to be a teenager. And I started thinking, you know, where is Dad and what happened to him? I came to really resent him. I didn't like him very much."

And Charles Ballard, the founder of the Institute for Responsible Fatherhood and Family Revitalization, said, "A father brings to a domain something no one else can bring. Mentors cannot bring it. They're all right, but mentors can never do what the biological father, who is a good lover and a good nurturer and a secure man . . . nobody can come close to him."

Not even stepfathers?

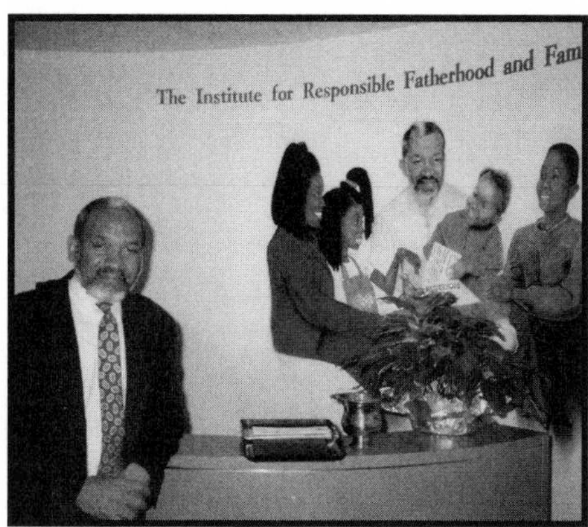

Charles Ballard

"No. Can't come close. They can do some things, but talk to the average child, they don't want that guy being their dad. The average child will say, 'No, man, get out of here with that stuff. I want my own dad.'"

* * *

Larry's father was the proverbial rolling stone, in and out of his son's life. He eventually went on to sire another family with a different woman.

"He was kind of a tough person from Louisiana," said Larry as we talked one afternoon in his office at his airy home in Bellflower. "He had a hard life himself. His mom died early, he was from home to home. So I don't guess he learned himself about how to be, what he was supposed to do.

"I would see him quite often. But he never did much for me whenever I saw him. I'd have holes in my shoes, but he'd have Stacy Adamses on. I'd be putting cardboard in my shoes to go school, he'd come by in Stacy Adams and a brand new car."

You resented him? I asked.

"Yes," said Larry. "The resentment was basically because he wasn't there when I needed him. A couple of times, I did things wrong, my mama called him and he came over and spanked me. That really upset me. I didn't understand how, him not being there, he could come over and spank me.

"I was a good athlete in school; I played football, ran track. He never came and saw any of the games I was in. That hurt me, too. I remember one football game, we had a father-son night. Everybody's dad came to sit on the sidelines with them while they played. And my girlfriend at the time, her father came to sit on the sidelines for me."

"It felt kind of odd. I appreciated his gesture, but I was really angry at my dad for not coming."

Larry was twenty-four when his first child, a daughter, was born. "Being [young] and having no direction, I just thought, 'I have a kid.' No big thing. I've got a kid now. I was a good father, as far as my perspective is, for the first five years. Then we broke up. I had two kids by [that woman] before we broke up."

It was a pattern that would repeat itself during his life. In all, Larry has seven children by five women. When I asked him to list his kids, he initially neglected to mention one of them, his daughter Ladonna.

"Sometimes," he explained, "I forget about her because I didn't know [she] was my daughter till she was like eighteen years old." Ladonna's mother, he said, gave birth after their relationship ended and Larry had gone on to the air force. Larry didn't learn about her until years later when he chanced to run into the girlfriend's sister, who told him he had a daughter he had never seen.

"I went through that thing about, should I get involved and all that kind of stuff. I'm the kind of guy, if I think a kid's mine, I want to know about it because I want to try to do what I can to help out."

Larry said that for a long time, he couldn't find the words to tell Ladonna he was her father. Eventually, the young woman had a child and Larry went to visit her at the hospital. "The kid's dad was there. I said, 'Gee, he looks like his dad.'"

Ladonna took Larry aside then. Told him that this guy wasn't the baby's father. And Larry saw the pattern of his life repeating itself in the life of his daughter. "I decided somebody has to talk to this girl," he said, "try to give her some kind of semblance of what was right and wrong."

So he introduced himself to Ladonna as her father.

Don't you think that harms a child? I asked. Not to know? To have to wonder, "Are you my dad?"

"Sure it does," said Larry. "I definitely know it does. Not to be able to know somebody that really loves you for the blood and would go to any lengths to

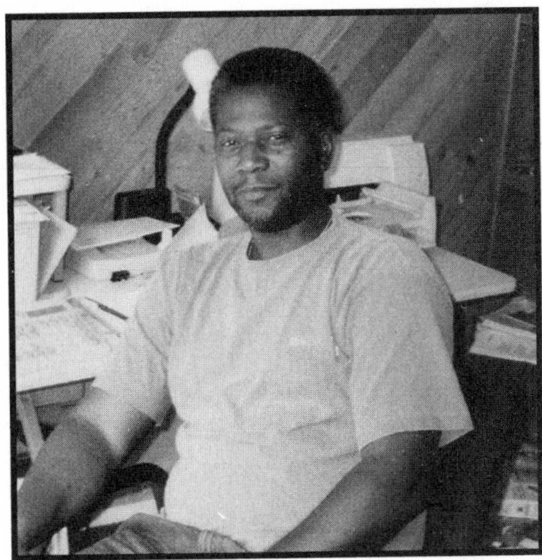

Larry

be there for you, to help you. You miss that. It's definitely harmful."

A sigh escaped him then. "Harmed me, too," he said. "I was hurt behind that. I didn't think there was no reason for her [mother] to hide the fact from me. I'm just that crazy about my kids."

Larry said he's always considered himself a good father. "Spent a lot of time with all my kids, even to this day." Granted, by his own admission, he didn't "grow up" till he was thirty-five. Until then, he said, he was more interested in partying hard, doing drugs, and selling them. Now, at forty-eight, he owns a non-emergency medical transport company and works from his home. He's been married six years and said he has great relationships with his kids.

In all, things seemed to have worked out well for Larry. And yet, he told me, he is living "the worst scenario" where fatherhood is concerned.

"It's terrible to have to go through all those different chains of all those different personalities to see your kids. I have to go to Alhambra, I have to go to Long Beach, I have to go Pasadena, to gather my children up or get to see them. I have to deal with various personalities. One of the worst things is that those women have a tie with me that I can't break, forever. I always have to interact with them whether I want to or not."

But is the alternative still realistic? Is it still practical (if, indeed, it ever was) for society to expect that two people will get married, stay married, and raise their children together?

Larry pondered the question a moment before he answered. "In these times, I'd say no," he said. "I don't think it's possible. So many variances come in to affect the family, and people seemingly run for any reason these days. I've come to the conclusion since I've grown up and gotten a little bit wiser that I may as well have struggled through that first relationship, that first marriage. I should have stayed with that first girl and just struggled it on through with her.

"The best is to [have] a single mom for whatever kids you're going to have. If I had to do it again, knowing what I know now, I wouldn't do it like this. I would either not have any other kids, or I would've stayed with the woman I had."

SIX

William never knew his father.

He saw him occasionally—William's parents were divorced—and went over to his house sometimes. But he never *knew* him. "We don't communicate," explained William. "Growing up, I was always kind of afraid to talk to him.

"I had a great childhood," he said, not wanting to leave the wrong impression. "It's just that some of the times, you're living your life as a kid, and people don't realize that kids have adult thoughts. I really wanted to be like my dad. I don't think of him as a bad person. I never really was able to . . . figure that we were the best of friends or anything like that."

Ask a man what makes a father, and if he's speaking *as* a father, he'll talk about providing and protecting. But if he's talking as a son, he's just as likely to talk about playing basketball or going fishing or just hanging out. Not for the activities themselves, but as a means of figuring out who his father is. As sons, we look for ways to get behind the masks our fathers wear in hopes, perhaps, of learning a little more about ourselves. Fathers don't make it easy sometimes.

"I could never contradict anything he said," recalled William. "If he was too pushy or bossy about something or if he was wrong about something, it was always, 'Don't tell me!' I guess the inflection in his voice was intimidating. When my mother died in '89, I guess I expected him to take her place or fill her shoes, for me and him to bond and be closer. And I don't think I've ever felt that."

Of course, men often don't do tender emotion well. We have difficulty getting the vocabulary down and even when we try, somehow it feels awkward in our mouths. So we work by inference and indirection. In the movie *The Great Santini* there comes a moment when Robert Duvall, as the swaggering title character, is bested in basketball for the first time by his oldest son. The father is churlish and abusive in defeat. He never admits to what has happened. Never slaps the boy on the back and says, "You're getting good. You're gaining on me." Instead, he takes the basketball and practices alone, deep into the night as the rain falls hard and his son watches from a window. Finally, the boy's mother comes to explain, "He's admitting to you that the gap is closing, that he's going to have to practice if he beats you from now on." In other words, this is the father's way of acknowledging that the son has come of age.

A Washington, D.C., man named Keith told me he'd had a difficult childhood because of abuse from his stepgrandfather, who helped raise him when his parents split. One day when Keith was an adult, he found himself on the porch with the man, who had become old, infirm, and, evidently, filled with remorse. But he still couldn't say he was sorry, couldn't express regret for all the mean things he had done. Instead, he said "something like, 'I just know you could get me back for the way I treated you all those years. If you wanted to get me back for it, I wouldn't be able to stop you.'"

Keith told the old man, "'I don't hold any grudges or bad feelings toward you about that.' You could see the pain and hurt in his eyes."

For some reason, manhood dictates that what we feel and who we are be buried deep beneath protective layers. Difficult for the world to reach. And oftentimes, impossible for our kids.

Even when we protect them and provide for them and show ourselves in their lives, there is this missing piece, this gap. And it persists until one or the other says, Enough. That's what happened to William.

He had never really had a conversation with his father until an incident that happened when the older man came down from Milwaukee to visit. "He was helping me move my washer and dryer; he ended up hurting his knee and he was just irritable from that point on . . . kept bitching about his knee.

"We went to a drugstore. I went back to the pharmacist to find out what was the best thing for his swollen knee. He got so irritable, he went up to the front counter and had the girl page me. He knew exactly where I was; I wasn't but in the pharmacy. Then when I got up front and said, 'Here's two choices. Which one do you want?' he snatched one out of my hand.

"I looked at him," said William, "and he just looked at me. It was a very, very quiet drive back to my apartment. When we got there, [I] gave him the medicine and the heating pad. I went in my room, watched television, and I'm thinking, 'Here I am, a grown man, in my own apartment, in my own room.' It was like I was in high school all over again. I finally went out in the living room and I told him, while he was sitting there watching TV, 'You're very difficult. And it's hard to talk to you sometimes.' And he said, 'I know. You're right.'

"Later that evening," said William, "[we] went out, probably for the first time, and had some drinks. We had a good time."

It had taken thirty-one years for them to reach that point.

"I think we as black men are kind of missing the boat with our nurturing of our kids," an Atlanta man named Phil told me.

Phil was the fourth of eight children, an army brat, born in Wurzburg, Germany. "We grew up on the move," he said. Phil's parents had just celebrated their fiftieth wedding anniversary when we spoke. Of the fifty years, Phil estimated that his father was gone for twenty on active duty with the military.

"He just turned seventy-five," said Phil, not without a trace of pride. "Just a hard working country boy from Saluda, South Carolina. Had a strong work ethic. He was in the army roughly twenty-seven years. Five or six years in the navy and then three or four years in the air force. And all that time, he was basically doing the same thing: cooked his whole life in the military."

Even after his father retired from the military, he didn't become any easier for his son to reach. "He was one of those guys who would work two and three jobs," said Phil. "He would be gone in the morning before we got up, come home from his other job, take a nap, go to his other [job]. So we basically never saw him, even after the military experience. He was just a hard worker. And with all those kids, I guess he had to be.

"Growing up, there really was no relationship because he was just Dad and he was always gone. Right now, we're closer than we've ever been because I've gotten to a point where we can relate about different things. I can talk to him about problems I'm having in my marriage and stuff like that. But when I was growing up, he pretty much wasn't there.

"My mother raised us and gave us all the love we needed. But there's some things that only a father can do. I saw a friend of mine walking. And he said, 'Watch this, watch this.' He started walking funny. And his son was walking behind him, walking the same funny way. I just laughed at him."

It struck a chord in Phil, this son imitating his father's odd step. "Growing up," he explained, "I had nobody to imitate and I don't know who I imitated. A son can't imitate his mother, so I must have imitated friends. I don't know where I learned anything. I don't know where I learned to unzip my pants and pee. I don't know where I learned it."

Phil, who is a thin six feet five inches tall, said he discovered sports while still in elementary school and began to use them as a substitute for the input of his father. "Basketball kind of took over about the tenth grade. Basketball took over everything. I was a good student up until I became a good basketball player." Basketball gave him what he needed: a way to be somebody . . . and a male to look up to.

"The point guard on my basketball team, Craig Geter, to me he was like an adult. He'd moved from Virginia, he had his own apartment. I mean, had a full beard in the tenth grade. And he was just kind of more streetwise than all of us. Even my big brother wasn't a father figure. There was no real strong male role model in my family. But Geter came along and he was hanging out with the older guys, so I started hanging out with Craig Geter. I learned a lot from him in that I saw a kind of mature teenager, which I had never seen before. We were trying to hit on the cheerleaders, Geter was hitting on the *teachers*. I was real impressed with this guy. He was really cool."

Cool he might have been. But there was something sad about the picture Phil painted. A boy looking toward another boy for instruction on how to be a man.

You can't say Phil didn't have a good father. His father provided. The home wasn't an abusive one. And yet, Phil never really knew the man. And the emptiness that left has been difficult for him to fill.

Phil told me that when he was about thirty years old, he had the chance to do some freelance sports consulting in Jakarta, as part of a cultural exchange in association with the American embassy there. One thing led to another, and Phil found himself spending two years traveling, giving basketball camps and playing abroad.

"I'll never forget, one day I was on my way to Argentina to go play some ball. My father was at the airport and I gave him a hug. I said bye and walked [through] the door. I looked back and my father was just still standing there, frozen. I realized," said Phil, "I had never hugged him."

* * *

What was your relationship with your father like? I asked.

"A good relationship," said David. "He did the best he could."

And then his face changed and he shook his head. "No," he said, almost to himself. "No."

Turned out it wasn't a good relationship and David's father didn't do the best he could. Indeed, David told me he had spent his life trying to get the older man's attention, trying to prove himself. And he never did.

We talked one day at twilight in the picture-lined den of his home in Lindenwold, New Jersey. His daughters were playing outside, the sound

David

from the television was muted. David told me he was three when his parents divorced. His father was abusive to his mother, though David had no firsthand memory of it.

After the divorce, he saw his father once a month. A little more frequently, perhaps, as he got older. David said there were many times his father promised to drop by but didn't. In fact, his mother stopped telling David about his father's promises as a way of shielding him from disappointment.

In the meantime, David was watching his father from afar, seeking to emulate him in every detail. Since Dad was a womanizer, David "wanted to be like him. You know, women liked me. Girls liked me. I was very popular."

So he played the girls and he waited for his father to notice. When he did, well. . . . "I was kind of happy he found out."

But it didn't matter in the end. The attention David was looking for, he never found. His father never quite knew he was there.

"I had a cousin, which is my father's sister's son. [My father] spent a lot of time with him. And I didn't know why. I didn't know why he didn't spend that time with me. I was over my cousin's house as a child, twelve years old. The phone rang, and it was my dad calling my cousin. They just were talking on the telephone. And he *never* called me. I was hurt. I never told him."

I asked David if he felt he missed anything from not having a closer relationship with his father.

"Absolutely. Your friends are out there playing with their fathers and you're playing with them and their father. Let's say I did a little bit better than their child. Then the child gets jealous, and the father favors his son. I was just out.

"I played sports all my life. My dad, I think he came to one football game when I was in senior high school. That was it. And I dropped the pass." The disgust in David's voice was still fresh all these years later. "I was wide open," he said.

David talked sports a lot, bragging about his ability in a wide variety of athletic endeavors. This, too, was in emulation of his father, a man given to horseback riding, motorcycles, hunting, farm chores, and other traditionally male pursuits. David wouldn't fit anyone's stereotype of a sportsman. He's a petite, wiry man—could pass for Prince's tougher, less dandified brother.

"I kind of thought [my father] thought maybe I was a mama's boy," said David. "As much as I proved that I wasn't. I've been on wild horses—I can ride my ass off. Stay on, [get] bucked off, get back on, right in front of [my father]. I've cleaned out pig stalls, horse stalls. I wasn't scared to get my hands dirty."

Do you think, I said, that you were doing this to prove to him. . . .

David cut me off with a laugh. "No, I was doing it because he made me do it. He had a farm and he was like, 'You want to ride, you've got to go clean out the stalls.' I wanted to ride."

But, I insisted, it also sounded like a way of proving to him that you could ride the horse, you could clean out the stalls, you weren't a mama's boy like he thought.

"Yeah," said David thoughtfully. "It could be. You know, I can't see why he would think that."

His eyes turned inward for a second. The question was obviously one he had struggled with many times before. "He's a big hunter," said David. "He took my cousin out and he got him his hunting license when he was sixteen or fifteen. I got mine on my own when I was twenty-five."

You don't know why? I asked.

"No, I don't know why he didn't do it for me or enable it to happen."

Did you ever talk to your mother about it?

"Yeah. I don't remember anything that she said."

And you never talked to your father?

David's voice was a near whisper. "Why would I talk to him about it? At this point, I don't care." He said it as though positing a possible answer to a perplexing question.

Are you asking that or are you stating it? I asked, confused.

David met my eyes. "I'm *telling* you that. I don't care. I mean, I have proven myself. I don't care."

You've proven yourself to whom? I asked. Yourself?

"Yeah," said David.

He spoke with conviction, as if he had truly struck peace with the irresolution he felt. But it was a lie, and I think we both knew that. I didn't call him on it, though. Just let it pass. Just let the conversation turn to other things.

We talked about raising girls and the need for boys to have role models and the things black men should do that they don't. He told me about his wife and shared a funny story of how frantic he was the day his first daughter was born.

At the end, I took his picture and shook his hand. He gave me directions back to the freeway. I said goodbye.

And it was then, as I was pushing open the door into the cool evening air, that David's lie broke of its own accord in a quiet murmur of disbelief that came out of nowhere, apropos of nothing.

"Even now, I still want his respect," said David in a soft, incredulous voice. "Even now."

SEVEN

Ray is my brother-in-law. When I asked him to describe his life, he started telling crime stories. Life on the streets of south-central L.A.

For instance, there was the time he and some of his homeboys knocked a hole in a liquor store wall with a sledgehammer, intending to rob the place. The breaking of the wall set off an alarm. Someone heard the police coming. The would-be robbers ran.

Later that night, Ray and his boys were smoking weed and drinking at a friend's house. "Me and this dude named Tim, we was leavin'," said Ray. "Tim said, 'Ray, come on, let's go off in that liquor store now, man. Police gone and everything. We can get away. We can get this beer and stuff and [sell] it to the Mexicans down the street."

So Ray and Tim went back to the store and crawled in through the still-open wall. They looked around for a moment, then Ray sent Tim back outside to wait for Ray to start passing him cases of beer. Tim was halfway out of the hole when the police said, "*Freeze!*"

Which is when Tim turned back to Ray, still hidden inside the store and said, "'You might as well come out, too. They know you in here.'"

Ray gave a rueful laugh at the memory. "Right then and there, that told me he was going to tell on me. I said, 'Fuck it. I'm comin' out.' I stuck my hands out and came on out.

"Told me to stand against the wall. Stood against the wall. Turned around, patted me down and everything. He told me to lay down on the ground. I laid down on the ground. He told me to put my face in the dirt,

Ray

I wouldn't put my face in the dirt. He reached down there and slapped my hat off my head and started kicking me in the back and stomping me. Then he put the handcuffs on me and snatched me up, slammed me against the wall, put me in the back seat of the police car."

All of Ray's stories are like that. Small-time crime with a hard-luck twist. You can imagine Quentin Tarantino eating this stuff up.

Many of Ray's stories end the same way, too. With him in the back seat of a police car awaiting transport to jail. His sister and I have been together more than twenty years and sometimes it seems as if Ray has spent at least half that time in jail. My kids don't even know their uncle. He's a collect call from a California lockdown.

Ray, a tall man with sleepy eyes, pouting lips, and the beginnings of a middle-aged paunch, was on parole when we spoke one rainy morning in an apartment where he was living with one of his other sisters. I've always liked Ray, always thought he was a lot smarter than the things he did—the drug dealing and the thievery. I used to like his younger brother, too. Ted was a garrulous, mischievous man who never seemed to take life all that seriously. He and I shared an affinity for soft soul vocal groups with romantic themes and falsetto leads: Stylistics, Delfonics, Chi-Lites and the like.

Unlike his brother, Ted got his fill of prison life after just one stretch. When he got out, he never went back. Instead, he went to work, and filled his after-hours with taking care of his two daughters. Not that his turnaround made a lot of difference in terms of his ultimate fate.

Ted was shot to death in 1993. Just walking down the street one night when some kid put a pistol against his nose and pulled the trigger. Random killing. Gang initiation or something. Even his sister, who grieves his loss mightily, concedes that he got back from life only what he had, as a wild teenager, put into it. Meaning violence.

Ted and Ray gave themselves over early to the slangin' and bangin'—drug-dealing and gang membership—that counts as career opportunity in much of black America. "Having ten in your family . . . your mother can't buy you that much," said Ray. "I can remember the time I'm walking around with holes in the bottom of my shoes. Want to go out, I've got to ask my brother can I use his shoes to go out with. It was like a money thing all the time, you know. Have to do what you have to do to survive in a big family like that."

Listening to Ray tell crime stories that morning, the thing that struck me hardest was the bland normalcy of it all, the incidental amorality of his life . . . the idea that you can just see what you want and take it, or sell what the government says is illegal and never mind the consequences.

Either he was crazy or I was. Or both. Or, most likely, we grew up in the same neighborhoods but worlds apart. I am naive, I know—the product of a mother who sheltered all her children from the worst of their environment.

Ray must have sensed he had a fascinated audience. The stories kept coming without pause, one right after another.

"We were over here on Avalon and Fifty-ninth," he said. "It was me, Jelly Jar, Sad and my homeboy Foster. We was at this corner, it was this Mexican bar. We was lookin' in the window. Sad had a gun. 'Man, come on, we can rob 'em.'

"We was on our bikes. So we told Jelly to go to the corner, look for the police. I looked up, I seen Jelly gone from the corner. So I looked behind us, and there was a car coming down the street with no lights on. I said, 'There's the police!' So Sad threw the gun and when the gun hit the ground, it threw all kind of sparks.

"Police had us against the wall, told us to freeze before they shoot us with our own gun. Handcuffed us, put us in the car and put our bikes in the trunk. Took us down to Newton [Division police station], asked us some questions and everything. My mother came and got me. We rode our bikes back. They gave us probation."

The recounting was matter of fact. Rote, even. He could as easily have been describing his résumé. Which I suppose he was.

I asked Ray about his father. Alcoholic, he said. "Didn't see him too much. The only thing I can remember is getting thrown from wall to wall."

His stepfather, he said, wasn't much better. "He was abusive too. [He and my mother] left one day and they had told us, 'Don't eat these pears.' We was off in there, looking around for something to eat, ended up eating the pears anyway."

As Ray described what happened when his stepfather came home and discovered this transgression, his voice grew tight in a way it hadn't while telling crime stories. "Told us to come outside one at a time, stand up against this tree, put our hands on this tree, drop our pants. Instead of whipping us with the belt, he whipped us with the *buckle* part. Bust my knee open.

"Went in there and showed my mother. She looked at my knee, started laughing. Said I shouldn't of ate the pears. Told her we was hungry, that's why we ate 'em. She just looked and laughed."

Ray fell silent for a moment. Outside, the rain drummed the building and splashed heavily to the ground.

We started talking about Ray's son, who was nine. His mother is a Mexican woman with whom Ray doesn't get along. His son is always in trouble at school, sometimes gets caught "trying to do things to the girls" as Ray put it.

He doesn't see the boy much. I asked Ray what kind of father he thinks he's been. "I try to do the best I can for him with the little money I have and the little time I can spend with him," he said.

It seemed an especially measured answer. A failure tacitly acknowledged, but not quite apologized for, either.

Everyone knows the statistic: On any given day, one third of black men between the ages of twenty and twenty-nine are under control of the justice system, either in jail, on parole, or on probation.

For many, that number is rationalization for ever more mean-spirited attacks on black men. This person thinks they justify her refusal to hire blacks. That one thinks they make it all right for the cab driver to pass up blacks of both genders and all ages. The other person thinks they prove the inherent savagery of black men. All interpret the number to the limits of their own personal fears and biases.

Hardly anyone calls the number what it is: a crisis. An *American* crisis.

Imagine for a moment that one third of all white boys were being lost to the criminal justice system. Does anyone pretend that this would not command attention at the highest levels of government? Can anyone believe we would not have our finest minds working hard on the question of why this was happening? We would not be content to simply rope those boys off for ever longer periods of time in some dark corner of society encircled by barbed wire and guard posts. We would make it our business to save them. We would understand that in saving them, we save ourselves.

But who makes that connection with black boys? Who speaks with urgency of the need to take them back from the forces that seek to destroy them?

In the face of their need, we have only excoriation and blame. We aim "justice" at them like a cannon. According to *The Real War on Crime: The Report of the National Criminal Justice Commission*, blacks account for 13 percent of regular drug users, but 35 percent of drug possession arrests, 55 percent of drug possession convictions, and *74 percent* of all drug possession prison sentences. A black male defendant pays higher bail than a comparable white one, is significantly more likely to suffer incarceration before trial, is less likely than his white counterpart to negotiate a lenient plea bargain, and can expect to serve more time for the same crime. A black defendant is also more likely to be sentenced to death than a white one who commits the same crime. The killer whose victim is white is *eleven times* more likely to be sentenced to death than the killer whose victim is black.

The Commission report points out that, though it is true that African Americans commit proportionately more crime than whites, it is also true that African-American crime rates have remained consistent since the middle '70s. In other words, blacks are committing about the same proportion of crime as they did a quarter century ago, but are being incarcerated *more.* A hell of a lot more. Indeed, after reviewing statistics from the U.S. Department of Justice, Jerome Miller, founder of the National Center on

Institutions and Alternatives in Alexandria, Virginia, has concluded that by the year 2010, the *majority* of black men ages eighteen to thirty-nine will be in jail.

This horror is not accidental. The Commission's report puts it bluntly: " . . . There are so many more African Americans than whites in our prisons that the difference cannot be explained by higher crime among African Americans—racial discrimination is also at work, and it penalizes African Americans at almost every juncture in the criminal justice system."

Under the guise of a tough-on-crime pose, we have built the foundations of a world without African-American men, imposed what amounts to a de facto criminalization of black manhood. We have become used to throwing away these men's lives without making even the first effort at redemption. At some level, we have come to see what is happening to them as normal. We cluck our tongues and mutter *tsk tsk*, but there is little sense of urgency, other than the urgency of our need to keep them under control, in check, away from decent people.

In the face of that complacency, we lose fathers. We lose sons.

Think of Clyde in Yonkers meeting his father behind bars and the picture it paints is enough to make you ache: the failures of the father reborn in the next generation.

Handcuffs and court dates have become part of a perverse rite of passage for many young men. And the economics of the drug trade have upended the traditional relationships between them and their parents.

In his heyday as a dealer, Ray was his family's banker. He paid overdue bills, handed out spending money, and supported his parents through lean times. They were eager to get what they could from him while the getting was good, he'll tell you bitterly.

Once, said Ray, he gave his mother three hundred dollars to hold for him. "Came back. Ol' Pops was down there, got his table fixed up, playing his music and everything, waiting till his card players come to play cards that night. Go upstairs and say, 'Mama, you got that money I gave you?' She said, 'Well, Daddy got your money.' I said, 'What he doing with my money? I gave *you* my money.'"

Ray said he went down and confronted his stepfather. "He reach in his pocket and pull my money out."

They knew how you were making this money, I said. Didn't anybody pull you aside and tell you you weren't supposed to be doing this?

Ray laughed. "They too busy enjoyin' the money, too," he said.

The irony is acute. A young man who was in many ways fatherless had been installed by drug money as a surrogate father to his own parents and siblings.

More and more, it seems, it always comes back to drugs, to the escape promised by their usage or the financial freedom offered by their sale. And either way you go, you run smack up against the same result: A tide of human wreckage and devastated lives that threatens to drown every decent aspiration and high hope we muster.

When I was a teenager in the '70s, the big threat was Phencyclidine, an animal tranquilizer known on the street as "sherm" or "angel dust." It was a powerful hallucinogen that, for a time, was all the rage among the young and foolish. Made them dance naked in busy intersections or leap from tall buildings under the delusion that they could fly. Preachers and teachers denounced it with a vengeance. Singer and social poet Gil Scott-Heron wrote a song in which he attacked it as a "dead-end street" and pleaded, "please, children, won't you listen." We thought dust was the end of the world.

Then came crack. Hit poor black neighborhoods like a bomb. Hooked the preacher *and* the teacher. Cheap and insanely addictive, it made mothers into ten-dollar whores, fathers into stick-up artists, and sons into wealthy men. It destroyed black neighborhoods one home at a time. My cousin Richard, who runs a home for at-risk youth, says boys like the ones he's spent years trying to save represent "the sum of our last generation and a half of an exercise in futility. We have allowed cocaine to infiltrate our community in overwhelming numbers. And now the drug of choice in the African-American community, every city and urban area, is crack."

It was crack that nearly destroyed Randy, who lives in Yonkers. Looking at him, you wouldn't believe it. He's a magnetic man, his handshake solid as the Federal Reserve, his bearing confident like a president among the party faithful, his speech full of more certainties and affirmations than a TV preacher. You like the guy on sight. Talk to him for a few minutes and you'd trust him with your last dollar.

How long have you been off drugs? I asked him.

"Five months," he said.

Randy

Only five months. I found myself wondering what a man like this might have become if he hadn't given ten years of his life over to crack.

When I met him, Randy was working and going to school, angling toward making a better life for himself, his fiancée and their two children. The other part of his life, he insisted, was over for good.

Randy told me he started using drugs early, right after his father disowned him, claiming—wrongly—that his mother had been fooling around with another man.

"I felt abandoned," he said. "Confused. I really didn't know which way to turn. And so I turned to drugs because of these problems I had with me, and I couldn't deal with them.

"It was a slow process. I gradually started smoking marijuana. I was thirteen when I first tried it. Then I started with the alcohol. And then the higher drugs. I went to cocaine, I went to crack."

And then Randy went into the military. He joined up right out of high school and did a six-year hitch as a communications operator for the army. He was clean while he was in the service. "And I was clean for a while after I came out. Then I started back using.

"It was like, 'I'll try it for a little bit. I'm not going to do too much of it.' Lo and behold, I was wrong. I started doing a little bit, then I'm starting to like it. Then as I started to like it, I got more into it.

"When I started, it was given to me. When you're not hooked and someone wants to get you hooked, they'll give it to you. My habit got worse and worse and I needed more and more to get high—to sustain me. I didn't realize it. I was blind to the fact that I was using more drugs."

For a while, said Randy, he was "what you call one of them functioning addicts. I would get up and go to work so I could make some money so I could go out there and get high. Anything else really didn't matter. Oh, I would take care of home a little bit, but I didn't give as much as I should. The rest was like, 'I've got to keep some money to myself, so I can see the smoke man, so I can see the cocaine man, so I can see the crack man. So I can get mine. I worked for this, so I should be able to enjoy this.'"

In that time, Randy and his girlfriend, Michele, started their family. The first child was their daughter, A'tia. I asked Randy about his relationship with his little girl.

"Tried to be a good father," he said, adding that he was also "trying to do drugs and drink beer. I was trying to do my best. I could have done better, but I was above average. I can say that much. I tried to do what I could for her when I could. I'd get Pampers if she needed it, some clothes if she needed it, always had her with me. I was a pretty good father."

It is, perhaps, an overly charitable assessment. As Randy himself told it, drugs began to overwhelm any desire he had to be a good father, to be a good man, to be anything, but high. "Seem like I just wanted to go out there and hang out with my friends, instead of doing what was right at home. We'd go to the park and play basketball and then after we'd have our basketball session, then we'd sit down and drink beer and start smoking. Right back into it again. Started doing the drugs all over again."

How did you treat your family? I asked. This time, the assessment wasn't charitable at all.

"Shitty," he said. "My intentions were always good, but see, intentions can be just that. Just good intentions. If you don't follow through, it leaves a hole there. My intention was to get high. That was my first priority—to get high, drink, and do whatever I wanted to do."

His kids, he said, never saw him using drugs, but they knew what was going on. "Daddy would come home all times of the night, two, three o'clock in the morning. They'd be in bed sleeping. Then I'd stay in the house a couple of days until I was ready to go on another run."

And then there were the times he jumped on Michele. "We'd have fights, cops would come and tell me to take a walk or whatever. I've actually stole things out the house so I could get high. Took my TV, took my VCR, sold them so I could get high. Giving my stuff to the crack man so I could get high. I didn't care. I just wanted that drug."

He wanted it so desperately that when Michele finally gave him the ultimatum—you can have the drugs or you can have your family—he had to think about his answer. Really had to think about it. "I looked in the mirror and asked what did I really want more? Did I want the drugs that bad, that I'm willing to risk my family and lose them?"

The decision, he said, wasn't as easy as it should have been. "I'd been doing drugs so long, I didn't know how it was like to be clean. I was afraid to actually do that."

Five months into his sobriety, Randy said his life was changed. "Me and Michele, we can sit down, we can play cards, we can do things together as a family now. She ain't got to hide things from me, thinking I'm going to take 'em and go out there and sell 'em. Or steal money from her to go out there and get high. All that's changed. My kids see a difference. And it makes them feel good because now I am able to be there, financially and mentally. My life is becoming stable again and I'm happy because of that."

There was, said Randy, only one piece of business left for him and Michele. A wedding.

"She's a special woman," he said, "because she's put up with my bull for so many years. She could have left me, but she loved me. And I guess she did see something in me."

It was, perhaps, the same indefinable something Grailyn's daughters saw in him. Like Randy, Grailyn, who lives in Washington, D.C., knows crack intimately. He's been both user and seller—in addition to other assorted criminal exploits.

"I was always a fast learner," he said. "Anything that I could make money, honestly or dishonestly, I gravitated toward. So I have committed crimes, just for the fact of getting money for the purpose of buying drugs.

"At first," said Grailyn, "it was like fun and games. I used to steal from stores at a young age just to be part of the crowd because my buddies was doing it. Just shoplifting. The first time I committed an armed robbery, I think I was around twelve or thirteen. Growing up, getting a pistol wasn't hard for me. I can remember having five guns at one time and I guess I must've been around seventeen. My mother had this old .45 around the house and when I first ran across it . . . that was a good feeling, to be in power. Carrying a gun makes you feel powerful. Made me feel powerful."

I asked him to tell me what it was like to rob a store when he was only twelve years old. "I guess a part of me was scared," he said, "but the other part was like, joyous. To take charge and have everyone afraid was a real good feeling. Just fortunately, I never killed anyone. [I got] about four hundred dollars. It wasn't much."

Grailyn said his first arrest was for bringing a shotgun to a party to back up an older brother who had been attacked there. This was followed by a series of other arrests, the most serious of them for armed robbery. I asked him where his father was during all this.

"He would criticize me, try to tell me that wasn't right. He used to come visit me whenever I was locked up. He was there for me. Made sure my little canteen had money in it. I couldn't say he was happy about it, but he didn't really pitch no temper tantrum or nothing. He didn't really go crazy. I guess he expected me to be a sour grape because he was kind of rough growing up himself. So it was just a natural thing."

Grailyn has three children, though he allows that he's "not sure" the middle one is his. The youngest, a toddler named Kanita, was playing at his knees as we spoke. He was an attentive father. Took her to the bathroom when she announced that she had to go, warned her back when she wandered over to play with an electric socket, carefully bundled her up when it was time to go outside, where it was rainy and cold.

Occasionally, Kanita contributed her own observations to the conversation. When her father mentioned at one point that he might like to find a woman and settle down, she ordered, "Don't get married!" in a voice that left no room for argument. We laughed.

Kanita's older sister, Angel—Grailyn's first child—was born when he was in high school. "Trying to be a man ahead of my time" is how he put it.

"I was scared," he said. "I didn't know nothing about being no dad. I knew that it took a lot to bring up a child. You needed money. That was a challenge, to take care of my habit and take care of baby, too. It was a good feeling, but it was a scary good feeling. I wasn't a stable guy."

His daughter's mother broke up with him soon after. "I took that kind of hard. You know how you say, 'I'm going to get you back,' and start doing damage to yourself? I really got into drugs heavily. Selling and using. All kinds of crazy stuff. Intravenous, smoking . . . any kind of way I could get it in me."

That was his life for most of the next fifteen years, much of it spent on the streets and behind bars. "I always did bits and pieces of time," he said. "Longest I did was about a year and a half. But I never done nothing like one-to-three or three-to-nine or five-to-fifteen. Just fortunate. I was doing the stuff to get that kind of time, but God was just looking over me at the time."

He was, he said, "very bitter at heart" toward Angel's mother. "So therefore, wasn't a whole lot that I did for my child. I think today my daughter has resentments toward me about those days, because myself and her mother used to fight a lot. And I think she remembers that. She loves me dearly, but I think she remembers bad things that I've done."

Angel, he said, is nineteen. And, he thought, relatively unscarred, all things considered.

"She really didn't want for too much growing up. She just wanted her dad, really. I'm very proud of her, because she went all the way through school. Right now she's going to college and working and we have a pretty good relationship. She's not mad, she just has resentments. She don't like the fact that her dad was an alcoholic and an addict. A lot of times she would see me on the corner with the boys or in a crap game or out there selling drugs. And she might be with her girlfriends. I guess I embarrassed her a lot."

Did you ever try to talk to her about it? I asked.

"Yeah," he said, "but it would hurt her and she would cry. I wouldn't press it."

Sooner or later, I said, you're going to have to talk to her about it. Do you know what you're going to say?

"There's not a whole lot I can say," replied Grailyn. "I mean, 'I'm sorry'? I'm not going to say that. What's done is done. 'I'm sorry' . . . that's a cop-out. I can only express my feelings to her, how sorrowful I am that it happened and try to make her understand that I will try not to live that way again.

"I can remember the last time that I used. [Angel] came into my room and I had just finished smoking some crack cocaine. She seen that look in my face, man. That pain right then and there made me want to stop using. But on the flip side of those feelings was the feeling of self-pity: She done caught me now, might as well go all the way."

Grailyn went into rehab not long after that. He said his daughter sent him a letter there one day. In it, she told him he was about to be a grandfather. And she enclosed a fifty-dollar bill. He had been clean for seven months when we met.

I asked him what had happened to change him.

"I just got tired of living like an animal," he said.

This bothered Kanita. "Daddy," she said, "you're not an animal."

Her father put his big face close to her small one and smiled a strange, sad smile that seemed filled as much with affection for her as with lamentation for all the awful things his life has seen. "No," he told her softly, "I'm not an animal. Okay. Thank you."

PART TWO:

Negotiating the Peace

Strong hearts just keep going.

— Crusaders

EIGHT

We were driving through a drizzly afternoon the color of gun metal when Lawrence asked me about my father. Lawrence was a counselor with the Institute for Responsible Fatherhood and Family Revitalization; I had seen him lead two men through a role-playing exercise that left the man playing the estranged son shaken and nodding with new understanding.

Which is why I answered the question warily. Told him the kind of man my father was and the life we lived as a result. Lawrence listened thoughtfully. Then he asked me something, "Would your father have done the things he did if he had known a better way?"

I resented the question a little. Found it presumptuous and intrusive. I had asked him to introduce me to fathers, not counsel me about mine.

I didn't stop him, though, and Lawrence went on, explaining what he meant. A hog, he said, knows only wallowing in the mud. You can take that hog out of the mud and put a suit on him, but that doesn't make him any less of a hog, any less prone to react to life in the only way he knows. Maybe, said Lawrence, my father was reacting to his life in the only way *he* knew, the only way he had been taught. Maybe he didn't have any choice but to be the man he became.

I wasn't buying it. Muttered something noncommittal as we pulled in across the street from our destination.

We darted through traffic to the front door of a modest row house. A man named Keith met us at the door. Physically, he reminded me of Fred Williamson, his face all hard angles and craggy good looks. But the looks were deceptive. Keith could hardly have been less like the macho Williamson, who used to swagger through action movies with a confidence that could burn concrete.

By contrast, Keith's eyes were haunted. He spoke in fits and starts, his thoughts often coming after long, painful hesitations. I had to strain to hear his voice. There was an almost animal wariness in him.

We sat there over his dining room table and he told me about his forty-five years. About the father who was violent toward the family and about the grandfather he lived with when his parents separated. The grandfather, he said, wasn't much better than his father had been.

"The grandfather was a very ignorant, uneducated and prejudicial man," he said.

Prejudiced against whom? I asked.

"Pretty much anybody other than his own immediate family. Always seemed to like my older brother Kirk more than me. Kirk was a little more acceptable than I was."

Why weren't you acceptable? I asked.

"Little bit different. Quiet." There came one of those long pauses. ". . . Just . . . quiet," he said, finally. "It would be a true statement to say the experience of living there wasn't good for me. Kind of gave me a sense of inferiority. It was always put before me that all the other kids and everybody was supposed to be better than me. All that crap."

Keith has two children. He's one of those men who speaks of his offspring in terms of mistakes and bad choices made. He was, he said, twenty-two years old when his girlfriend became pregnant with his first child, a son named Kamau. "Last thing in the world that I wanted at the time was a child."

Keith and Kamau's mother were broken up at the time, after a relationship that had lasted more than four years. "I had become interested in somebody else and I was trying to work things out there. I came home one Saturday or Friday night from being with the other girl. Didn't go well. Didn't say the things I wanted to say the way I wanted to say them."

When he walked in, he said, he found Kamau's mother lying in his bed. "I was very mad that she was there. I thought of rudely waking her up, telling her to get the hell out. I didn't do that."

Instead, he had sex with her "to fulfill unfulfilled needs. To the best of my recollection, it seemed to me that I had protected myself by not releasing any semen in her.

"It wasn't a very romantic kind of thing at all," he added. "It was an anger thing. I don't think I saw her or talked to her again until a couple of months later when she comes over one evening, and she tells me that she's pregnant.

"I was very hurt when she told me that. It was a tone in her voice, expression, body language and all, that [said], 'I've done something I know you didn't want. And I know it hurts you, and I know it's nothing you can do about it.' I didn't let on to that's how I perceived it, because this particular female was supposed to be so sweet and passive and nice and all that and not devious and all these things that women can be." Keith's voice was heavy with sarcasm and reproach. "I know if I'd tried to get support from my mother or sisters or family or anybody, I was going to be the heavy and the bad person," he said. "I'm the bad male."

Similarly, he told me, he didn't ask the girl to get an abortion because he knew she wouldn't. She wanted the baby to "hold over" him.

"I hated with all my heart having a child with a woman I wasn't married to and wasn't going to be a family. But I couldn't stop her from having the baby."

So Keith joined the army, married Kamau's mother, and went to his posting in Germany, leaving her behind. He wrote home, asking his wife to find an apartment for the two of them to live in when he returned. "I'd get all these letters about the baby this, the baby that, the baby the other. All these pictures of the baby. The baby this, the baby that, the baby the other."

Keith returned to Washington two and one-half years later and met his son for the first time. "I'm not sure," he said, "but I think I didn't like the way he looked."

A couple of months after his return, Keith filed for divorce. "That was after making another mistake, though," he said.

This "mistake" was a girl—Aeisha—by another woman who, said Keith, "came over to my mother's house when I was there. I started messing with her, see how far she'd let me go and she didn't stop me, so I went on. Thought again [that] I had pulled out. Next time I see her, she tells me she's pregnant. I screamed and hollered and cussed that time. I was really pissed off that time."

How many kids do you have in all? I asked.

"Just those two."

On the mantle was a picture of a young man with large, frightened eyes, wearing a soldier's uniform that seemed to swallow him. This was Kamau. "He don't look like me," said Keith. I wondered about Kamau in that moment. I felt sympathy for him.

When you look toward the future for these kids, I said, what do you want them to be able to say about you?

"That they know I loved them, cared for them, did what I could for them, was there for them as much as I could."

Was there a conscious effort on your part not to be the father that your father was?

"Definitely," said Keith. "[When] I was in high school, we heard a lot about the black matriarchy. [Senator] Patrick Moynihan had did his report and all that. We talked about that in social studies. I was bound and determined not to be part of the statistic. I didn't want to bring any children into the world who were going to be disadvantaged and be a trouble to the world more so than a benefit."

I asked him if he felt he'd achieved that goal.

"Despite it all, yeah. [Aeisha] is more than I could ask for. She turned eighteen last month. She's finishing up high school now. She's been on the top of her class ever since she's been in school. There's a tenth of a point difference between her and the valedictorian. She's a captain of the majorettes, she's in a sorority and the step team."

And Kamau?

"He did all right in school," said Keith. "His mother kind of messed with his head too much in order to get back at me. And with all the killings and the shootings and stuff that was going around in high school, I think he was very much intimidated by all that. He didn't assert himself as much as he could, as opposed to just trying to make his way through without drawing too much attention and all."

I get the feeling you don't fully believe he's your child, I said.

Something flashed in Keith's eyes. There was another of those long pauses. ". . . I guess there's always going to be a little seed of doubt in the back of my mind if the paternity thing is never done," he conceded.

And again I felt sympathy for Kamau.

Moments later, as we were crossing the street back to the car, Lawrence asked what I thought of Keith. I told him the truth. That he struck me as a man eager to blame others for his failings. And that he struck me, too, as a man imprisoned by his own past. Lawrence gave a satisfied nod.

So here's the question, then: How do we get there from here? Where does the road on which two scarred men both travel diverge, so that one finds his way to functioning fatherhood and the other is left traveling circles in a fog of unfulfilled potential and failed efforts?

I posed that question to several successful fathers. Mike said he modeled himself after his ex-wife's father and a neighbor across the street. "Fortunately, I had two older men that were very directly involved in my life and kind of helped me do the right thing and show me what the right thing was, being that I wasn't getting any help from home, from my dad. Those two men were very influential on making me the person that I was."

Andrew said he found what he needed in the Bible and in an uncle who lived across the street. "The thing that impressed me most about him was that he was always there, whether his kids liked it or not. And they didn't like it because he was a strict disciplinarian. He was always there for them and he was always in church. He was in church every Sunday."

Jerry told me he mimicked an older brother, and also men he saw in his neighborhood. "I was able to pick out some unique things about them, qualities and attributes. I said, 'I want to be like that.'"

Charles credited his mother. "My mother never spoke ill of my father, even though he did all the things he did. When he would do certain things, she would say, 'That's not how you treat a woman. You treat a woman like this. . . .' When we were little kids, she would talk to us about what we wanted to be when we got older. The neighbors used to say my mother raised us like white folks raise their kids, and would tease her. But that didn't matter to my mother. She just extracted from everything good she saw around her. She was a maid, but she was a smart woman. The stuff that white folks did that she saw working, she did that. And the stuff that black folks did that she saw working, she did that."

If there is a common denominator among them, it seems to be this: Each felt he had somewhere to go, a resource he could turn to for comfort and advice in making himself Dad. None was forced to pick through the barren fields of his meager experiences with his own father, trying to figure out from that what to do.

As we drove away from Keith's house that rainy day in Washington, Lawrence was talking about another factor: The ability to close the books on the past, to come to terms with what happened back there and then move beyond. It is, as he sees it, a crucial element in the making of a whole man. It's also an element men often ignore.

Instead, we do what we are taught that men are supposed to do: Sweep the emotions into a dark corner and pretend they don't exist, pretend they have no power to affect us. I'm reminded of David, being caught in that lie he told himself, one minute saying he no longer cared about his father's approval and then whispering the contrary as I left his door. "Even now, I still want his respect," he said. "Even now."

That kind of self-deception seems to find its echo in the pained faces and strained voices of a dozen other men, all saying emphatically that they don't think about their missing or abusive fathers, don't care where they are, are ambivalent about them. And all the while, their bodies are calling them liars.

As Timothy puts it, "For all of those that went bad, that found themselves with six or seven illegitimate children, or maybe find themselves in trouble with the law, for all of them, they never came to grips with their situation. Before they went into the world, they never accepted where they were, where they came from, and who they are."

It's not enough to want to do things differently, to promise you're going to avoid your father's mistakes. Those mistakes hold greater sway over a man's destiny than we think. And here, I think again of Cleveland, the father I met in San Diego who grew up watching his stepfather abuse his mother. You will remember that when Cleveland got older, he did the same thing to his child's mother. She left him and that tore his heart out. So when he finally entered a new relationship, he renewed the promise that he would avoid the patterns of abuse. Yet when I met him, Cleveland was only a few months out of jail for beating his stepdaughter's mother.

Twice he'd tried to break the cycle. Twice he'd failed. I asked him why. Cleveland said he didn't know. He'd been trying to find out himself by searching his family history. What he'd found so far was a grandfather who was abusive to his own wife. So the violence went back at least three generations.

Cleveland was in counseling when I met him. He said he could already see the changes. "As far as me hitting my wife right now, I don't do it. I talk to her in a lower tone of voice, I respect her. My daughter can see it. A good loving conversation with your spouse is a good environment to your children. That's what I'm learning."

He nodded toward the stepdaughter sitting beside him. Having a father who's involved in your life makes a big impact, he said. That's something else he's discovered. "I can see it as I raise her. I'm selling candy for her, I help her with her homework, I go to the school meetings, just being there for her. I can see it in her. It's a *shine.* You can *see* it. It's a glow. I mean, mother's always going to be there, but it's just different with fathers somehow."

Different. In ways social science has scarcely begun to quantify. But you can feel it. You can *see* it.

My daughter's kindergarten class held a "tea" for fathers and their children one day. A bunch of men taking the morning off from work to have breakfast with their children at a picnic table under a shade tree behind the classroom. It was a happy morning. Every kid's father—or in one or two cases, a grandfather—showed up. You could see the children beaming in the undivided attention of these men. Everywhere you looked, boys and girls were climbing jungle gyms, running across the lawn, and the air was alive with the sound of them all saying the same thing, "Daddy, look at me! Look at me!"

Different somehow.

Which is what makes it so crucial that a man do whatever he has to do to become a functioning father. Even if it means coming to grips with those emotions and memories we cast to the side, the ones we tell ourselves have no power over us. Because the fact is, they do. A hard past doesn't die. Not ever. You look at children of the Great Depression—rheumy-eyed and wrinkled now, yet still inordinately cautious with money, still consider waste the greatest sin there is, still live in thrall to a nightmare of want and deprivation that ended a lifetime ago.

A hard past doesn't die. But you can, if you are willing and brave, sit down with it and negotiate a peace.

Lawrence knows all about negotiating that peace. A few days after we left Keith's house, the counselor and I met again in his office. He wanted me to ask him some of the same questions I'd asked Keith. So I did. And Lawrence

Lawrence

started telling me about his life, some of which I've already recounted here. He talked about how his parents split up because his father was abusive to his mother. He spoke of beating his own wife and raping her, about the daughters he abandoned and about the day he got so sick of it all that he decided to end his own life.

"I remember getting a gun that I owned and I drove around the city of Cleveland looking for a place to get up the courage to take my life. I really am not sure to this day why I did it, other than it was meant for me not to die: I called a worker from this Institute at home, *not* to have them talk me out of suicide. I had the gun to my ear and as I was talking, I was going to pull the trigger. It was at a pay phone at the intersection of Lomond Boulevard and Lee Road in Shaker Heights."

This was not too far from his father's house. "That was the place that I had picked. So I had the gun to my head, I was talking to this worker and I began to use profanity and curse out my life. I said, 'Man, this is unbelievable, this is unreal, to have to be going through this kind of blankety-blank-blank.' And the worker, in a calm voice, said, 'How your wife treats you is not your business, and it's not your problem.' I said, 'Man, you better get out of here! She does this, she does this, she does this!' The worker said, 'What you're going through has nothing to do with your wife. Because if you leave her and go to another woman, you're going to carry all that mess with you.'

"And he asked me this question: 'What would happen if you could learn to give up all your selfish desires and dedicate 100 percent of yourself to pleasing your wife? And what would happen if your wife could learn to give up all her selfish desires and dedicate 100 percent of herself to pleasing you?' I said, 'Man, we'd have a relationship with an ecstasy beyond belief.' He said, 'Well, you don't have any control over her, but you've got control over [yourself].' And I said, 'But this pain that's inside me over these two children I can't be involved with, it's just eating me up inside.' The guy said, 'The best thing you can do for these two children is to learn how to show love and respect to their mother, even though you're not involved with her.'"

Lawrence's voice was touched by wonder as he spoke. "It was like a tremendous burden was lifted off of me," he recalled. "If you've ever heard people talk about a religious conversion experience, I would equate what I went through at that moment, to that. I remember my hand coming down from my head and then, *boom!* I pulled the trigger on the gun. Not like I intended to shoot it, but that's what I did. And the bullet lodged in the dash of the car."

He had begun to negotiate a peace with his pain.

As Lawrence tells it, he has largely blocked his father from his mind. He says he has only six childhood memories of the man, all of which revolve around themes of abandonment and abuse. In one memory, his father has promised to come by and pick him up for a visit and never does. In another, he's beating him for misbehavior. Six memories, said Lawrence, and all of them negative.

"At age thirty-seven, I decided I was going to reach out to him. Which was painful. What comes to mind, I think it's in Malachi, Chapter Four, verses five and six: 'In the last dreadful days of the Lord, I will send the prophet Elijah. And he shall turn the hearts of the fathers to their children and the hearts of the children to their fathers. Lest I smite the Earth with a curse.'

"Look around and see what's happening with our society; the curse is taking its effect. But I decided that if my father is not going to be what I needed him to be to me, I'm going to do my part to become the child to him that I should be. I remember calling him up and saying, 'You know, I only have these six childhood memories. I'd like to get together with you and talk and find out what life was like for me as a child.'"

Lawrence made his voice into his father's then, rough and impatient: "'What do you want to talk about?'

"'I don't know,'" he told the older man. "'I don't remember anything.'

"Well," said the father, "if you can't tell me what you want to talk about, I don't have anything to say."

"I'm thirty-seven," said Lawrence, "and I'm holding the phone and I'm crying. But I didn't want to let him know that that's what I was doing. He said, 'Man, just call me back later.' And he hung up the phone. About a week later, I called him again. 'Hey, how you doing? How are things going?' And then I said what was the most difficult thing to say to my father. As I was hanging up the phone, I said, 'Okay, just wanted to let you know I was thinking about you. And Daddy, I love you.'

"Next thing I heard," said Lawrence, and he completed the sentence by banging his knuckles against the desk—the sound of the telephone receiver being slammed back into the cradle. For the better part of a year, that was the pattern. "Daddy, I love you," followed by a phone going back on the hook and then the empty hum of a dial tone.

"It became easier and easier for me to say it," said Lawrence. "When I relocated from Cleveland, he called me and left a message on my answering machine. He says, 'Son, as you always say to me, I just wanted to see how you were doing. And Son, I love you.'

"Our relationship is not as bad as it was," said Lawrence, "but I wish I could be closer to him."

So, I'm wondering, what does all of this mean to me? My father has been dead for many years. And besides, what he did and who he was, these things don't affect me anymore, do they?

Do they?

I hadn't planned it, wasn't even thinking it as Lawrence spoke. But a seed was planted then, and grew in the weeks that followed.

What if my father didn't know any better? Lawrence had said. And if he *had* known a better way, would he still have done the things he did? I didn't know.

Did I love him? Didn't know.

Did I hate him? Didn't know.

And I *wanted* to know. Wanted to escape this ambivalent place. Wanted to negotiate a peace.

A seed was planted and grew to fruit one hot night several months later as I walked across a tarmac and climbed aboard a small plane bound for Mississippi. I went in search of someone I never knew, a farm boy whose name and face were the same as mine.

NINE

Macon is a town in northeast Mississippi most people have never heard of. So small that if you lean down to adjust your car radio, you might miss it altogether.

Mashulaville is a *suburb* of that, lying about ten miles west. There's almost literally nothing to see. Unpaved roads branch off into the woods from a two-lane blacktop and cows graze peaceably in the fields.

This is where my father was born.

"My people got land," he used to boast. In our minds, I think, it assumed a nigh-mythical status.

This afternoon, as the mercury climbs past the middle nineties, I've asked an old man named Walker Hill to show me to this land. We are proceeding down the blacktop in his truck when, without warning, he veers sharply to the right. Next thing I know, tree branches are slapping at the windshield of the truck and we are bouncing roughly along what once, evidently, was a road. Several minutes later, we reach a small clearing where someone has dumped an old stove and refrigerator, both coated now with rust.

This, says Hill, is about where the house stood. This is the land of my father's pride. Sixty-one acres of Mississippi trees and soil.

It used to be more. As far as the eye can see, says Hill. It all used to belong to my family. That was before it was sold off and mortgaged away in pieces that reduced it to its present size. What's left is overgrown now, reclaimed by nature. But when my father's three surviving sisters talk about it, it is a

Walker Hill

thriving farm of dairy cows and corn, hens and greens, supporting a large colored family in the South of the '20s and '30s.

The land came into my family in November 1899, when Richard and Lavinia Cook paid the British American Mortgage Company, Ltd., six hundred dollars for 340 acres. The Cooks had only one child, a daughter named Annie. In 1904, when she was nineteen, Annie Cook married a minister named John Wesley Pitts, the son of a black landowner named Dennis and a white Irish wife named Louise. John Wesley was ten years his wife's senior. When her father died, the land became theirs.

They certainly needed the space. Annie Pitts bore nine children over the next seventeen years. Leonard Garvey, my father, was the tenth of an eventual thirteen. He was born on May 5, in 1924. His middle name was probably an homage to Marcus Garvey, the great black nationalist who was then at the height of his fame in New York City. My grandfather was of a political bent; some of the old men who were children then remember him as doing civil rights work before that term even came into being.

As a seventy-three-year-old named Nelson Short puts it, "He was teaching, way back yonder, things that I'm coming across now: That you need to get up, instead of feeling sorry for yourself. You get up and look around and it's plenty things you could be doing helping other folks [instead of] sitting around pitiful. He would make talks on Thanksgiving and holidays like that, all about how they come about, what was you celebrating. Until I got to know him, I didn't know really what [Thanksgiving] was about. I just knew it was a time when you didn't have to work!" said Short with a laugh.

"He was real smart. He would talk about things. And sometimes, he wasn't liked by the white people too well because he was enlightening black people [about] what they needed to know. It's all right to work on where you're working, but you need to know how come you're there. That's the main thing. You find out that you could be at home farming, just as well as you over there plowing that [other] man's crop."

John Wesley, in other words, argued that black people should own their own. This, at a time when a ruinous sharecropper system was the norm for black farmers. He was a man ahead of his time.

"My daddy was no dummy by a long ways," is how my Aunt Annie puts it. She is the oldest of my father's three surviving sisters. Adoration softens her features when she talks about her father. "[He] went to school and he wrote a beautiful handwriting. He was a scholar. But he never got the chance that his children had, because he moved from place to place. And he did not take nothing. Feisty. Stand up to them white folks. I seen my mother just [fearful] because she was scared somebody was going to hang him."

One incident tells the story.

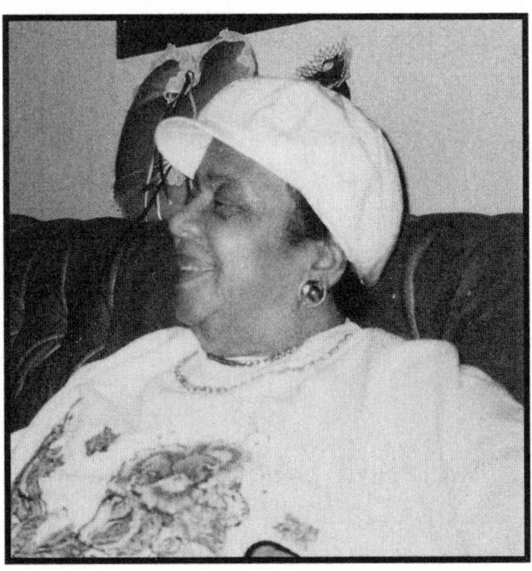

Aunt Annie

My aunts were children, riding the wagon with their parents to church on a Sunday morning. And the white man who owned the adjacent land came out to confront them, bearing a long shotgun.

As Aunt Annie remembers the story, the man accused my grandfather of letting his cows cross the property line. "My father said, 'No, it wasn't my cows.' And I think he said, 'Are you calling me a liar?' And my father let him know, if that's what you call it, if that's what it is, that's what it is. Because he knows this was not his cows. His fence was not broken anywhere where his cows had been out.

"And anyway, an argument ensued and Papa jumped out of there, and this white man told him, 'I will shoot, I will hang you.'"

He raised the rifle and my aunt says there's no doubt that he would have carried through on his threat. "That's the way they were doing at that time. They were killing black people just like they were dogs. Didn't make them any difference."

My grandmother knew this, too. She jumped down from the wagon and got between the two men, the rifle barrel pushing into her stomach.

My father's next youngest living sister, my Aunt Ruth, takes up the story. "Mama started crying," she said, "and said, 'Don't shoot him! Shoot me! Shoot me!' She got in front of it and told the man to shoot her. And he told him, 'Wesley, I ought to blow your goddam brains out.' Whoo! I will never forget that."

"[My father] did not step back," said Aunt Annie. "He ain't moved. He would die. If he was going for what was right, he didn't care. My mother told him, 'Come on, Wesley, come on.' She's just pleading with him. And I guess she prayed, [because the white man] just turned around and walked. And Papa wanted to still get up and get this man. Mama got him in there and cooled him down, talking to him and we went on to church.

"See, my father did not work for none of them. He never knew nothing about no sharecropping. His children didn't have to work for none of 'em. And so they kind of pick on you. They call you crazy when you stand up."

This is, of course, the way the world was constructed then. In the year of my father's birth, there were sixteen recorded lynchings of black persons. And this represented a significant *improvement* over the tallies of previous years.

As seventy-seven-year-old Beatrice Walker, a childhood friend of my

Aunt Ruth

father's, puts it, "They was very, very much prejudiced then. If you see 'em coming, you have to get out the way.

"We was coming from the show one day," she said. "Five of us girls. And about three white young folks told us, 'Get out the street!' And Riley Allen—that was a man from New Salem—he told them, 'They don't have to get out.' They stopped and looked at him. They didn't go to him. But we said we was gon' get 'em. We all said that. 'If [they] touch him, we gon' whip them today.' But they didn't bother him."

In owning their own farm, said Walker Hill, the Pitts family had something of an advantage over those blacks who had to sharecrop or were otherwise economically beholden to whites. "They had all that land up there and they didn't do too much [hiring themselves] out or nothing like that. They had their own."

It was a life of predictable rhythms. Up before the dawn to milk the cows and put the big five-gallon cans of milk out on the highway where a dairy truck would pick them up every morning around eight, dropping off the empties in the evening.

This, said Aunt Ruth, was my father's chore. "I know him and [the youngest son] Carl had to get up and go and milk the cows in the morning and put the milk on the highway. We sold milk. In the evening, Carl and Leonard had to go get the cans from the highway." In between the farm work, there was school, church, and, of course, play.

"We did little devilish things like drink milk out of the cows' titties," recalls Aunt Mildred, youngest of the thirteen children, "scoot milk at each other. Just things that children do. We made Jake ladders and put cans on the end and walk around, *clop, clop, clop, clop.*"

A Jake ladder, she explained, was a contraption with a long board on each side, a ledge for your foot and cans tied to the end. "We'd walk on it—we'd be way up in the air, walking on those things. At that time, we had to make our toys. Our parents were poor; they didn't have no money, so we made everything we played with.

"Christmastime was the biggest time of our lives. It was just a happy time. We didn't get anything but maybe an apple or orange, raisins, prunes, peppermint candy. I'm just talking about the fun we had on simple things in life that we made ourselves."

Aunt Mildred

Friday was washing day. Saturday was the day to go town, meaning Macon, where the young people spent the afternoon walking around, seeing and being seen. Maybe they'd slip off to a movie—"the show," they called it—when their parents weren't looking. And then, of course, there was church on Sunday.

They were good days, recalls Nelson Short. Then he catches himself and adds, with a wry laugh, "But I did a mighty heap of walkin' for them to be good days."

Walking, it seems, was an inescapable part of life. Bad enough Macon was ten miles away. But if a fellow grew sweet on a girl, that meant even more walking, what with escorting her from and back to her front door. "Walk home with the girls yonder way, then have to walk all the way back. You be walkin' near about all night! Before you get home and get in the bed, time to get up and catch the mule."

My grandmother is remembered by all as a quiet woman with a kind heart and an even temper. A great fisherwoman, too, according to Beatrice Walker.

My grandfather is similarly well remembered.

"He was a nice guy, a nice man," said Curtis Walker, yet another childhood friend of my father's.

"A hard working farmer," said Aunt Ruth.

"Very sweet man," said my Aunt Mildred.

And my Aunt Annie said he was "A good man. God ain't put none here no better."

A decent man, then, by all accounts. But invariably, there comes a coda

Curtis Walker

to that judgment, an offhand suggestion of something darker also at work.

"He had a temper," says Aunt Annie.

In this, too, everyone concurs. And then the stories start coming out. The old people who were his students at the little country school say he didn't really have the patience a teacher needs. "He was a pretty good teacher," said Nelson Short, "but he'd tear you up, boy. Hickory switch, whatever come up."

"Beat our butts if we didn't do right," said my Aunt Ruth.

My Aunt Annie sought to correct her. "He didn't whip the girls, he whipped the boys," she said.

"Yes he did," retorted Aunt Ruth emphatically. "He whipped *my* ass." She recalls a time when she was fourteen and staying in Memphis with Annie, who is seven years older. Aunt Ruth returned to the farm for a visit that summer and got into a row with her youngest brother. "Carl busted a watermelon," she said, "and he put half of it down over my head. An old rotten watermelon. And I came to the house just hollering, crying. I'm a big girl; I didn't want nobody puttin' no watermelon on my head. And he whipped Carl for doing it and whipped me for hollering. With a *stick!*

"I called him an old bald-head something, and I said, 'This the last time you going to hit me. You will never hit me no more, because I ain't coming back.'"

It reminded me of a story my father used to tell. He and his father were on the roof, doing some repairs. My grandfather hit his thumb with the hammer. My father, thinking this the funniest thing he'd ever seen, broke out laughing. In response to which, my grandfather took an angry swipe at him, knocking him off the roof. I asked my aunts if that story was true, if my grandfather had actually done that.

"He might have," said Aunt Ruth. "He might not have intended to knock him off the roof. He might've hit him and he fell off the roof, you know?"

It's difficult to know how much to make of it. Certainly, it would constitute child abuse by the laws and mores of this time. But it didn't happen in this time. It happened sixty or more years ago, happened at a time when physical punishment was common and parents ruled with iron fists. Even today, black families are more apt than others to sanction corporal punishment. It's worth noting, too, that my father was usually laughing when he told that story—never seemed to regard the episode with anger or resentment. My mother had similar stories to tell about her parents and *she* laughed, too. I take it as a reminder to beware the presumption of judging their lives by our standards.

And yet, even granting those caveats, I can't help but wonder if it doesn't mean something that everyone who recalls John Wesley Pitts invokes that dichotomy: his goodness and his willingness to use violence.

"He had a razor strop," says Aunt Ruth. "You know what a razor strop is? It's a big thick leather, about that wide"—she held her hands maybe a foot apart—"and they'd sharpen straight razors [on them]. He whipped them boys with a razor strop."

Aunt Annie told me that when she was little, she would cry and run away when the whipping of her older siblings started. "I swore that if I got up big enough, they wasn't going to whip me like that; I would run away. I had that so strong and I was so against it in my little mind that I dreamed that they whipped me to death and put me in a pint jar. This is what I dreamed."

Aunt Mildred remembers my grandfather tying his sons to a peach tree with a rope when it was time to administer punishment. The picture she conjures is stunning to me. The grandson of a slave tying his children to a tree to beat them.

"It wasn't nothing that critical," Aunt Mildred assured me. "He just wouldn't tussle with them; he had a tendency to tie Carl and Leonard to the tree. Get through with Leonard, he'd tie Carl. Big tree. And he'd go round and round the tree with a rope. He would whip 'em and I would just stand back crying and asking Pop, 'Please don't whip my brothers.' I just used to have a fit over it. I didn't like it."

There was an elemental harshness to John Wesley Pitts. And a schism. The same man who was capable of tying his boys to a tree and whipping them didn't allow cursing in his presence. Walked through his days governed by a moral code that could be—and often was—unforgiving and astringent. He was the prototypical Papa who didn't take no mess. In those days when all was "yes ma'am" and "no, sir" and children were to be seen but never heard, he was the unquestionable authority, the ultimate unknowable father. But at the same time, there was a certain rough tenderness to the man, a jagged sweetness. His daughters recall him with as much fear as affection. Indeed, the two emotions seem to mingle into some indefinable third thing.

For Aunt Mildred, he's a bald curmudgeon, yelling for her to come find his glasses when they were perched right on top of his head all along.

For Aunt Ruth, he's the dad who came home fussing to beat the band the day the kids killed one of his pigs and tried to cook it, without knowing how to clean the thing.

And Aunt Annie recalls him coming to visit her once after she was grown and married. Her husband was away and she out went to visit a girlfriend, only to return home to a disapproving lecture from her father. "He acted like he was my husband," she told me. "He said, 'Where have you been? I never thought I'd have a daughter that would be out in the streets. That does not look nice.'"

Formidable as he was, John Wesley's daughters can recall only one occasion when he raised a hand against his wife, whom he called Sugar. "Every Sunday," said Aunt Ruth, "Papa used to take a walk over his land. And the little ones would be running and playing along. Papa was taking his Sunday evening walk down to look at his corn or whatever it was, and him and Mama got to arguing. And that was the only time I ever saw Papa start to slap Mama. He didn't hit her, but he *started* to slap Mama. I remember that. Leonard and I said, 'Never saw that before.'"

When John Wesley was provoked to violence, it was likely to be my father who did the provoking. His sisters and friends all use the same word to describe the first Leonard Pitts: devilish.

"Look like he would always be doing something," said Aunt Annie.

"He got a lot of whippings," said Aunt Ruth.

"That was just his nature," added Aunt Annie. "He did things. He was busy keeping something going."

"He loved to fight and things like that," said Curtis Walker. "He was kind of mean. He'd fight in a minute. He'd fight schoolteachers and everything else if they make him mad enough."

"He was kind of devilish," said Nelson Short.

I asked him to explain. "Some boys is quiet," he said. "Some of 'em not quite so quiet."

My father, then, was one of the not-so-quiet, though Short was quick to put that in context—rowdy country boys, they could be scrapping one minute and friends again the next. Don't read too much into it, he seemed to say.

"He was a real nice young man. Very intelligent," said Walker Hill.

Duly noted. But there was this other side as well. This "devilish" side that kept him in trouble, kept him running afoul of his strict and moralistic father. This side that used to compel him to sit in the trees, pissing down on passersby. The side that once drove him to hide under the house with a pile of rocks. He spent an afternoon chucking those missiles at his brothers and sisters. No one could get close enough to drag him out. Charles Hayes, who was married to my late Aunt Edna, said that when my father was ten or eleven, he somehow convinced some naive kid a few years younger to pull his pants down, take a stick and use it to hit a wasp's nest. "Those wasps," said Uncle Charles, "like to stung the poor boy to death."

There was, said Aunt Mildred, a "demon" in Leonard Pitts.

My father left the farm at nineteen and enlisted in the army. The year was 1943, a turning-point year in racial relations, according to historian Lerone Bennett Jr. America was two years into World War II in Europe while at the same time fighting Jim Crow wars in the streets of its major cities. There were race riots that year in Harlem, Detroit, Mobile, and elsewhere.

Uncle Charles Hayes

Though the demand for men and materiel was crushing, the nation's military continued their tradition of segregation, with black units routinely drawing dirty, menial duty. "A black man didn't do no fighting when they first went in World War II," recalled Curtis Walker, who also served during that war. "[Later], they had to have 'em. But they tried to keep 'em from fighting as much as they could. They didn't want a black man to fight if they could help it."

My father was assigned to Camp Van Dorn, just north of the Louisiana border, not quite forty miles southeast of Natchez. It was while he was based there that he met my mother.

She would have been seventeen that year. Photos taken around that time show a dazzling young woman—dark, luminous skin, smoky eyes, full lips. I imagine that the rakish young soldier never even knew what hit him.

Agnes Rowan was the second child of five born to Pearl and Rachel Rowan, who lived in Natchez. Isabel Gordon was a girlhood friend so close that she and my mother considered themselves sisters. She can barely remember a time when they were not friends. As children, they were inseparable.

"[Agnes] used to have to go take lunch down to the box factory under the hill to her daddy. She wouldn't want to go by herself and she always would come and ask Mama could I go. And we would take her daddy lunch and have it down there for twelve o'clock.

"Her daddy used to pay her fifty cents a week to bring it. And she'd ask her daddy, 'What can I do with fifty cents?' He said, 'Fifty cents will buy a lot. And you better save some for the next day.' Lot of times, I didn't have money to buy lunch at school and she knowed it, 'cause she would always buy my lunch. When I had money, I would buy her lunch. Me and her, together."

My mother, she said, was a spirited and feisty girl. "She didn't take no foolishness off you. White nor black. She didn't care who were, she'd give you a piece of her mind."

I was surprised. These were not years when a black person could easily tell a white one off, I said. "Well, *she* did," insisted Mrs. Gordon. "She was working for one, Miss Burns. And her and Miss Burns got into it and she just told Miss Burns off. Told her what she wanted her to know: 'If you want me to work for you, you let me do my work like I know how to do it. You don't get in here and talk to me no any kind of way, 'cause I'm human just like you.'"

According to Mrs. Gordon, young Agnes got along well with her folks.

Agnes

"She loved both her parents, but she was crazy about her daddy. For a little girl, she was kind of fast, too," said Mrs. Gordon, invoking the old slang term for a girl who is womanish beyond her years. It made me laugh.

"Oh, she was a whip," continued Mrs. Gordon. "That Agnes, she was something. Cuss you out in a minute. Didn't care who you was. You cuss her, she'd cuss you back. And the teachers at school couldn't fool with Agnes. She got her lessons, she done what she had to do, but they didn't bother her.

"Agnes was tough. I would stand sometimes and look at her, listen at her. And I'd say, 'Agnes, why you do that?' 'Well, they had no business saying what they said to me. I would have never said it to them.' And we'd laugh and walk on off. [When] she met your daddy, that's when she really kind of slowed down some."

They met at a dance on a warship. An open house thrown by Camp Van Dorn. My mother, too young to be there and, of course, "fast" beyond her years, snuck onto the ship along with her friend Isabel. They also took along my aunt, Kate, who was all of eight years old and whom they had been saddled with baby-sitting.

"[Isabel] says all the time that they took me on there so I wouldn't go back and tell Mama they had been on there," recalled Aunt Kate with a laugh. "Even though they were young ladies, my mom probably would have gotten upset if she had known they had been on there."

Leonard and Agnes apparently hit it off right away. There was an instant and mutual attraction. Then my father's orders came through and he was shipped out. Agnes told him that if what they felt was real, then it would survive his absence and once he was out of the military, he would come back and find her.

While he was gone, though, my mother married someone else. And divorced him.

"It was the quickest marriage," recalled Mrs. Gordon with a laugh. "They met, got married and I don't know whether they stayed together a month. I said, 'Well, why did you marry him?' She said, 'I don't know. I married him, I guess, just to get out my mama's house.' I said, 'Well, Agnes, you didn't have to marry him to get out your mama's house. Your mama wasn't doing nothing to you.'"

My mother's reply: "I know, but I just wanted to see how it felt to be a woman."

Curiously enough, Mrs. Gordon said that first marriage broke up because the man was a wife beater.

In the meantime, Leonard Pitts was gone to war. He was, he later said, assigned to the Transportation Corps in France, which became famous as the Red Ball Express. The Express was six thousand trucks manned by drivers who worked grueling thirty-six hour shifts to shuttle food, ammunition, and other supplies to advancing Allied troops during the invasion of France. The drivers, many of them African-American, followed a route that had been marked out for them using signs with red dots—hence, the name. They were renowned for their recklessness. The speed limit along the route was twenty-five miles per hour. The Red Ball drivers were often clocked doing twice that, much to the chagrin of soldiers and civilians trying to use the same road. But the Express got the job done, delivering over twelve thousand tons of materiel in the first five days of operation. Seven days later, the total was eighty-nine thousand tons.

Discharged from the Army in 1945, my father went to Chicago, where his sisters and brothers were beginning to migrate. He went to work at Argonne National Laboratory. Was fired before too long. The reason, according to one of my uncles: drinking on the job.

John L. Johnson, a distant cousin who spent a lot of time with my father in those days, said he was a nice guy who liked to have fun, liked to laugh, and loved to drink. "He did, he drank quite a bit."

"Your daddy was a happy-go-lucky," said Uncle Charles. "He'd get a job a little while—wouldn't keep one long. Drank two hundred proof alcohol and Coke on the job."

The chronology is difficult to pin down, but it was probably not long after he lost the job at Argonne that my father returned to Mississippi and found the girl he'd met at the dance several years before. They were inseparable after that. For a time, they lived in Holly Springs, a small Mississippi town where my father and two of his siblings—Ruth and Carl—tried to make a go of a small restaurant. As my Aunt Ruth recalls it, the enterprise failed because her feckless and irresponsible brothers kept using the cash register as their personal reserve, dipping out wads of money to support their good times.

From there, Leonard and Agnes went to Memphis where he drove a cab and she worked as a soda jerk in the train station and also was a domestic for a white doctor. In 1952, my father re-enlisted in the military—this time, as a Marine. Shortly after he completed his recruit training, he was granted a two-week leave. It was during that period—on October 1st—that he and my mother were married. Isabel still remembers receiving the letter.

"She wrote and told me they had gotten married and she said, 'In order for you to believe that I am married to Mr. Pitts'—that's what she always called him, Mr. Pitts—'I will send you a copy of my marriage license.' And I wrote back and told her I didn't want her marriage license. What I'm going to do with it?"

In his second stint with the armed forces, my father was a cook, first at Parris Island, South Carolina, then at Camp Lejeune, North Carolina, and, finally, at Camp Pendleton in California. He was discharged two days after Christmas, 1954.

Through it all, my mother always kept in touch with her old friend back home. The letters were happy ones. The occasional visits, even more so.

"Him and Agnes used to kill me fussing," recalled Isabel with a smile. "He'd tell me, 'Sis, it's not me, it's her. She's always starting something and don't know how to end it.' I'd say, 'Well, why is she picking at you?' 'I don't know. She's just mean . . . with her black self.'"

Isabel shifted into my mother's voice. "'That's all right. I'm black. You got me. You love me, don't you?'"

The recollection resonates. My mother was dark-skinned and my father loved to make fun of it, though in later years there was none of the affection Isabel heard. None of the affection that led him to reply, "'If I didn't love you, I never would've married you.' They used to tickle me," said Isabel, still beaming.

There must be a couple dozen pictures of them taken during those years, and they all tell the same story: an attractive couple, often seen clustered together with friends around a nightclub table heavy with drinks and smokes. Everyone smiling, everyone lost in good times that seemed endless. You gaze into black and white prints from four and five decades ago and you can almost hear the chatter of voices and the clinking of glass, almost smell the smoke, almost see the people crowding the floor to swing it to the earthy testifying of Ruth Brown's latest record, or hold to each other for dear life through the pleadings of the Platters.

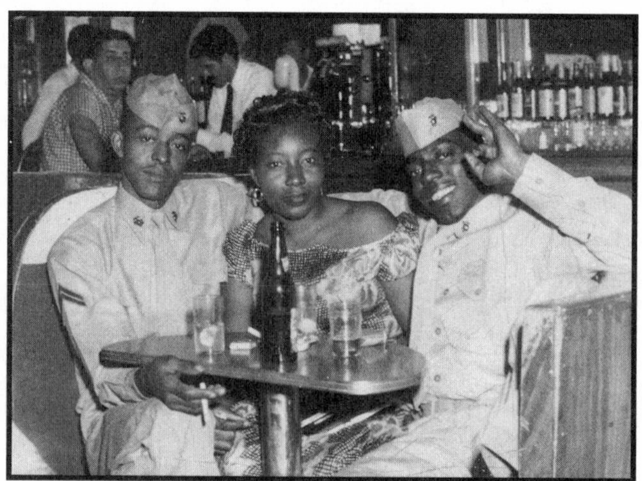

Leonard, Agnes, and a friend

Agnes and Leonard Pitts

Sometimes they were photographed alone, studio settings against painted backdrops. My father proprietary and proud in his uniform, my mother a beautiful mystery nestling into his arms. She used to say that in those years, Leonard Pitts was a sweet and solicitous gentleman of the kind they don't make anymore. Indeed, even at the height of production, they never made more than a few.

Kate, my mother's sister, recalls a time when my parents were staying in a rented place that "didn't have the necessities that we have today, like go and turn the gas on or the central heating or whatever. And he paid someone to come and start the fire in the heater, in the house where she was staying at so when she got up, it would be nice and warm. Just beautiful," she said, shaking her head in admiration and memory. "Beautiful, beautiful, beautiful."

"Leonard was a sweetheart," recalled his sister Mildred adoringly. "He was the life of the party. He brought laughter to you. He'd just do anything foolish to make you laugh. I wonder sometimes was he ever serious, because he always carried on foolish."

It was a good time. But for Agnes, at least, it was also an incomplete time. She wanted a baby. Wanted one badly. Twice she became pregnant, twice she miscarried. Her friend Isabel still recalls the pain my mother felt.

"That really did something to her. She said, 'Oh, children are just not for me.'"

It was early in 1957 that Isabel got a call that her friend was expecting again. "It's going to be my first baby," said Agnes.

"Oh, what you want [it to be]?" asked Isabel.

And Agnes responded as women have often responded, especially when they've known the cruel agony of losing a child. "Long as it's a healthy baby," she said, "it don't make me no difference." She got her wish.

I was born on October 11, 1957, a fat and hungry baby who came into the world gnawing his own fist.

It wasn't long afterward that everything began to change.

TEN

In my favorite picture of the two of us, I'm a baby on his lap. A chubby-cheeked boy, probably not much more than a year old, if that. And he is the proudest of proud fathers. So young, so clear-eyed, and ever so handsome. He wears his pencil-thin moustache atop a mouth that seems to have been caught between smiling and outright laughter. He is so happy.

I never knew the man in that picture, at least, not that I can recall. He was someone my mother reminisced about from time to time. "You should have known him before," she used to say, sadly, softly. "He was a different man, before."

It was a hard thing for me to picture, this idea that he had ever been other than he was. I've always wondered what it was that changed him. His sister Annie has long clung to the belief that the things he saw in the military somehow shattered him. "Shell shock" is her all-purpose explanation.

But my father's last experience with combat was during World War II. By all accounts, he was a decent—if often drunken—man until the late '50s and early '60s, when his children were born. So "shell shock" seems, at best, an incomplete answer. You begin to wonder if the change didn't have something to do with the fact of the children themselves. For the ten years before my arrival, they were a childless couple. For him, at least, I must have signaled an unwelcome change. Especially since his family grew so rapidly after that. Linda was born in 1959, just twenty-one months after. Keith followed two years later, in 1961, and Rachelle came in 1964. This was, I suspect, more responsibility than my happy-go-lucky father truly wanted or knew how to handle.

The Pitts children, 1965 (clockwise from top):
Linda, Keith, Rachelle, and Leonard Jr.

"To tell the truth," said Linda, "I don't think he really wanted children. I think he felt children were an intrusion. Mama always wanted kids, but he wanted her to himself. I think when she cut out all the drinking and partying and started being a mother and doing the right thing, he felt, This is not the woman I married, this is not what I wanted.

"You can look at some of the pictures, they were always together and smiling. They were like the couple of the year. They looked like they were so happy. I don't think he really liked that responsibility, and then her turning into Miss Goody Two-Shoes. Some men are like that."

His rages, she thinks, grew from a resentment as simple as that.

"He didn't really mean the things he did," said his sister Mildred. "Leonard, deep down, had a tender heart. Very tender. He had a kindness about him that a lot of people don't have. It was a demon in Leonard and it caused him to clown and drink too much."

It could not have helped matters that his wife was sickly throughout much of the '60s from high blood pressure and heart disease. She had a medicine cabinet full of pills, seemed like she was on the bus out to what was then called General Hospital at least twice a month. I went with her on a few occasions. It was a sad place—an endless line of poor people sitting all day on hard benches, waiting for their names to be called. This was probably not the future the handsome young soldier in all those nightclub photos had envisioned just ten years before.

Aunt Mildred explained: "He wanted to be the life of the party, you know? Leonard wanted to be jovial. He wanted to kick the responsibilities out of the way. This is how he reacted to life. It was as though he was still a child. He preferred this carefree way of life to this responsibility of family and children and the responsibility of paying bills."

So his response was to retreat. Deeper into indolence and violence. Deeper into rage. Deeper into the bottle. And we did what we could to cope. He couldn't hold a job and soon stopped trying. My mother went on welfare. When the checks arrived on the first and the fifteenth, she had to go shopping right away, because to tarry a day or two was to have the grocery money taken away to be spent on alcohol and good times. Even at that, he made it a point to follow her to the supermarket, where he'd heckle her as she shopped, demanding that she not spend everything on food. When they got back home, he'd order us children to unload the car, invariably saying the same thing: "I bought it. Y'all can bring it in."

He actually seemed to believe it. To think that *he'd* bought the food by the sweat of his brow. As if this money the government dispersed to indigent families like ours was his salary or his entitlement. "*My* money," he used to say.

A few times, I reminded him that he hadn't bought anything—welfare had. This didn't endear me to him. But I hated welfare so much. I didn't understand why he didn't or couldn't work.

I remember one time when we'd had angry words, I ended the argument by yelling, "At least I won't be like you. When I grow up, I won't have my family on welfare!" Then I stormed off to my room where I laid on the bed and kicked the walls.

And yet . . .

In the words of the Al Jarreau song, we got by. My sisters, my brother, and I. Got by, grew up, went out, made productive lives.

Funny thing is, we never talk about where we came from, never mention those days we clustered behind mother's skirts and begged him to leave her alone. It was as if a mutual conclusion was reached without anyone ever saying a word: This was a topic we would not discuss. We would pretend it didn't exist. We would pretend these things never happened. Rachelle, though she was eleven when he died, used to go so far as to claim she couldn't remember him at all.

I never believed her, but I never challenged her on it. Never pushed it. Never said a thing to any of them about him. They went their way and I went mine.

But we are not kids anymore. My fortieth birthday is behind me now and I find myself tired of pretending. Moreover, I find myself wanting to know what they saw and felt, needing to have my own perceptions validated. I had buried him so deep, pushed him down so far that some things about him seemed more myth than memory, something I had made up or embellished. Like when something happens before your eyes and it's so incredible you begin to doubt your own senses. You turn to another witness and say, "Is that true? Did that really happen?"

In just the same way, I made a conscious decision to break the silence. I turned to my witnesses—my sisters and my brother—and asked them if they had seen the same things as I.

* * *

I met Linda, the older of my two sisters, at her home in a middle-class Compton neighborhood. Linda is blunt, plain-spoken, and bossy as hell—as kids, we went a few rounds because of that. She's a nurse now. Between that, her family, and her myriad duties to her church, she's almost never at home. I got her to spare me a precious few minutes one morning as she was on her way to work. She got her husband and their three daughters out the door on the way to their various destinations, then sat with me to talk about our father.

"He was a bad boy," she said. "He really was."

But at the same time, he got along well with her, relatively speaking. "It's

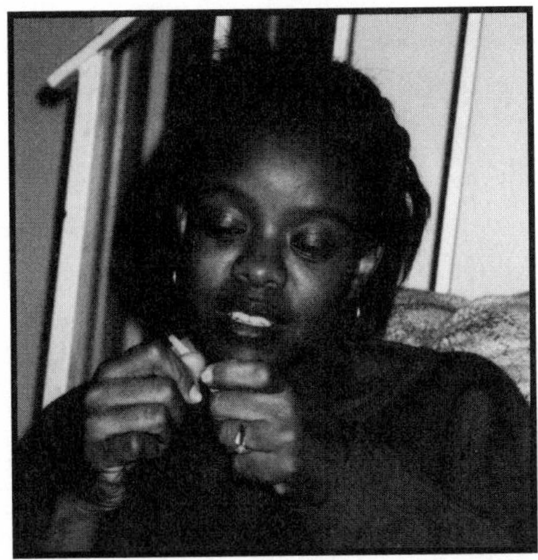

Linda

like he kind of took to me or something. Daddy's girl, that kind of stuff. [I was] the defender: always trying to break up fights, 'cause I was determined that they weren't going to fight, he wasn't going to hit her, and that I could influence him to calm down, sit down, and be quiet. And he respected me, I think, because I maybe reminded him of Aunt Annie. That's probably why. I think he listened to me.

"Those were anxious times for me," she added. "I can remember not getting a lot of rest because I was always so scared that when he comes in, he's going to come in ready to fight. I couldn't stand the fighting and the arguing. I still don't like all that. If I see two people arguing in the street now, I go another way. I don't like confrontation.

"And he'd always come in ready to pick a fight. She wouldn't be doing nothing to him. I remember he used to like to kick her when she was down on her knees praying. I think all that was because of his guilt. He felt so guilty. *He* was the demon. He was doing just the opposite of how he was raised. He was raised in a Christian home with a minister as parent, and he was just this devil. He had this quality in him, and he was just so negative and so anti. Rebellious."

I told her that my own theory is that he was spoiled by his sisters, especially by the idea that they would send him money whenever he wished. Linda agreed.

"Yeah, they spoiled him. I think—and I don't have anything to prove this—they may have spoiled him because he took a lot of heat [as a child]. He always was getting his behind whipped. He just went above and beyond to be rebellious and mean. Mama was trying to do right and he was just the devil trying to inhibit her. He had no reason to be mean to her, but he just was hell-bent on making her life difficult. He was the one out partying all night and she was at home being the good little wife, never threatened to leave.

"I couldn't understand it. 'Why is she taking all that? What is *wrong* with her?' I'd have left. That was my attitude. I would never put up with all this mess. I would be gone."

Linda's always been a nervous person—can't take too much arguing, even when there's no threat of violence. She considers this a legacy of our father.

As we were talking, my sister reminded me of an episode I had forgotten. Our parents were fighting and he was yelling at the top of his lungs, threatening to move out, threatening to walk away from us all. From out of nowhere, Linda piped up with deadpan seriousness, telling our mother, "Give him some dishes."

"They laughed at me," she recalled. "He had to stop. He couldn't even leave, he just stopped and started laughing."

But Linda wasn't joking. "I didn't care. I was really hard-nosed. You were crying," she told me, "foaming at the mouth. And I was like, 'Did you give him some dishes?'"

With all the abuse I took from our father, I thought it strange that I'd have been the one crying for him to stay while Linda, though she enjoyed a relatively easy relationship, was eager to see him go. "I think at that time maybe you were still at that stage where you really wanted his approval or him in your life," she theorized. "But I remember that distinctly. I meant it: Even back then, I was sick of it. I was sick of the ruckus. I didn't want to hear all that. He wasn't doing nothing noway, and we're struggling and he's coming in acting a fool everyday. It's like, 'Bye. Go.'"

And yet, she said, there was that other side, those moments of rare calm that offered a glimpse into who and what he had been before the children came. "When he stopped drinking, he was the sweetest thing in the world. I could see where she fell in love with him. He'd sit down and listen; he and

I used to love to watch all those different programs. He loved wrestling matches. He liked [the TV show] *Divorce Court* and I did, too."

I was a little jealous when she said that. She had known him—enjoyed his company—in ways I never did. "He traumatized all of us," Linda told me, "but I think he more or less affected you because he didn't reciprocate that love. He didn't show you any love in return. Matter of fact, a lot of times he put you down and he talked about you, told you he didn't like you in certain ways. So it's harder for you. But see, he didn't put me down."

I asked Linda what she thought of our mother for staying with him. Her answer surprised me. "When I was a kid, I thought she was crazy. Now I just think she was weak. Not only was she weak, but she probably, primarily wanted to keep the family together. She wanted all of us to stay under one roof and be raised by both parents. She felt a strong obligation to her children to keep us all together."

I've always thought the same thing, but I never thought any of it grew from weakness. Is that really what you feel? I asked.

"It just looks like weakness," said Linda, "because she endured too much. But she was a strong woman. She was strong in that she took that little money, she made it work, she held the house together, she held the kids together, she held the family together. She also withstood a lot of his abuse. So she was strong in that way and she had a lot of qualities in her. I guess she was looking at the bigger picture, but it looked like weakness to me because like I said, I wouldn't take that."

Linda said she never understood why our mother put up with him. Especially since his abuse took an obvious physical toll on her. "Mama was taking, like, twenty pills at one time, you know? A whole handful of pills she was taking because of *this?* All I could think of, it was because of him. And if he would leave, the house would be so much better. And actually, it was. I still missed him [when he died]," said Linda, "but I guess I could say I was a little relieved, too. I wasn't happy to see him go, but it was a burden lifted."

* * *

Rachelle didn't want to talk about it. Kept dodging my questions, insisting that she had no memory of our father.

Finally, she admitted, "I remember a few things."

"You remember more than a few things," I said.

"He made our life a living hell," she said, with sudden venom. "He made our life a living hell and it didn't have to be that way."

My youngest sister and I were driving in Los Angeles. I was taking her to see some of the places we had lived as children in an effort to jog her memory. Rachelle hardly ever gets to those neighborhoods. The house where she and her fiancé live is a spacious split-level in a middle-class area; it's far from the old places in ways that don't measure on the odometer. Rachelle, who is a legal secretary studying for a degree in psychology, was visibly uncomfortable as we rolled through the familiar landscape of liquor stores, motels, and churches.

I tried to draw her out, mentioning something a counselor had told me about the need to forgive a bad father and get past the pain. It seemed to work. She told me about a conversation she'd had with her fiancé.

"We started trying to put some things together. Black man in the '60s, four kids, apparently the kids were coming too fast, a lot quicker than maybe his money was, and he still had that party mentality where he wants to hang out and do what he wants to do with his money, yet he had all this major responsibility."

It was as close as she was willing to come to trying to understand him. "That still doesn't justify or excuse his behavior," she added, emphatically.

Do you remember when he was fighting with Mama? I asked.

"I remember one [fight] they had," she said. "They were in the front yard with knives or something. I remember that."

I knew which fight she was talking about—that last big one where he pulled the gun on us and I jumped on him and started punching him in the head. I got scratched on the face with the knife that night. Rachelle's eyes widened as I told her the story.

"I remember that," she repeated. "I remember when he used to get dressed up in his suit and go out drinking. He fell in a hole or something?"

Again I helped her with her memory. Told her he was coming home drunk, missed a step on the porch, fell, and ended up in the rose bushes. Sprained an ankle or something like that.

"I remember that," she said, yet again.

How did those things affect you? I asked her.

"He used to make me really nervous. Everything was fine till he was on his way home, you hear him coming in. He used to be drunk, 99.9 percent of the time."

What kind of relationship did you have with him?

"I didn't," said Rachelle. "I didn't have a relationship with him. He never did anything for me.

"He used to be whoopin' and hollerin' and carrying on and I'd be shaking like a leaf and [Mother] would try to console him. He thought it was funny. [He laughed at] my behavior. He just couldn't believe that his ranting and raving and hollering made me tremble like that."

Like Linda and me, Rachelle believes our father was spoiled by his sisters. She recalls how we, as children, looked forward to having Aunt Annie come to visit. Not simply to see our aunt, but also because we knew we'd be going to fun places we otherwise never got to see. Places as exotic as Disneyland and as pathetically normal as McDonald's. But they were both the same to us: places we watched from afar. Places we never got to go.

Until I was well into my teens, I understood a "vacation" as a person coming in from out of town to treat you to a good time. Rachelle did, too. "Think about it," she said. "A person is coming out here on vacation . . . they bring a certain amount of money for *their* entertainment. Basically [Aunt Annie] came out here and took us places we had never been in our lives. And we lived here all our lives, had two parents—one wasn't working and one couldn't work—and they came out here and provided entertainment for us."

Our visiting aunts, she said, provided us with "lovely" childhood memories. "But as far as my father and anything he did for me, he didn't do jack for me. When he passed and he was in that casket, I felt sorry for my mother, that being her husband and a part of her was gone, but I was *relieved.* Because I knew that it would be no more fighting and there wouldn't be any more whoopin' and hollerin'. And even though she had lost a part of her, she would find it again. She would find it again with somebody else. Only this time, she really and truly would be happy."

I asked Rachelle if she loved her father. She said no.

* * *

Did you realize that you were Daddy's favorite child, that he took you on as a project early in life?

In response to the question, my brother rolled his eyes and heaved a heavy sigh. "Yes," he said.

We were sitting in his car, parked in downtown Atlanta while he ate a McDonald's breakfast sandwich. It was a Saturday morning and the streets were quiet.

"When did you first realize this?" I asked.

"When he started showing me how to shoot dice," said Keith. "He always used to tell me that I was his favorite."

"He actually said that?" I asked, surprised.

"Yeah," said Keith. He mimicked what Daddy used to say about him. "'*He's* the one that's gonna be something. *He's* the one that's gonna be the man.' And . . . *surprise!* " said Keith, making his voice fey and insouciant. "Yoo hoo, Daddy!"

There was a time Keith didn't laugh about being gay, a time when it was a secret he held closely, even from himself. In the hypermasculine world of black men, gay is the last thing any guy wants to be.

Leonard and Keith

"It really didn't hit me that 'I'm gay' until my first year in college," said Keith, a telephone company account executive. "It was like leading a double life, being a double agent. I mean, I knew my Mama knew. She just wasn't confirmed. Just trust me, she knew. The last thing she said to me before she died really cracked my face: That I don't need to get married, I will find someone—*someone* . . . not male, not female, *someone*—who loves me for me."

When Mama died, Keith was still trying to figure himself out. Still getting engaged to a different woman every spring and breaking it off every fall. One of those relationships produced a son who carries the same first and middle name, eerily enough, as my own child: Marlon Anthony. During the time she was pregnant, the boy's mother learned that Keith was gay. When her child was born, she kept it a secret. Keith never knew about his son until a few years later, when he was informed by the woman's brother.

"From there, I got to spend three months with him, one on one. Picking him up from daycare. I'd go pick up the car from her at her job and pick him up from school. We'd go to Burger King, go to Mama's house, sit there and chill and wait till she got off."

Then one day, the child and his mother were gone. "I did the same routine. Go to her job to go pick up the car: 'Marsha doesn't work here anymore.' Go to the day care to pick up my son: 'She took him out of school. He's no longer in this school.' Disappeared. I don't know where he's at."

It hurts, he said, to have that young man out there somewhere and not know where he is, not know if he thinks his father abandoned him, not even know what surname he's using now.

My brother has searched the Internet, gone through intermediaries, come up dry every time. He jokes that if he ever found his son, "I'd probably be broke. I would try to do everything I could to make it up. I would take every picture I could, take him everywhere I could. I mean, introduce him to each and every family member. I would smother him. He'd probably have to tell me, 'Get back, Jack.'

"All I would like to do is see him. And I would like to hold him in my arms. Just give him a hug and say, 'Hey, I'm your daddy.'"

I asked Keith what he thought his own father would have done if he'd known his favorite child was gay. "I would have been beaten down," he said.

They had a strange relationship—more like drinking buddies than father and son. Keith said the old man taught him many "manly" arts. Showed him how to drink, for instance: "He was really big on that." Keith was around nine or ten years old at the time. Our father also showed him how to smoke a pipe and to cook. And then there were "sexual things," as Keith puts it. "Panties and coochie and all that."

"Your dad was nuts," I said, disgusted.

"Yeah, pretty much so," said Keith.

To a degree, our father was successful in his campaign to mold Keith. Of the four of us, my brother is the only one who drinks, the only one who smokes. He resembles our father, too, in less superficial ways. "I am like him," Keith conceded. "I have his hot temper. But I don't have his rage. I learned to control that early.

"Some people, when they're subjected to that atmosphere of being hit, abused or whatever, it tends to overflow into the next generation or what have you. But I'm controlling it. I'm fighting 100 percent to control it, because it wasn't something that I liked. It wasn't something that brings back good memories. It's just awful memories."

But my brother added that allowing himself to be molded by our father also carried with it a benefit, at least as he perceived it at the time. "If I could please him, I'd keep the confusion and trouble down. I'd be the one to go run and do something for him before he had to call one of you guys. Because you guys would get the brunt of the hell and I would get the easy part. That didn't feel right.

"He used to kick Rachelle when [she was] taking off his socks because Rachelle wasn't taking them off fast enough. I remember he used to hit you all the time. He used to hit Linda. But I used to try to keep the peace by doing what I had to do to help. To do my share."

Keith was the entertainer in our house. Used to shimmy in the middle of the floor in imitation of Tom Jones. Used to stagger around in imitation of our drunken father. Used to regale the men with tales of all the panties he had seen. He was the best dancer in the house, the best joke-teller, the best clown. Anything for a laugh. Anything to keep the mood light and bright. Anything to maintain the peace.

"It didn't feel right that my sisters and brother were getting chewed out, kicked, stomped, talked about, and 'You ain't worth this' and then, 'Come here, [Keith].' It just didn't feel right. It felt like either you guys should get what I get or I should get what you guys get."

When Keith's best efforts failed, when the cursing and the fights came anyway, we would often have to go looking for Keith afterwards. Found him sometimes, curled up on the floor beneath a table in the pantry.

It was Keith who ended the last big fight our parents ever had, the one everyone seems to mark as a watershed. He called the police. Dad was stunned, said Keith. "He said to my face, 'I never thought [you] would call the police on me.' He was hurt, 'cause he never imagined that I would do it. But he was in the bathroom with the shotgun, choking my Mama. And with a knife."

I asked Keith if he loved Daddy.

"I loved him," he said, "but he wasn't one of my favorite people. I loved him because he was my Daddy. I have no choice but to love him."

It struck a chord with me, because it reflected my own ambivalence. It seems, I said, that if we say we love him, we ought to have a better reason.

"But we don't," replied Keith. "We can't. He was gone in a younger part of our life. What if he was here now? Yeah, he's still drinking . . . maybe he might've slowed down. There's so many avenues he could've went down. But I can only stop him at when I was fourteen. I was young, I loved my Daddy. It hurt that my Daddy was gone, but I really didn't miss him after he was gone. Not as much and as deeply as I miss my Mama. No. No. I don't. I mean, it became more peaceful."

It's unanimous, then. Our father died and we, every last one, sighed with relief.

* * *

As I remember, it was in 1973 that my mother gathered us on a couch in the living room and explained that Daddy had cancer of the throat. Apparently, he had been suffering symptoms for some time. My Uncle Charles told me a story that dated from 1971, when my father went to Chicago for the funeral of his oldest sister. "He couldn't drink hardly," said Uncle Charles. "I bought him a bottle of Chivas Regal. He said, 'I can't drink it. My throat won't let me.'"

Still, when my mother gave me the news of his diagnosis, I'm not sure I really grasped the import of it.

So much was happening in my life then, not least of which the fact that I started college that year under an honors program that skipped students directly from their junior year in high school to their freshman year in college. The only catch was that you had to live your first year on campus. Because I had also been skipped a couple of times prior to that, I was all of fifteen years old the day my family drove me across town to the University of Southern California and moved me into the dorms.

Mama's chest was poked out with pride. Even Linda—my perpetual nemesis—seemed for once to have nothing cutting to say. And my father, he just watched me with something unfathomable in his eyes. Like he was taking my measure. Like he was proud or something.

Even then, you could see the effects of the cancer that was killing him. Maybe it's because I only saw him once a week or so during that school year, but the deterioration seemed to come so quickly. One day, he was the father I had always known. The next, he was a stick figure with red eyes and sallow, gray skin.

It was as if we lived our lives on intersecting planes, one ascending, the other descending. I was becoming stronger, surer, moving in a new world of college girls and higher education and white people and a nascent black pride. While back at home, he was becoming smaller and weaker. Back at home, he was dying.

I needed him less. And he needed me so much more.

One night, he had to be rushed to the emergency room at General Hospital. My mother had long since given up driving—too nervous, she said—and I was still on my learner's permit, but she put me behind the wheel of our 1963 Cadillac anyway.

I got them out there just fine. But in the hours that we sat waiting, my father lying on a gurney in a hall full of the suffering poor, a fog settled on the city. A fog thicker than any I had ever seen before or have ever seen since. Must have been close to midnight when we left the hospital. And there I was, creeping at ten miles an hour through a sheet of impenetrable white. No landmarks. Couldn't see traffic lights even when you were right up on them. Dad was semi-conscious in the back. And my mother, terrified like me, coached me softly. "It's okay, take your time. Just take your time."

We got home safely. I remember feeling a flush of pride at the accomplishment. And I remember realizing something else: They needed me. *He* needed me, as he had not before. Intersecting planes. My role was changing. His was, too.

He raged at the thing that was killing him. He was angry and felt sorry for himself. Later, he just seemed resigned.

And I began to see more and more that thing I had seen the day the family dropped me off at USC. It stole into his eyes over time, seemed heightened by the resignation. I'd look at him and see something that was wizened and melancholy and much older than his fifty years. I'd catch him looking at me sometimes as if he were trying to memorize me.

As if he had only just realized that there was something he needed to say and could not begin to find the words.

I was talking to Keith once about the fact that our father never seemed to think too much of my academic pursuits. "You have to remember," replied Keith, "Daddy only had . . . what? A sixth-grade education? Maybe he had an inferiority complex that you were his namesake and you were outdoing him at your early age. Have you ever thought about that? That he had a complex about that. He can't help his son [academically]. His son is, what, four years old and in the twelfth grade!" joked Keith. "You know what I'm saying? Maybe that's how he felt."

"Felt what?" I said, incredulous. "Threatened?"

"Yeah," said Keith softly, "maybe he felt threatened."

Maybe he did.

I wasn't the only one who saw him change. My mother's sister, Kate, saw it, too. She had always had a difficult relationship with him; once, he forbade my mother to see or talk to her for three years. Then one day, during the illness, my mother went to her with a request from my father for a small kindness: Would she cook him a plate of collard greens and cornbread?

Aunt Kate told me my mother begged her not to turn my father down. "I said, 'I wouldn't *dare* tell him no.' Even though he was being fed intravenously—his throat was so messed up—he ate a bowl of those greens. I cut 'em up fine and cooked them for a long time."

My cousin Nathaniel said Daddy began surveying his life and regretting

Aunt Kate

what he saw. "One day, he and I were sitting out on the porch and he started rattling off about all the mistakes he had made trying to bring y'all up, and what he should've been doing. That he should've been working and providing instead of just sitting on his ass, getting a check."

"He called us all in the room," said Keith, "and apologized for all the bad things he did. 'I loved you all, but it was just me drinking. I really apologize. I'm so sorry.'"

I must have been at school, because I never heard those words. I wish I had.

But every now and then, I would catch him watching me with those eyes.

After my freshman year was finished, I moved back home. He had a tube in his nose by then. Received his meals through another tube in his abdomen. It always smelled of sickness and decay. His weight was down to nothing. His hair was as thin and fine as a baby's. He had no voice.

My father had always mocked my mother for her Sunday pilgrimages to the little corner church out near Watts. Now he prayed. Now he sought the face of God.

We saw horrible things. Vessels in his throat burst and blood came gushing out. Rachelle remembers him—probably in the throes of dementia—exposing himself in the front window. "That was the first time I ever saw a penis," she said. "It scared me to death." And I remember something that has stayed with me—something so awful that I'm half-convinced I didn't really see it, half-believe I must have dreamt it. But I *remember* it. Us sitting there in the living room when suddenly he jumped to his feet like the chair was on fire, fumbled his zipper open and began to urinate blood. Everywhere, blood.

I'm not much for interpreting divine design into the everyday sufferings and triumphs of women and men—every life knows joy and pain. But I swear, that cancer seemed like a torment. It seemed like a punishment.

And as his voice grew silent, his eyes became more intense. Watery and red, they watched me. They watched us *all,* with such infinite regret. You could feel them on you.

"His eyes would follow you wherever you moved to," recalled his sister Mildred, who visited during the illness. "It was so sad. I had a problem with it, looking at him like that. This good-looking man that was so full of life, sitting there as though he was already dead. Like in his eyes, there was . . . something he wished he had done and didn't do. It was just so much in his eyes. I would usually have to go and get away from 'em. It just got to me. I can still feel his vision now."

Nineteen seventy-five was just a god-awful year. It was a crucible.

My mother's father died suddenly in February. A few days later, she flew to Mississippi to bury him. That August, her mother died. Mama kicked and cried on the bed when that happened. Then she returned home for another burial.

Linda helped care for Daddy in both absences. "It was hard to watch him," she said. "I felt bad. I felt sorry for him."

By December, my father's condition had deteriorated to the point that we could no longer care for him. Nathaniel took him out to a Veteran's Administration Hospital. "Y'all are taking me out here to die," he whispered accusingly.

Nate told him that it wasn't like that at all, but of course, it was.

We visited my father on Christmas. Brought him a robe. Kept up a stream of forced chatter to which he did not contribute. He was semi-conscious, moaning occasionally in pain. I don't think he even knew we were there.

We left before long. I was the last one out of the room, as I recall. As I was walking out, I bent over the railing of his bed and kissed his temple.

He made a small sound. His skin was warm and soft.

Two days later, a nurse at the hospital called. My father was desperately weak. He had asked the nurse to tell my mother that he loved her. We were on our way out to the hospital, but the nurse said we shouldn't rush, because he wouldn't be alive when we got there.

He wasn't.

ELEVEN

We buried him on the last day of the year. I don't remember much about it. A few words at the church he never attended. A flag from his coffin folded into a triangle and presented to my mother by a military man who then stepped back and gave her a crisp salute. I don't recall crying. I don't think I did.

That afternoon at the house, I cornered a lady from our church about a girl she had brought to a service some weeks before. The girl used a wheelchair; she had been shot as a child. I thought she was cute and I told the woman I wanted to meet her.

Strange enough I was making dates at the reception after my father's funeral. It was also, under any circumstances, an uncharacteristically bold move for the shy, reticent boy I had always been. But things were changing. In part, it was because I was older. And in part, it was because his control over me, the fear he instilled, had been slipping away these last years. And now, with his death, it was finally gone. I was free.

The timing of my conversation with that woman has always struck me as telling and not at all coincidental. If 1975 had been a crucible, the year that dawned the day after his funeral was, in many ways, a rebirth.

I dated a few girls over the next years, but never with the sort of carefree recklessness and freedom from commitment that you think of when you think of young bachelors. "I want to be married," I told my mother one day when we were shopping together in the produce section of the local market. I was only seventeen years old at the time. To this day, I have no idea where the desire came from, but I meant it: I wanted to be settled, wanted a marriage. So I wasn't out there just looking for fun—I was looking for a wife.

Found her in 1978 when I crossed paths with Marilyn Pickens, a girl I had known in grammar school; she had been the subject of one of my earliest and fiercest crushes. Marilyn was a beautiful woman with a dazzling smile. We had fun together—she laughed at all my jokes. And she was touched by small things I did for her. Bought her flowers one evening on a whim and when I handed them to her, she asked me why. I said, "Because it's Tuesday." She started crying. It was, she said, the first time anyone had ever bought her flowers.

I fell like rocks.

Some members of my extended family were less enthusiastic. Marilyn was a year and a half older than me. Her brothers were roughnecks, constantly in and out of trouble. She was married to a man who beat her; they were separated then and a divorce would soon follow. Finally, Marilyn had two kids: Markise, who was four and the result of a teenage liaison, and Monique, who was one, and a product of the marriage.

That last probably bothered them more than anything. "Why do you want to take on an instant family?" they asked. "Why do you want to take on another man's responsibilities?"

I didn't care what they said. I loved her, walked more proudly when she was on my arm, thought of her without ceasing when she was away. If I'm to be honest, though, I have to admit that I was also drawn to her by the prospect of saving a damsel in distress—attracted by the fact that she needed me.

We dated off and on for a long time and I became close with her children; that first Christmas, when she told me she didn't have money for gifts, I went out and bought small toys for both of them. After about a year and a half, we moved in together.

Although I liked the kids and they liked me, I tended to steer clear of them in those earliest days. Didn't want to discipline them or even tell them to do things. I was acutely aware of the fact that these were not my children. It was as if I was operating in some strange limbo of near fatherhood, but not quite.

Marilyn was not much help. She didn't, I think, understand this position I found myself in. "Just tell them what you want them to do," she said. "If they misbehave, give them a spanking."

So much easier said than done.

But then, the whole thing was awkward. The kids called me by my first name, even though by this point it was apparent to all of us that I was now a permanent part of this family. But what else could they call me? "Mr. Pitts" seemed far too formal and the alternative . . . well, it simply was not a part of the equation. I shuddered just thinking of it.

Then one afternoon, Marilyn came to me with a request from the kids. They wanted to know if it was okay to call me "Daddy."

Oh, man.

Oh, man.

My heart split, going in two directions at once. I was flattered to the skies. And I was frightened beyond words.

I think I nodded numbly and said something brilliant like, "Yeah, okay. Sure. If that's what they want."

Oh. *Man.*

I didn't know anything about being "Daddy." Hadn't a clue what new obligations and responsibilities this entailed. It was as if I had just agreed to walk blindfolded through a minefield.

They started calling me this and I would dutifully nod and respond as if I knew what was going on. Lived in that limbo for a long time.

Was still living there, in fact, the day Marilyn and I got married. I had been after her for months to say yes. After ditching one husband, though, she wasn't all that eager to risk her heart on another one. "Why can't we just leave everything the way it is?" she kept asking.

But I was persistent, and eventually she caved in. We stood before family and friends at the altar of a beautiful chapel in a quiet neighborhood near Hollywood and recited vows I had written. I had the first lines:

"On those days when right things turn to things all wrong,
Light is out, hope is dead and despair kills the song,
I can go on because I remember you love me."

In memory, I still see that day as if shot through a gray gauze. As if it happened in a dream.

It wasn't long after that, as I recall, that there came a Saturday morning when I woke up early to find Markise's bed empty and the front door unlocked. I panicked. Dread formed like ice on my heart. I went up and down the street, calling his name.

Nothing. Birds chirping and my own voice coming back to me. *Nothing.*

I was ready to give up, ready to go wake Marilyn and call 911, when I saw him, sitting on a neighbor's porch. Markise was always a child who liked to wander; never could see any reason why he should keep his parents apprised of his ramblings. So he looked up at me with this milky bland face that held no concept of the fact that he had nearly given me a heart attack.

In that instant, I felt it all. Relief, exhaustion, gratefulness, anger. Anger was the strongest. I marched him across the street, took him to his room, and I spanked his behind. It was the first time I ever did that. The first time I really knew I loved him. The first time I felt like a father.

It is, of course, telling that I drew those feelings from that action.

As anyone who has seen a black comic work in the last ten years knows, black parents are great believers in corporal punishment. They spank. They whip ass.

There's a telling sequence in the Spike Lee movie *Get on the Bus*. Several black men en route to the Million Man March are laughing in reminiscence of the times they crossed their moms and paid for it with the skin of their backsides. Then one of them, a cop named Gary, offers his own story of the time he shoplifted some candy from a store. His mom was *soooo* mad, he says. "Man, she must've lectured me for like two or three hours!"

Laughter freezes on the faces of the other two men. They are incredulous.

"*Lectured* you?" asks Jamal, the former gang member. "You didn't get a beatin' or nothin'?"

"His mother is white," says Flip, the aspiring actor, by way of explanation.

At which, Jamal nods in understanding and Gary becomes annoyed, wanting to know what his mother's race has to do with anything. "*Our* mothers whip ass," says Flip. "Your mother lectures."

And so it goes. Indeed, it's a rare African American who can't spin at least one "worst-whippin'-I-ever-got" story.

This is not, I know, the corrective measure preferred by the experts who preach to the white middle class. But me, I wasn't raised in the white middle class. I was raised in black south-central Los Angeles where the kid who did wrong was directed out to the backyard to get a switch from a tree, the application of which was designed to show him the error of his ways. If no switch was available, brushes, belts, and tracks from Hot Wheels toy sets were suitable substitutes.

The older I get, the more ambivalent it makes me feel.

There are those who call what black parents do child abuse. Which strikes me as a singularly specious argument. Tell a child who has been burned repeatedly by cigarettes or beaten bloody by fists that an occasional whack on the backside with a Hot Wheels track is an equivalent experience and that child will, with justification, look at you as if you are quite mad.

I saw my mother raise four children from the worst neighborhoods in Los Angeles—with abundant amounts of love and firmness—and watched them all become productive citizens. That would not have happened, *could not* have happened, had she been a woman we felt free to trifle with.

Which leaves me ill-inclined to listen to experts who say parents should rely exclusively upon "time outs" and other negotiations with terrorist tykes. The parent-child relationship is not a democracy and a parent who has never been fiercely, albeit momentarily, hated by a child probably isn't much of a parent to begin with. I've seen too many embarrassed mothers and fathers—almost always white—out in public helplessly pleading with these tiny tyrants to think otherwise.

And yet . . .

I keep seeing my father tied to that tree by *his* father and I'm lying if I say it doesn't make me wonder if black families have not historically suffered the opposite failing of some modern whites. Meaning that if they tend toward an excess of leniency, perhaps our sin is an excess of inflexibility, a too-willingness to employ force, and an inability to listen sometimes, bargain sometimes, and respect the personhood of the child.

Not that any of this mattered the day I spanked Markise. I wasn't trying to reinvent the wheel. I was just trying to learn to use the one that already existed. Just trying to figure things out, to survive this rite of fatherhood by sudden immersion, with the least amount of damage to myself and the children. So I would do what I had seen work. And I came to a decision: If I couldn't model myself after my father, I would model after my mother.

Throughout my life, after all, she had been an anchor in the midst of turbulence.

So often, we act as if the child raised with a dysfunctional parent in the midst of upheaval faces a situation that is hopeless. But I look at her and wonder if, in feeling this way, we don't underestimate what it can mean to have just one person in that child's life who is solid, dependable, and unwavering. One person who creates a cocoon of stability, a space in which a child can be simply that, a child.

That's what my mother did. That's how we were raised.

All hell might be breaking loose around us. Drunks might be laughing till all hours on the front porch. Police helicopters might be circling low overhead looking for this felon or that.

But bedtime was still the same time, every night.

The same chores always had to be done by the same kids, every day.

The same naughty words were likely to elicit the same stern punishment every time they were uttered.

In the middle of chaos, she gave us the comfort of order, the gift of predictability. Hedged us around and protected with a fence of rules. Adults were always to be addressed as Mr. or Mrs. or Miss So-and-So. Children did not interrupt grown persons' conversations. And God help the child whose teacher called to say he'd been acting up in class.

We knew where the boundaries were. We knew what was expected.

Children, I think, thrive in such a situation. Even children who seem to have every odd stacked against them.

For kids of the inner city with an alcoholic father, we were remarkably sheltered from the seamier aspects of the world that surrounded us. As a result, none of us ever went to jail, none of us drifted into behaviors that might have endangered us. You had the understanding that a certain standard was expected of you and you'd rather walk through the lion's cage with raw meat strapped to your tender parts than disappoint that expectation.

Mama had a sense of herself and her children as being too good, not for the people she lived among, but for the conditions she lived in. There was something in the way she carried herself, some offhand haughtiness that told you this was a person of substance. If you'd met her in some neutral setting, you'd never have guessed she was a small-town girl living in a bad neighborhood in Los Angeles. You'd have thought her the queen of some unknown land.

"She carried herself with airs," is how my Aunt Mildred puts it. "Little uppity ways. And I liked that. She had this serenity about her that touched you. That almost literally reached out and grabbed you. She was like a breath of fresh air."

"She taught us etiquette," recalled Keith, "taught us proper diction, fear of God, education is the key. I mean, she taught us values. I think those values she instilled in me made me the whole person that I am."

"We were her life," said Linda. "She sacrificed a heck of a lot for us. She went without. She spoiled us, she protected us. She dedicated her entire life to us. You didn't know you were in the ghetto, you didn't know you were poor, you didn't know a lot of things. She made things fun."

And me, I've always thought her simply the most amazing woman who ever lived.

Of course, every boy loves his mother. But even granting that truth, she was special. The kind of woman to whom people tended to gravitate. Neighborhood kids from bad families, young women raising their children alone, grown men far from home, they all came to her, all called her "Mother."

So when I was trying to decide what kind of father I wanted to be, hers was the example I copied. I established bedtimes, handed out chores, exhorted my stepchildren to do better in school. Tried to be like her.

Wasn't easy. Her patience didn't come naturally to me. I had to work at it. Had to force myself to stop what I was doing and give them my attention when Monique or Markise interrupted me at some solitary pursuit. Had to remind myself to smile and make them feel welcome.

Markise was a serious, reticent child who kept a lot inside. Monique was the opposite; a garrulous little girl with her mother's incandescent smile, she could talk the bark from the trees.

I kept trying to get close to Markise, to have the kind of buddy-pal relationship that, in my mind, sons and fathers were supposed to. It never happened. There was some core part of him that I never could reach. Or maybe it's just that I was trying so hard and didn't know what I was doing.

Monique, on the other hand, craved attention; in fact, never seemed able to get enough. I was always after her about her grades, which were usually pretty bad. On those occasions when her report card showed some small improvement, I made a big fuss about it and gave her special privileges and rewards in hopes that she would be encouraged to continue doing well.

I sought to be creative when it came to discipline as well, though the results were sometimes less than I'd hoped. Markise had a habit of sneaking out of bed in the middle of the night to watch television. One time, I sentenced him to sit on a couch for forty-eight hours straight with the TV on. Suspended the sentence after one sleepless night when I realized that the only way to make sure the punishment was met was for me to keep getting up during the night to check on him. The child remained an inveterate night owl.

Monique had a habit of stealing jelly when she wasn't supposed to have any. I made her spoon the stuff out of a jar and eat it. It wasn't long before she was cried uncle. That punishment worked. The jelly thieving stopped.

At Christmas, I struggled to faithfully recreate the holidays I had known; Mama used to bake to exhaustion, scrimp and save her money, and hide gifts with devious care to make real for us the fable of the fat man in the red suit who magically left toys under your tree in the middle of the night. It was a delicious luxury for children raised in an unforgiving place where a child's faith in magic fades faster than morning mist. I still remember all the Christmas Eves I lay in bed tingling with anticipation of the glitter and hard plastic the morning would bring. It was a night when all things seemed possible.

I wanted my children to know that feeling. So I raided memory, then tried to photocopy it. Hid the toys as she did, told the fables as she did, served the same foods she did. Made a Christmas Eve tradition of her favorite holiday carol, Nat "King" Cole's "The Christmas Song."

And it worked. We had great Christmases.

Marilyn and I would get up early, so Monique and Markise didn't beat us to the tree, so I wouldn't miss seeing the delight in their eyes. Sitting there in the chill of the morning, watching eager children tear the wrapping off fantasies made flesh, I would sometimes feel pretty good about this father thing. Feel as if I had figured it out, become for them what my father never was for me.

I never talked about him, though. Never even thought about him that I can recall. Felt that I was past him, that I was shaping my own life and he didn't have a damn thing to say about it. If you had asked, I'd have told you that I was free now.

But a strange thing happened one day. We were at the home of one of my wife's sisters, where a barbecue was in progress. I had brought a book with me and holed up with it in a corner. I hadn't wanted to come and had only agreed after a nasty argument with Marilyn. The book was a pointed, albeit childish, statement to her: *You made me come, but you can't make me participate.*

Marilyn ignored me. But my mother-in-law didn't. She saw me sitting there with my nose in a book while everyone else was telling jokes and waiting for the food to be done and she lit into me, demanding to know what on earth was wrong with me. A strange thing happened then: Her mouth was moving, but my father's voice was coming out. His words. His anger.

Reminded me of how he always hated to see me reading. How he used to curse me for it, make me feel awkward and small.

It shook me.

When we left, I had no conscious plan to go to the graveyard; it just happened. Before I knew it, I was pulling through the gates. I hadn't been there since we buried him and it took a while to find the spot, which had not been marked with a stone. When we finally reached his grave I knelt there, absently fingering the grass that poked up from the hard, dry soil.

My wife knew what was coming before I did. She gently shepherded the kids away, using her body to shield me from their eyes.

I was about to ask her why, but suddenly I was crying, my body heaving, breath leaving me in shuddering gasps. It just hit me, this ton of grief falling out of the sky. Some disengaged part of my brain saw the kids shooting worried glances at me. I wanted to go to them and reassure them that I was all right, but I couldn't move. I could only sag to the ground and cry. I cried for the times he hit me, cried for the times he came home drunk, cried for the pain he gave. And I cried because he was gone, escaped into the loam beyond retribution and tears.

I cried because I missed him, because I loved him. And, I think, because I hated him, too.

I cried, feeling lost and bereft and realizing with a sudden shock that I would never, not ever, be free.

PART THREE:
The Sunrise Drums

Can't you see
While you're picking on society
That the leaves on your family tree
Are calling you to come home?

— Four Tops

TWELVE

How, then, do you become Dad? How do you do it when it's something you've never seen? How do you do it when you're beaten up inside by the failures and absences of your own father? Worse, how do you do it if you're one of those men who is busy just trying to get out of each day alive?

One day at a time. This is the answer life has taught me. There is no finish line. One is ever a work in progress.

The sobering truth is that parenthood is a conundrum: You can never know for sure how good a job you've done until it's too late to do anything about it. That is, until you're finished raising the child and you step back to see what kind of adult you're sending into the world.

That day I fell atop my father's grave, I grappled feelings I never even knew I had. The years since then have taught me that I am not the first who ever did nor the last who ever will. This sense of irresolution, of being at odds with a father's failings, is a distressingly common thing.

So at some point you simply have to deal with it. Suck it up. Because life doesn't come with a pause button. And in the meantime, there are children to be raised, kids looking for the guiding hand of a committed man. They deserve this, and there's no excuse for the man who brought them into life not to give it to them. This is not a need that can wait on a man to get himself together. This is a need that must be met *now*. So you pick yourself up from where you've fallen, and you get on with it. You do the job.

I rose from my father's grave and rejoined my family. My wife's eyes asked after me—was I okay? I told her I was all right. And I was. We gathered the kids and took them home.

* * *

Fatherhood, like any other difficult commitment worth undertaking, is a process of reward and regret. A sense of having triumphed over adversity balanced by a sense that adversity has you pinned and is kicking the living daylights out of you. This is just the way it is, something else I have been taught incrementally—sometimes painfully—over the years. There are no perfect fathers, no perfect children.

It is liberating knowledge.

I am, I like to think, a pretty good father, all things considered. But then, I've had plenty of practice at it. After that day in the cemetery, Marilyn and I went on to have three children together. Marlon was born in 1982. Bryan followed in 1985. Onjél came in 1990.

The joke around the house is that the influx of new faces wore me down. There's some truth in that. Maybe it's just advancing age speaking, but I find that I have less of a need to always be in control than I did when fatherhood was still new. I still believe in parental authority—a benign dictatorship, if you will—but I've come to realize that not every issue is life or death. It's not crucial to win every argument every time. Somewhere along the way, it has become easier to surrender to them—or at least forge a compromise—without feeling that this represents an abdication of parental prerogative.

I suppose I'm a little looser now. More at ease in the role of father.

I wish I had been that way when Markise was younger. He's in his middle twenties now. He's a good and decent man and that makes me proud. Still, my relationship with him is touchier, more prickly than I'd like. We get along well enough, but we're still not as close as I've always desired. After all these years, it feels like we're still circling one another, still trying to get the range. We live by truce, the space between us too often a DMZ of hurt feelings and misperceived gestures.

His teen years were rough on us both. He wanted autonomy, I wanted control. I wish we had met somewhere in the middle. Instead, I made a habit of putting my foot down and closing the door on discussion. I think

I was more intimidating to him than I realized or ever wanted to be. Too stern too often. Didn't bend enough.

So here is one of fatherhood's regrets: I wish my oldest son and I could talk more easily than we do.

Monique is another story. She never found the attention she sought. I don't think she ever could have.

We used to shower her with one-on-one time in hopes that would fill this ravenous need of hers. It was never enough. And it probably didn't help matters that her natural father was a ne'er-do-well who kept making promises—as big as a new bike, as small as spending an afternoon with her—that he never fulfilled. She wanted him in her life and he never really understood that. Or else never really cared.

As she grew older, Monique slipped further and further out of control. She became a chronic runaway, began to steal from other members of the family, ditched school, failed classes, shoplifted, and covered it all with a web of flimsy, inexplicable lies. Counselors counseled her; preachers prayed for her; aunts, uncles, and grandparents reasoned with her; and I spent hours—literally, two and three hours at a time—pleading with her, trying to reach her to let her know I loved her and was desperately worried about what she was doing to her life.

But she was some place I couldn't reach. Nobody could.

When Monique was eighteen, her mother noticed that she was putting on weight and had begun going around the house in big, shapeless blouses. "Are you pregnant?" Marilyn asked. Monique said no. Insisted on it indignantly. In fact, she even swore to us that she was still a virgin.

Marilyn was dubious, but me, I wanted to believe. Needed it, I suppose.

One morning before dawn a few months later, her water broke and she crept out of the house. She ended up giving birth in an ambulance. Her mother and I have been raising the baby, a boy she named Eric. Eric's father is not in the picture. Monique, who doesn't live with us, visits her son about once a week. She says she wants to study nursing.

So here we sit with this uneasy compromise. It's not what I want, certainly not what I envisioned. But perhaps the most difficult lesson fatherhood has taught me is that sometimes what you want and envision don't matter. Sometimes there is nothing you can do.

I suppose I began learning that when Monique was sixteen. That was an especially bad time for her. So bad that we had decided to send her to stay with her maternal grandparents in Louisiana.

We were at the airport. Monique's flight had been called and the good-byes had all been said. She was moving toward the ticket taker. I looked at her—sixteen years old, her cheeks still pudgy with baby fat—and saw her as she was when I met her, a toddler I called "Monkey" for her bright eyes and infectious giggle. I used to throw her in the air and catch her just to hear it. "Do it again!" she'd cry. "Do it again!"

I loved to make her laugh. One time she went to the emergency room with a bad asthma attack; everything she tried to eat was coming up, including a jelly sandwich she'd had right before the illness struck. I walked in on her, sitting weepy and miserable on the gurney, twin trickles of regurgitated Welch's coming from her nostrils. Took one look, said two words: "Jelly boogers." She laughed uncontrollably through her tears.

Years later, those words were still a private joke between us, guaranteed to end any bout with the blues. Years later, that still made her laugh. "Jelly boogers."

I saw her handing over her boarding pass and I walked away.

Went to the other corner of the room and landed heavily in a chair. Thought of all the time, all the love, we had been given to reclaim this girl, to turn her around. And in the end, we hadn't been able to change a thing. Not a damn thing.

Now we were giving up, it seemed. Conceding defeat.

I just lost it. Broke down in tears.

Another regret—the biggest one—why weren't we able to reach this child?

Watching her slip away over the years had a devastating impact upon me. Made me painfully conscious of the limits of parental power. But at the same time, it made me more determined than ever not to lose another child. *Never* to lose another child.

My youngest sons and daughter and I have very good relationships. We laugh and joust and enjoy one another's company. Marlon's a stringbean teen with a ready smile and a quick wit, an affable charmer who is most at home as the life of a large party. He has some of my father in him, I guess.

Or his mother. Both of them sociable people who never met a stranger. With him, I am like a big kid sometimes—video games, comic books. He keeps me young.

Bryan is a shy and dreamy kid, thickly built and something of a gentle giant. Wants to direct movies. Enjoys softer pursuits than his brother. Like his father, he tends to keep a lot inside, to move comfortably in his own company. I suspect he has a very active internal life we know nothing about. The boys are unalike, but where that was once a source of friction between them, it seems more and more a glue of companionship as they get older.

And then there's Onjél. She's a spirited little girl, all arms and legs and heady joy. Never walks when she can run. Never runs when she can fly. Smart as a new suit and doesn't mind showing it. Wants to do everything at one time. When I come back to town from a business trip, Marlon or Bryan will usually be too busy with girls or video games to accompany their mom out to the airport to pick me up. But Onjél is always there, always yells, "Daddy!" as I step into the lounge, always throws her arms around my neck in a way that makes me less tired than I was a moment before, and causes other passengers to smile as they step by me.

Between the three of them, I am reminded every day of what an imposing trust it is to raise a child. When I started, with Markise and Monique, I did just what the psychologist James Cones says you shouldn't: I worked to be the father I wanted for myself as a child. But Cones is right, isn't he? We need to minister to our children's needs instead of using our children to minister to our own.

They're not here to help me fix what went wrong with my father. They are here on their own terms, as their own persons. I try to look at my kids and really see them.

But again, having lost a child, I also look at my kids and worry. There are so many forces that can steal a child's future away. And this is particularly true for black children. Worse, on top of all the pitfalls and obstacles black boys and girls confront as a whole, each gender also faces its own distinct and complex set of challenges.

Black boys worry me. I'm frightened to death by the anti-intellectual ethos which many of them have embraced, the one which holds that the only way to be authentically black is to spurn education, involvement, and achievement. One doesn't get A's in school or embrace the King's English; these things constitute "acting white." "Keepin' it real" is the battle cry of this nihilistic generation.

It is, of course, ahistorical and ignorant to argue by implication that such well-educated and well-spoken Americans as W. E. B. DuBois, Maya Angelou, Malcolm X, and Martin Luther King Jr. were somehow less than truly black. But then this attitude, which one sees and hears with frightening regularity, is in itself a relatively new thing. And you wonder how we came to this point.

Not so long ago, African Americans prized those among their number who demonstrated academic excellence and elocutionary legerdemain. The man or woman who could "talk that talk" and back it up by a command of relevant facts and figures was held before children as an example and before the outside world as tangible proof that all the lies about black intellectual inferiority were just that. Lies.

But something has changed and it feels very much like surrender. Nor is it difficult to understand why. For all his excellence and legerdemain, after all, Martin Luther King Jr. ended up before his time as a slab of cold meat on a coroner's table. More to the point, those who looked to academic success to gain them access to the Promised Land of equality, where color matters not, have been rudely disappointed.

There's a bitter old joke that illuminates this disappointment better than I can. It goes: What do you call a black man with a Ph.D.?

Nigger.

For all the doors that have opened in the more than thirty years since the end of the Civil Rights Movement, there remains a core of cold truth in that joke. Go to college, play by the rules, do as you're asked, and at the end of the day, it's as if you never did any of it. Oh, you might get the job, the title, the salary, and the nice car, but you still won't get a cab to stop for you. The white woman who sees you standing before the hotel in a tuxedo will still automatically hand you her car keys. You will still be asked, every day, to prove your right to belong.

And it will be exhausting.

This truth, gradually glimpsed, has settled across African-American aspirations like a cold, wet blanket. And those in the underclass, those who were exhorted to go to school, better themselves, join the mainstream, and become part of the American Dream, could not fail to notice the heartbreak in the eyes of some of those who went out and did just that.

So, for at least some, the answer was a familiar one. Opt out. Choose black nationalism, black gangsta-ism, or just black apathy. Either way, the result was the same: You stood to the side, too "smart" to play in a rigged game.

In the last fifteen years, what was once an option for some in the underclass has become a fashion statement that crosses all demographic lines. Boys like those my cousin houses in his facility for troubled youth live this as life. And even boys like my sons—products of a middle-class home where books are read and ideas discussed—adopt it as style, something heard in the rumble of the music and the droop of the pants, a rejection of mainstream mores, a surrender of mainstream hopes.

I watch all this and struggle for the proper balance in my response. You don't want to be the stereotypical panicked parent. You make yourself remember how your own mother thought Marvin Gaye and Parliament-Funkadelic, long Afros, and bell-bottom jeans were going to take you to hell in a rocket ship. You tell yourself to breathe deeply, calm down, it's only youthful rebellion, only a phase, only music, only fashion.

But it's easier said than done.

My boys fill their ears with music of "bitches" and "ho's" and "niggers" and guns, affect the swagger and attitude of hopeless boys in hopeless 'hoods, all the while assuring me that it's just a pose, just a thing they do to connect with their buddies. I nod and try to take them at their word.

But I also take them to museums, leave them interesting newspaper articles to read, use objectionable behavior modeled by some of their idols as a springboard for discussion. For so many African-American children, the world is such a small place, bounded by familiar streets, people, and attitudes they never get to see beyond. It is important to me that my boys understand that the real world is huge, offers more opportunity and challenge than what you see immediately before you.

All things are possible to the person who learns to open his eyes, engage his brain and *question.*

Not to create the wrong impression. My boys have never given their mother or me even a hint of serious trouble. Their biggest offenses run along the lines of missing the curfew by ten minutes or nagging their sister to hear her whine. They are good boys.

But they're also black boys. And black boys are allowed fewer chances, have less margin for youthful error. I'm trying to make men here, I told Marlon once, and that's not easy. Especially knowing that in a few years, I'll be sending them into a world that fears them on sight.

It was different for me. One of the few blessings of being raised in the segregation of the inner city is that you grow up relatively free from direct encounters with white racism. Granted, the segregation itself represents an encounter with racism, but what I mean is, life was mercifully clear of one-on-one episodes that served only to remind you that people like you were lowly and despised.

I had no white neighbors. In fact, when I was young, I was of the impression that Los Angeles was a predominantly black city. Indeed, the Los Angeles I knew was. White people were visitors in our lives. They were the cops who cruised by in patrol cars, the welfare case worker who came snooping into your business, the principal at the school, the cowboy on television. There was something about them that was not quite real.

I wasn't called "nigger" by a white person until I was eighteen or nineteen years old. A group of coworkers and I had gone to the tony Westwood district for dinner and a movie. A carload of white kids zooms by and someone yells the word from the window, and orders us to "go home." It was over before I realized what had happened. And when I did, it was like a slap across the face, one that stings all the more because you never saw it coming.

My children, all of them raised in integrated middle-class neighborhoods, all had similar experiences at much younger ages. Sometimes it's a bully in the neighborhood. Other times it's a person my child has always thought of as a friend; they have a falling-out as children will and the white kid chooses to "go there," chooses to escalate what was trivial and childish into something ugly and indescribably demeaning.

One of Bryan's friends did that and his grandmother was so mortified she spanked him, made him apologize, then marched over to apologize herself. I always respected her for that. Far more often, the parent feigns ignorance, professing to have no idea where the child might have picked up such awful language. Bryan had another playmate who lived across the street; she was forbidden by her father to play with him because he is black.

And Marlon had an ongoing dispute with a white girl at his high school that culminated with her boyfriend swerving a car toward him on three separate occasions while someone inside the vehicle yelled racial slurs. Marilyn went to discuss the matter with the young lady's parents, only to be met by a large group of white kids jeering at her from the front porch while the mother stepped down as if to fight, declaring herself "tired of you people."

It's heartbreaking.

So I guess I shouldn't be surprised at the change I've seen in my boys as they get older. Where once they ran with a rainbow coalition of kids, these days, they pretty much hang out only with other black kids.

I can't choose their friends for them. All I can do is remind them that it's a fallacy to judge a group of people—whites included—by a few of its less civilized members. But at the same time, how can I not understand why they've chosen to do this? How can I not understand any person who decides not to put himself in a position to be hurt again?

Once Marlon, Bryan, and a group of black friends were sitting in a parking lot waiting for a ride home after a movie let out. A police car pulled up and an officer began to question them. When Marlon challenged him, the officer claimed that he'd just wanted to say hello.

To which my boys reacted with sneers of derision. They knew why he stopped. They knew exactly why.

So young and so cynical already. It doesn't help that the cynicism happens to be well-founded.

It is exhausting work, making a black man of a black boy. Sometimes you feel like you're fighting to hold a position that has already been overrun. But other times you swear you can see, behind the facade of teen arrogance, the wheels turning, the words finding purchase in the hard soil of youthful minds. And you think maybe they're going to be okay, going to do just fine.

I worry about my daughter as well, though for different reasons than I do the boys. If childhood is a minefield for black boys, it is much the same for girls, period. I look into the light of my daughter's eyes and I think of how we lost Monique and there was nothing we could do to save her. Makes me want to hold my little girl in my arms and keep her safely enfolded there until adolescence has come and gone.

In her compelling 1994 book, *Reviving Ophelia: Saving the Selves of Adolescent Girls,* Dr. Mary Pipher illuminates a topic that's too-little discussed: the difficult passages of adolescent girls, the ways in which they are emotionally brutalized by a pop culture that treats them like meat and a world that refuses to quite see them. She describes girls who live in castles of wishes, girls who amputate their own personalities to conform to social pressures, girls who have no sense of self except that which is reflected in the approving gaze of some boy.

I recognized my oldest daughter in what she said. And I feared for the youngest.

In an interview, Dr. Pipher told me she lays much of the blame at the feet of American junk culture. "The ways girls are portrayed by media could not be more discordant from their actual lives," she said. "Almost all young women you see are very beautiful, their roles are very sexualized and most girls, in fact, are really struggling with appearance and do not enjoy being in a situation where they are very sexualized. The ways in which we present young girls is very harmful."

It's important, she said, to help your daughter see herself in dimensions that have nothing to do with her popularity or physical attractiveness. "Make sure she has good sources of identity that have nothing to do with how attractive she is, like music and sports."

Onjél has a purple belt in karate (can break a board with her bare foot!) and is a good student in school. I try to make sure she hears praise based on those achievements more than on the fact that she's a pretty girl. One day, I've told her, someone's going to tell you that girls cannot do karate and girls cannot be smart. When that happens, you tell them, Tough. Too bad.

She promises that she will. And I pray that she does.

So many times girls get lost on the way to womanhood. What was spirited and adventurous about them gets hammered out by a world that prizes neither spirit nor adventure in women, favoring instead a numbing, one-size-fits-all sexuality. Big hair, big chest, big smile, small waist. For a girl, it must feel not unlike trying to squeeze one's entire being into a shoebox. You can't. And so you learn to leave things out. To become a truncated version of who you really are.

As a parent, you wonder what happened to the fearless and multifaceted girl you once knew. You wonder why she has turned into the sullen and unhappy young woman before you. You think you are alone, think yours is the only home where such a thing is happening. And you wonder where you went wrong. Good people sitting there in the aftermath wondering what happened and why they didn't see it coming.

The interesting thing is we tend to think of raising daughters as woman's work. Men, we seem to feel, are more important to the upbringing of sons. But I find myself questioning whether it's anywhere near that cut and dried. Onjél needs me, needs perspectives only I can give. I've become convinced of this.

Phil, a father I met in Atlanta, has reached the same conclusion. When we talked, he had been separated from his wife and three daughters for several months for work-related reasons.

"And I'm seeing, in this period, how important I am to them," he said. "They're all girls, and they need a man in their life. My fifteen-year-old is having problems right now with the boy thing. I go home and there's an eighteen-year-old calling my house. That's naiveté . . . she doesn't get it, because I'm not around. My wife, who's very stern, is not getting across to her like I would get across if I were there."

It was, I told him, surprising to hear a man speak in terms of being needed by his daughters. "It surprised me, too," said Phil. "A woman just can't give a young lady that male perspective. All she can do is be strict. Right now is a tough time to be a teenager, because you're taught as a boy to be a dog and to be overly aggressive and to get into the panties by any means possible. And as a girl, you're taught to play the game and tease the boy."

It is important, said Phil, that a girl see her father treat her mother with love and respect. By this example, she learns how she herself should expect to be treated.

I agree. One recent Valentine's Day, after buying a red rose for my wife, I went back and picked up a pink one for Onjél. You never saw such a surprised and delighted little girl. I don't want her to be a "Daddy's girl" in the sense that she is spoiled beyond anyone's ability to endure. But I want her to learn from her Daddy to value herself and to demand to be treated in a certain manner.

I want to save her from becoming lost on the way to womanhood.

For the most part, my wife and I have been lucky with our children. We've done well. We have been blessed. For me, at least, my mother's example is still the one that guides.

My mother passed away in April 1988 after a long battle with breast cancer. About a week before she died, she asked me to bring her "babies" to her bedside so she could say goodbye. When we arrived with the kids later that night, she was in and out of consciousness. The damned cancer had emaciated her, shriveled her up, and stolen the fire from her eyes. The kids stood over her without really knowing what to say.

Marlon was five then, Bryan only three. She really doted on those boys. Got a kick out of the way Bryan used to meticulously inspect his food before he'd eat it. Laughed at Marlon charging around the house in a basketball jersey yelling, "Take it to the hoop, Coop"—meaning Michael Cooper, who was then a member of the Lakers.

When she died, I felt so alone. Felt as if there was no one left in the world. Friends patted my back, Marilyn held me when I cried, but I saw them as if from a great distance. I was in a cold place all by myself.

I've done my best to keep her alive for Marlon and Bryan, but their memories are so sketchy. The only thing Bryan recalls about her now is that she used to make scrambled eggs for him. Onjél, of course, never knew her at all.

The only thing I can give them is her example.

They say that a woman can't teach a boy how to be a man, and in some respects, this is true. I found myself nodding in commiseration with Robert, raised by a single mother in Atlanta, when he said, "As a father today, the thing I wonder about is how would it have been to have grown up with a man in the house. I think that men and women, they're totally different and they react to certain events differently. Because a man was never in our house, I always wonder do I, today, act the way a man would act."

Sometimes I wonder too. It's a wondering that has nothing to do with sexuality—gay versus not gay—and everything to do with traditional male rites of passage and bonding. I don't hunt or fish, I know and care nothing about the mysteries of the internal combustion engine, I have never played poker in a smoky room, and—outside of developing a rather late-in-life addiction to Lakers basketball—I have precious little interest in sports.

Throughout my life, most of my closest friends have been women; I find them easier to talk to and more apt to be discussing things that matter to me. Of my few close male friends, most are just like me: products of absent or abusive fathers and strong and persevering mothers.

So yes, you wonder. You feel again the absence of missing pieces.

On the other hand, some things know no gender. Like fidelity and compassion. Like toughness and soul. Like love.

I don't know where I would be, or even *who* I would be, without the woman who spent her life trying to impart those things to me.

There's an old gospel song that says in part, "My soul looked back and wondered how I got over." I recall a day when I lived a tempest and she was a harbor in the midst of it. And it occurs to me that my soul has never had to wonder. My soul has always known.

I am here because of her. And it buoys me when I look at this family I have raised, these young men and women who are here because of me: Markise wending his way toward a law degree; Marlon finishing high school and making his own plans for college; Bryan standing on the cusp of his middle teens and the challenges of high school; Onjél zipping frictionless through her elementary school years; and even Monique seemingly in the process of turning some invisible corner, becoming a responsible adult at long last. They do me proud.

And I realize that while I have known plenty of fatherhood's regrets, life has a way of balancing these things. Because I have also enjoyed more than a few of fatherhood's rewards.

THIRTEEN

The problem is that too many men—too many black men in particular—never get to fatherhood's rewards. They get the regrets instead, so many regrets coming so fast and piled so high that a man buckles under their weight. And seeing nothing to the contrary in his life or the lives of men he knows, seeing only other men bent under the same cruel mass, he convinces himself that this is the way it is, and the way it will always be. That he is helpless to affect his own life or circumstances.

We'll never know how many men we've lost to that pernicious assumption. But it's easy to understand why a man succumbs. So much of what we as black men see speaks only to the hopelessness and despair of people like us. Acts as an inducement to surrender. We are an "issue," a "problem" for the country to solve. It gets wearying sometimes.

I was driving one night in Chicago with Richard, my cousin who runs the live-in facility for troubled young men. "Today is a very sad day for me," he said. "One of my boys is going up for murder."

Richard says something like this almost every time I see him. Every time we talk, it seems like his heart has been freshly broken by some young black man he wanted to save.

This latest was a tormented teenager who had once tried to throw another young man out of a third-floor window. Richard sought to have him placed in a psychiatric institution for observation and assessment. Authorities refused, saying the young man was simply acting out his aggressions.

"A week later," Richard told me, "he robbed a guy at a gas station. Shot him point blank in the face *after* the guy gave him the money."

Richard will tell you straight out that he doesn't have a lot of hope for the young men he refers to as "my boys." Too many mothers lost to crack joys, he says. Too many fathers missing and unknown.

"If they're a microcosm of our society, our future is very dim. They are without hope, they are without direction, and they are without a sense of purpose. The most alarming thing is, when I ask them what they want to be twenty years from now, they say, 'Mr. Pitts, we only want to make it to our seventeenth birthday. All our friends were killed early.' That's pretty sad."

I looked over at Richard and knew exactly what he was feeling because I felt it, too. An ache that struck all too close to home. It wasn't the first time I'd felt it. Not even the first time that day.

Black men don't speak of that ache very often, but it's always there. You catch it in another man's eyes on the street sometimes just before one or the other pulls away and tugs the mask carefully back in place. Even a man who has won the badges and prizes of mainstream acceptance is not immune. He may wear a suit to work and drive a luxury car, but he still looks into a dead-eyed corner boy like a mirror and marvels at the turns that put one on this side and the other on that side—yet didn't quite separate, didn't quite sunder, didn't quite make it possible to turn away.

We are closer than heartbeats. We are closer than brothers.

And we struggle with the same questions. Where is our father? Why did he leave us like this? Why did he orphan us in this hard world?

Not that those questions are unique to African-American men, of course.

Hardly anyone would dispute that many children of other races also know what it is like to grow up in the absence of a father's love or in the presence of his violence. This is important to keep in mind.

But it is also important to acknowledge that African Americans suffer these things in disproportionately large numbers. And, more to the point, that African-American families are the ones that can least afford to absorb the pain. In virtually every major quality of life indicator—education, employment, crime, health, housing, and life expectancy—blacks rank at or near the bottom of American society. And black males often rank below blacks as a whole. The lowest of the bottom.

So a sense of desperation attaches to the plight of the young men who represent, in some eyes, the death knell of a people's hoped-for redemption. Those young men are in a hard place from jump street, beset from within and without, damned if they do, damned if they don't. News media that focus disproportionately on black male crime have, in concert with very real and distressing crime statistics, made the young African-American male a national icon of fear and dysfunction, the bogeyman that haunts America's dreams.

The result is a kind of national hysteria where the specter of the criminal black man eventually overwhelms virtually any discussion of who and what black people are. In his book *The Rage of a Privileged Class*, Ellis Cose recounted an episode where he shared a cab with Benjamin Bradlee, the former executive editor of the *Washington Post*. In the course of their conversation, Cose mentioned that he was at work on a book about race. To which Bradlee responded with a story about how his home had been broken into more than once, the result being that he now found himself frightened all the time.

Cose said race, Bradlee heard crime.

Take it as an emblem of what has happened to the dialogue between blacks and whites in this country. Some time ago, an overheated white man left on my voice mail a message ranting about black crime. Blacks could hardly expect empathy for their struggles with racism, he reasoned, so long as they continue to prey upon innocent whites. A white woman is *sixty-five times* more likely to be raped by a black man than by a white one, he proclaimed. It was a fact, he said. He challenged me to look it up.

As it happened, I had just finished doing some research on crime statistics and still had the material close at hand. The picture the numbers revealed was quite different from that painted by my caller. According to *Criminal Victimization in the United States, 1993*, published by the Justice Department's Bureau of Justice Statistics, 10.4 percent of white rape victims for that year reported that their assailant was black. But *22.6 percent* of all black rape victims told police that the person who attacked them was white. The numbers indicated, in other words, that a black woman was better than twice as likely to be victimized by a white rapist as the other way around.

My caller didn't leave a name or number, and I don't know if I'd have contacted him even if he had. I have learned from hard experience that the fact that his statistics were demonstrably wrong would be useless against the fact that he so passionately believed them to be unassailably right. The image of black men as predators preying upon white people in some twisted rite of racial revenge is a hardy one, impervious to contradictory truths. Indeed, whenever statistics documenting the disproportionate participation of young black males in violent crime are released, fearful white observers frequently ignore the corollary—that the overwhelming majority of their offenses are committed against other blacks, particularly other black males.

These things are inconvenient—and thus, easily ignored. Where black men and crime are concerned, rage washes away reason. "I fear for young black males in this society," is how Phil, a black executive in Atlanta, puts it.

And it's important to note that the demonization of black males comes not just from whites and from media, but from other blacks. Contrary to popular opinion, the black community is not some barrier impervious to the bombardment of mass media imagery depicting young black men as, in essence, beyond civilizing. African Americans are, themselves, influenced by this depiction. Indeed, I wonder sometimes whether our acceptance of this image doesn't become a self-fulfilling prophecy.

Black comedian Franklin Ajaye used to tell a story in which he and his brother were walking along behind an elderly white couple who kept turning around nervously, scared the two young black men were going to rob them. "Me and my brother were insulted," goes the punchline. "So we robbed 'em."

You laugh, yet at the same time, you wonder how often that actually happens, how often a man reasons that if he's going to be treated like a criminal regardless, he might as well become one and enjoy the spoils of the trade.

"I was coming from the store one day last year in Albuquerque," said Phil. "This young black kid was walking toward me. I felt myself clutching my keys and I'm ready to jab this guy in his eyes. Totally intimidated by this young black guy. As he walks by me, he says, 'How you doing, sir?' And I realized: If I'm afraid of this young black male, I can't imagine how white people feel."

No one wants to talk about the fear young black men instill in other blacks, I said.

"They don't," agreed Phil. "And I'm telling you, I'm scared to death."

As a citizen of Atlanta, Phil said he even understands the city's trepidation over Freaknik, the black college bacchanal that descends upon the Georgia capital every year. "If you're riding up the street, say you're in Fort Lauderdale, and the white kids are out there acting crazy and drunken, that's one thing. If they pull in front of you, you can give them The Look. You can't give The Look to a young black male. It'll go nowhere. That's why the city is really at odds with that Freaknik thing. White kids out of control is one thing. Black kids out of control is terrifying."

But objectively speaking, I said, is there a lot of difference between white kids out of control and black kids out of control? *Yes,* said Phil. He actually thought that out-of-control white kids might go to *greater* extremes of destructive behavior. But it was the black kids he most feared.

Makes no sense. Until you understand that black kids—and in particular, black males—frighten us even *before* they become out of control. This is the way we—blacks and whites alike—have been socialized. And at some level, young black men understand this.

"A young black male knows when he's intimidating people," said Phil. "So there's a certain braggadocio that you walk with or you carry yourself with. A young black male, especially when he's with four or five other young black males, he knows he carries a lot of . . . I don't want to say clout, but just intimidation."

It reminded me of something a friend named Wallace once told me. In his mid-1960s youth, Wallace was a Black Panther whose towering Afro—a rarity in those days of processed hair and conservative cuts—struck fear in black and white hearts alike. And this was exactly the effect he desired. "That was the only way we knew to get respect," he said. "Through fear."

It is the same today.

The problem is that fear is a dead-end road. Any respect it inspires is counterfeit and is quickly followed by resentment. Because anything that causes a person to fear soon earns that person's enmity.

At some level, this must be obvious even to young men who work hardest to instill that fear. Even they must know that what looks like respect is really just hatred waiting for an opening. But when you are starved for validation, desperate to have someone see you and say that you matter, you'll take what you can get any way it comes.

I wonder about that sometimes when I consider young black men like the ones my cousin works with. When I was a child, even the baddest among us had some connection to something larger. A sense of "we" and "us."

I see no such connection in Richard's boys. Instead, I sense in them a desperate fatalism, a sense that they have moved beyond the sanction, not just of society, but of family and friends and peers. That they have gone to a place of despair where they are all but unreachable and suicide is practiced by degrees.

All of us as black men know where that distant place is. Some of us live there and careen toward death every day on the razor's edge of our own lives. Some just whistled past it on the way to productive manhood. And some live suspended between the two, never fully one or the other.

Doesn't matter.

The differences aren't as important as the similarities. And the questions are the same for the corner boy as for the man in the luxury car with badges and prizes.

How do you escape the pull of the distant place? How do you salve the ache and heal the wounds? How do you pull it all together and become the father, the dad your children and community and nation need you to be?

But the answer is as sobering as it is obvious.

Sometimes you don't.

And when you don't, the failure is left there for children, community, and nation to deal with. So it would seem to be in all our interests to take what has been called a black problem and redefine it as an *American* one. Moreover, redefine the way we view black men and their passages.

We must find ways to make family once again a possible dream for black men. And the men themselves must and should take a leading role in that effort. Their task—our task—begins with a single revelation:

We matter.

You sense that this is something many of us have never fully understood in our relationships with our children and women. But it is true nevertheless.

We matter. And not solely because we can make the money to buy Pampers or food, though these things are important and, indeed, integral to a man's vision of himself. But we matter more because we bring to the family perspectives and experiences women do not have. We matter because by our presence, we secure a household, lend it stability it would not otherwise have. We matter because without us, a child is never quite whole in his own mind.

And we matter because we love and are loved. When we allow it, at least. When our ideas of what is manly and what is not aren't filtered through the protections and barriers we have learned to erect to hold ourselves safe from the battering we experience on a daily basis. It's exhausting to go through life always playing defense, your guard up from the moment you open your eyes in the morning to the moment you slip into sleep at night.

Indeed, some black men reported that the most revelatory aspect of the Million Man March in 1995 was that it was the first time they had ever felt free enough to walk with their guard down. The first place they were ever able to let themselves feel and confess without fear. Every hour of every day we play this role—black man—acting out our lives against the often-demeaning expectations of others. Suddenly, walking in a throng of hundreds of thousands of men just like yourself, you found expectations that felt less like weight than wings. You cast aside the role you had played for so long and it felt like you were . . . *flying.*

Tracing figure eights against the clouds. Free. Able, if only for a few transcendent moments, just to *be.*

If it's impractical to think black men will, in our lifetimes, know that feeling on a daily basis while acting and interacting in the streets and suites of America, perhaps it's not so far-fetched to think they can at least find a way to carve out some semblance of it in the comfort of their own homes and the safety of their own families. If not in that place among those people, then where and with whom?

Families are required to provide a love different from that ordinarily shown black men. Not simply love that nurtures and accepts, but love that does them the extraordinary honor of holding them to high expectations. Meaning expectations of a financial contribution when that is at all legitimately possible, yes. But meaning, also, expectations that they will share the other gifts they can bring into a household—and that the family will value those gifts.

Successful fatherhood is a hell of a lot more than keeping a baby in Pampers. By basketball in the driveway and lectures about the value of money, by spiritual instruction and help with homework, by bad jokes and checking the doors at night, by reining in the reckless misbehavior of children with the glance that could freeze magma . . . by all these things and a thousand more, black fathers—like all fathers—validate and prove themselves.

We are more than the sum of money we are able to earn. Indeed, sometimes, what a child needs can't even be quantified by dollar signs. Hell, I never went hungry a day in my life; my mother did wonders with a welfare pittance. But nevertheless, I had needs, requirements my father didn't meet and money could not. My mother saw this, knew how important it was, and kept trying to find an adult male for me to spend time with.

She finally approached my cousin Nate—Nathaniel Davis was his given name—and asked that he take her kids, me in particular, under his wing. He wasn't comfortable with that. Nate and I talked about it in early 1998, a few weeks before he died of cancer, and he said, "I used to tell your mom, 'I can take 'em up under my wing, but I wouldn't want them to turn out like me.' I thought I was a player. That wasn't really a very good image."

But he did as she asked anyway. And you know what? He was often *awful* at it. The first advice Nate ever gave me about women went as follows: Don't get serious about any of them. Don't let any one of them tie you down. Follow the "four F's": find 'em, feel 'em, fuck 'em, forget 'em.

The man was far from perfect in other ways, as well. Most glaringly, Nate had three children of his own whom he seldom saw. Until a memorable Thanksgiving dinner when my sister Linda piped up in her usual blunt way and asked why he was always squiring his girlfriends and their kids around but never had time for his own. Mortified by this mouths-of-babes indictment, Nate left the dinner table, went and got his kids, and brought them to live with him.

The point being that Nate was not exactly a role model straight from Central Casting. But he was there. Always there. And we could talk about anything.

One day, when I was still just an adolescent, I called Nate and woke him from a sound sleep with this question: What do you think of oral sex? I swear, the poor man must have stammered for a full minute.

And then he answered.

Might not have been the best answer, but in a very real sense, that was beside the point. Just the fact that he was willing to be there, willing to be awakened for such an intrusive question, meant more than anything. It was certainly more than I'd ever had from any male relationship before that.

We became very close over the years. Nate was my sounding board, loan officer, driving instructor, friend, and shade-tree mechanic who kept a series of my old cars running long after the time they should've been consigned to the junk heap. I remember how he used to take me with him to see kung fu movies. Me, I was never that big a fan of martial arts flicks. But again, that wasn't the point. I'd sit through a whole Bruce Lee marathon without complaint, just knowing that he was willing to make space in his life for me.

I've never forgotten how it felt to have a good man's time and attention. Some boys—and girls—have never known.

What is required of black men, then, is a courage different from what we ordinarily think of when that word is invoked. Not physical courage in the face of danger, but spiritual courage in the face of love. Courage enough to shed masks and armor before the women and children who love us and need us. Courage enough to understand that the mores we have adopted, the methods of defense that have come to seem like second skin to us, are not nearly that natural.

After so many years, we have come to take as normal a whole array of destructive ideas about black men in particular and black people in general. For instance, at some level, some of us have come to accept that poverty and want are a black person's normal lot in life. Why else is the man who desires to leave the dirt and danger of the inner city automatically derided as having forgotten his roots? But of all the dangerous ideas we have internalized, none is more destructive than this notion we have that it is unremarkable for black fathers to leave their children or to make themselves emotionally unavailable.

We have to find it in ourselves to challenge these suppositions. Have to find it in ourselves to challenge the idea that black people must always get the leavings, the crumbs, the leftovers of life's good things. Or that black fathers must always be stragglers drifting in and out of the lives of their children.

Says *who?* We are shaped by the past, true enough. But where is it written that we are *imprisoned* by it? What is there that says we cannot flip the script, revise the paradigm, change the game, if only we can make ourselves dream something new? And if a man who would become Dad needs examples of how that's done, they are—contrary to popular opinion and media portrayals—there. Fathers, black men, *family* men who came up on hard streets, sired by disappointing dads, yet get up every morning and do the hard work of raising and supporting their children. Men whose names history will never know and whose work media will never see nor celebrate. Men who are in our offices, on our blocks, at our stores, upon our streets. Men who understand that there is nothing predestined about fathers who physically or emotionally leave their children behind.

"I don't think it's natural," said Enrico, a black father who lives in Yonkers. "I think it's a wimp mentality. Not being man enough to stand in there and make a difference."

Enrico told me the first time he ever saw his father, he was eight years old, playing behind an apartment building in his native Panama. "It was me and a bunch of other little guys playing out there. We were all about the same age. My father walked right over to *me.*

"He picked me out of a bunch of kids, playing, because I looked like him."

Lawrence in Washington had a similar experience when he went to a classroom to meet his ten-year-old daughter, whom he hadn't seen since she was three weeks old. He had no idea what she looked like, "but when I looked in the room, I said, 'Is that her?'" The girl's mother said yes and

Enrico with sons Adonis (left) and Alexander

Lawrence, standing in the doorway, gave a little wave. "She jumped out of her seat, ran to the door—'Daddy! Daddy! Daddy!'—jumped up on me. I tell you, man, that was a Kodak moment."

There is, then, something sacred in the bond between a father and his children.

"Being a dad, I think, has saved my life," said Enrico. "There's a lot of things I think I would have gotten into [otherwise]." It's something he feels so strongly that when he and his wife divorced, he fought for—and won—custody of their two sons, Adonis and Alexander.

"Because I grew up without a father," he explained, "I wouldn't have my sons be raised without me. I also did not have another sibling that had the same two parents [I did]. That's why I had to have at least two out of the same woman. I made a vow that all my kids would come out [of] the same woman. I don't want to have kids all over the place like I saw a lot of guys do. When we grew up, there was a lot of guys talking about, 'Oh yeah, man, I got her pregnant.' They were having babies all over the place.

"I wasn't down with that. I wanted something different for my sons. I wanted to be there for them. I didn't want to miss anything, I wanted to see myself in my children—and I do."

It hasn't always been easy for Enrico to stay with his boys. To the contrary, there have been times when it might have been easier—even more practical—to leave. He recalled a time before the divorce when he was out of work for six months, desperately searching anywhere he might be able to find a job. "I'm throwing out résumés—the wrong thing to do when you're going for a McDonald's job."

Not surprisingly, the same response kept coming back over and over again: overqualified. "I don't want to hear that," he told them. "I've got kids, two dogs, and a wife at home. I need a job.

"I remember when I was eighteen years old, I had a girlfriend [whose] aunt told her I was going to be nothing but a welfare patient. Because I didn't have a car, I didn't have a job. And I turned up on welfare when my kids were little. All I could hear was in the background, 'welfare patient, welfare patient.' That ate at me."

It was, he said, a despairing time. "Me and their mother had bought this life insurance and paid it up for a year already. I was like, 'I'm worth more money to my family dead than alive.' And it was sick. It was really sick. I saw myself driving off the bridge."

Making matters worse, said Enrico, was the knowledge that the government would give his family more money if he left. For a "split-second," he said, he thought about it. But in the end, he couldn't go through with it.

"I said no. I said to myself, 'I will never leave.' I said, 'Wow. Is this the reason other men leave? And have these women on welfare like that?' Because the women do get more money if the man is not there. I couldn't do that, because I couldn't live with myself.

"I mean, there are some guys that have grown up without a father and all they do is repeat the cycle. But I was not going to let it happen with me and my sons. There were times I thought I was weak, but when I look at that situation, I feel that, wow, I must have been very strong to come through that. I had a 1969 Chevy Impala, man. When I got it, it was already ten years old. We went through the time when we didn't have nothing in the cupboard but some macaroni and cheese. We were eating peanut butter and jelly sandwiches. And I *still* stayed. I felt that what I had to give my sons was far more important than them getting some extra money."

That understanding is the first step in becoming Dad.

That understanding cost Robert, who lived in Pontiac, Michigan, his very life. As his brother Ernest tells the story, Robert was in a common-law marriage with "a third-generation welfare girl who never worked. Just a baby machine, had six kids. [He was] struggling, working all the time and she had a crack habit."

Robert's family implored him to leave, but "Robert wouldn't leave those kids for nothing," said Ernest. "The girl wouldn't marry him because she knew that was her welfare, her money train: 'You can live with me, but I can't marry you, 'cause I'm third-generation welfare, and that's the way we always made money.' He would do laundry, he would cook," said Ernest of his brother. "He's working all the time and she's at home doing drugs. And consequently, that situation happened."

The "situation" was a horror that, according to newspaper accounts, unfolded as follows. Robert's common-law wife, Jackie, a self-confessed crack dealer, became embroiled in a dispute with another dealer, Anthony. He wanted to sell his product from her house and she wouldn't allow it. And so, said prosecutors, Anthony decided to take revenge. One night in September 1995, he took a bottle—a forty-ounce malt liquor bottle, according to Ernest—filled it with gasoline, attached a fuse, lit it, and heaved it into the house where Robert, his wife, and their six children were sleeping. The night exploded in flame.

Robert managed to get Jackie and three of the children to safety. Then he went back for the others. The house was fully engulfed, said Ernest, but "he went back in, and had run a tub with some water, was trying to wet some things down and looking for one of the kids that had hidden up under some laundry.

"He died in the house with the three children."

You wonder why someone didn't stop him from this act of suicidal bravery. But as his brother puts it, "You would've had to kill him on the street" to do that, to keep him from his children.

Ernest

The first impulse, perhaps, is to think of Enrico and Robert as exceptions, the proverbial good men that are hard to find. But the only thing that is exceptional about either man is that they chose not to go along with the program, chose not to buy into the prevailing vision of themselves as congenitally helpless.

There are those who argue that slavery ruptured the black family and of course, it did. But who is to say that this tear was either permanent or irreparable? Indeed, one of the most poignant pictures of the world in the days immediately after the Civil War is of black families—very often black *fathers,* their lives torn asunder by the trade in human flesh—choking the byways of the defeated South, often traveling on foot, searching for sons and daughters who had been lost to them days, years, *decades* before.

Sometimes they had only bare scraps of information—the name of a county a son was living in five years ago, but still they walked.

Sometimes so many years had passed that the lost child had almost certainly become an unrecognizable adult, but still they walked.

Sometimes they were footsore and hungry, weather-beaten and lost, separated from their destination by counties, mountains, *states.* And still they walked.

In that pre-computer, pre-telephone world, the searches were often doomed to failure. But they walked anyway. Because they knew how important it was to get back. They knew that this was life and breath. They knew that there was healing to be found in the arms of kin.

And African Americans today, what do we know? Are we still as tough of mind and body as we once were? Or has toughness been beaten out of us by racism's everyday indignities, seduced from us by a responsibility-shifting society in which everyone is a helpless victim and our very dreams are stolen away, then sold back to us on easy credit terms with low monthly payments? Are we willing to do what it will take to get what we want?

"We're expecting things to come easy," is how Andrew, who lives in Los Angeles, puts it. "Everybody wants a good-looking woman on their arm and to drive a nice car; you'll see guys who'll go out, get the raggediest apartment they can find, just something to keep the rain off their heads, and have a really flashy car and think, Now I can go out and get women and have a great time.

"But there's more to it than that. There's steps we want to just bypass in order to get to the fun part. We look at TV and we see all you need to do is brush your teeth with Ultra-Brite and you can get all the babes. Buy a real nice car with no money down and you don't have to start payments until next year.

"I think society makes things easy for us and we tend to always want to take it a step further. Welfare is another situation that kind of makes life easy for us without having to put any effort into it. You've got folks who [say], 'All I've got to do is have a kid, and I can get money. I don't really have to look for a job. The white man's not going to give me one anyway, so why put myself through all of that?' That's that lack of responsibility thing. And of course, the white man is the root of all evil and creates problems for us."

His sarcasm resonates. Makes me remember how my son Markise told me once about a fourteen-year-old black male friend who complained that he could never get ahead, because "the white man" was keeping him down. I was stunned. Just fourteen years old and this boy was already beaten where it counts most—meaning in his soul and spirit. Beaten before he ever entered the game.

The hell with the white man, I wanted to tell him. What are *you* doing for yourself? How are *you* working to flip the script? Because until and unless you do that, any white man interested in keeping you down is going to be spared the effort. The same holds true for black people as a whole.

"I know blacks folks have been treated badly for a long, long time," said Andrew. "But I think we're continually treated badly because we don't want to assume responsibility for the things that are done to us. If we put ourselves in a position to be treated badly, then we *will* be treated badly and then we want to look at the person who treated us badly as the culprit. Which in fact it is, but [we] don't have to be in that situation."

He offered as an example the story of a cousin who was "always going to jail" for smoking crack. Andrew said his cousin was raging against the often-discussed disparity in federal drug sentencing guidelines whereby the sale of crack cocaine (whose dealers tend to be black) draws mandatory sentences significantly stiffer than the sale of powdered cocaine (whose dealers tend to be white). "The white man is always looking for ways to keep us down," was the assessment by Andrew's cousin.

"And I said, 'Well, why are you smoking the crack?' Why you want to blame the white man because you have to spend more time in jail than the white guy who snorts the coke? *Let the crack alone and you'd be all right!*' Don't want to assume responsibility for their actions, but want to blame everybody for their predicament."

The issue isn't whether black fathers and black families have been damaged by white racism. Of *course* they have. But if the repair of those fathers and families has to wait until white racism is gone, then we're likely to be waiting a very long time. More to the point, much of what black fathers must do to reclaim their families requires no repeal of racism. Much of it is in our hands now, requiring nothing more than a commitment and a toughness and a will.

Ernest is one of the fathers who already knows this, who is already moving on it. He wonders sometimes why more black men don't do the same.

"I look at some [men]," said Ernest, "they're drunks. Some people out there doing drugs. And I [say], 'Hey, man, why don't you get your boy involved in sports? You've got a *son,* man, and your son went to the school counselor and said, My dad don't never do nothing with me. Why don't you do something with your son, man?' I don't see how folks can't do it. I don't know why they won't.

"I just have a zest and a zeal to be a father. I want the full package of husband and dad. I couldn't think of two greater titles a man could have than being husband and father. It's a privilege and an honor."

It's a sentiment Jerry, who lives in Los Angeles, echoes. "Anybody can make a baby," he said. "But being a father is a whole different situation. Every once in a while, my kids call me Dad, I stop and think about it. That title is something else. It carries a lot of weight to it. For the child to relate to you as their dad is an honor. Because usually when fathers don't meet their responsibilities, it's very difficult for a child to refer to their father as Dad."

Ernest, whose father died when he was just five, describes himself as "an active dad. I'm the disciplinarian in the house. My wife tends to be more the cuddler. I know it's tough out there; I love 'em, but I'm tough on my children in terms of having responsibility. I do spank. Some people say you shouldn't spank, you should talk to them. They're little people and you should talk to them and give them all the privileges of being a person and never spank them. But I don't believe in that. I believe in spanking if need be."

His daughter, he said, is involved in dance. "I go to her recitals, I brought her flowers for the first time and presented them to her." The little girl asked who the flowers were for. Her dad said, "'This is for you, sweetheart. You performed at a recital, so you deserve roses.'" Ernest's son is involved in athletics—"Any kind of sport, he wants to play it"—and his father coaches his teams.

"I'm not a drop-off kind of dad. I want to be there for him as well as the other twelve little boys who might not have fathers. I coach basketball for six and under, I go to the rec centers and give time and help work with kids."

Like Ernest, David, a father of three girls in New Jersey, is also a coach for his children's teams. He's found that in that role, he's had influence on more kids than simply his own. "I took two kids on my team that nobody else wanted. I didn't see them, I just heard their names: 'This child is bad, he's a problem child.' I said, 'I'll take 'em. I'll take *both* of 'em.' And they turned out to be good kids. They just needed discipline. They just needed somebody to step up and spend time with them.

"That's what I think [is] the problem with the younger kids now. The ones that are bad, they don't have the father figure. If you're raised by your mother, then most of the time she's gone at work. She does the best she can. With a father, I guess, a son expects him to help him hit the ball or have a catch with him. Interact with him. Even my wife, she doesn't do hardly anything I do as far as interacting with the kids."

Charles, the minister in Los Angeles, is another dad who makes a point of involving himself in the life of his child. "I'm there for my daughter," he said. "I participate in my daughter's life daily. Just moment by moment. My wife and I, from the time she was born, shared responsibilities. There's no such thing as one person gets up all the time throughout the night. We took turns getting up and feeding and changing and bathing. For the most part, the stuff my wife would do more of would be the stuff I can't do—like hair and that sort of thing. I'm just lousy at doing hair."

The point isn't that it's easy, getting around the debits of a bad upbringing, but that it's *possible.* If a man wants it bad enough. Like Charles, Mike grew up in a violent home. He admits that when his son, Jarrett, was born, it was difficult not to let that affect his relationship with him. "The hardest part was, when I was very upset with him, not to bring forward the abuse that I suffered as a child, not to beat him with a stick, not to beat him with an extension cord, but to talk with him about what happened verbally, prior to using any type of physical discipline. That was very hard," said Mike, "because all my life, I've always been physically abused. Now I'm a father, and I don't want to do that. I never, ever, wanted to be like [my father]. I never wanted my son to cower down to me.

"I hit Jarrett one time in anger, when he was probably four years old. He took off down the street and no one knew where he was. When I caught up with him, I whacked him on the butt really good and hard. Not beat him in the face or anything, but I really hit him harder than I would've probably any other time. And when that happened, I told myself, 'I'll never, ever hit him in anger.' That was the last time I ever hit him in anger. After that, I would talk."

We are not prisoners of what we were, not bound by awful things we once saw or the emptiness we have felt. Not to deny the power these things can exert upon us. But too many men who knew too many harsh times have been too successful as fathers for us to buy the idea that a man is helpless before the inadequacies of his past.

Take Timothy, as a final example. Not because his is the perfect story, but rather, because it is the imperfect one, the story of a man who came of age shouldering pain that is still largely unresolved, yet who manages on a daily basis to do the work of being a stepfather to his wife's two children.

Timothy was born on the move. Air force family. By the time he was in the second grade, he had already lived in South Dakota, Holland, and Illinois. Finally his father brought the family—three boys, five girls—to Mather Air Force Base in Sacramento. Ask Timothy about his father, and he'll tell you that the main thing he remembers is tagging along behind him and his two older brothers on fishing trips. "I was there just to carry the tackle box," is how he puts it. His brothers were six and seven years older. "So they were really close with him. I kind of tagged along because maybe they felt sorry for me."

It was an uneventful life that ended with brutal suddenness. Timothy was ten years old and in the fifth grade—had not a clue anything was amiss—the morning his father went to the door in his dress uniform. "Normally when he left, if he was going on an extended business trip, he would always say, 'I'll see you later.' But in full dress uniform that morning, it was 'Take care of the family.'

"The way it was supposed to work, he was going to be stationed in Panama. And we were going to follow him shortly thereafter. But it never

Timothy

[happened]. He went and was stationed in Panama and retired there. I never saw him again until I was twenty-four."

Timothy didn't immediately understand what had happened. Comprehension didn't come until the morning his mother sent him in the station wagon with his two brothers to do some shopping at the commissary. As Timothy remembers it, the older boys—sixteen-year-old Terry and seventeen-year-old Eddie Junior—were very angry that morning. "Man, that really sucks," said Terry.

At which, Eddie cautioned him. "Be quiet," he said, pointing toward Timothy in the back seat. "He's not supposed to know.'

"That's when I stuck my head up and said, 'What am I not supposed to know?' He said, 'That Dad's gone.' I said, 'Yeah, I know. He's in Panama. We're going to go see him pretty soon.' That's when my brother Terry really, really belligerently said, 'No, we're *not.* We're not going to see him. He's never coming back.'"

There had been, said Timothy, no warning that he can remember. "I can count maybe on one hand the number of times I saw my mother and father fight with each other. They really never showed a great deal of affection towards one another, either. So just as I say I can count on one hand the number of times I saw them fight, I can also count on one hand the number of times I saw them embrace. There was never any real rocky relationship-type thing going on with them. As a matter of fact, growing up, I just thought that's the way couples interact with one another. They were cordial, but distant. No physical abuse. I saw my father lose his temper one time and he punched a hole in the kitchen wall and walked out of the house."

Even after his brothers told him what had happened, Timothy didn't quite grasp the ramifications of it. "I didn't know that it was going to have far-reaching consequences on my life. So I just said, 'Really? Oh. Okay. What are we going to get from the commissary?'

"It started becoming a reality when Terry ran away. He was close to my dad. So was Eddie. They were really tight with my father. They couldn't wait for him to get home after work. He taught Terry how to play chess and he and Eddie would hang out and watch westerns and war movies well into the night. All I wanted to do was wait till I got old enough, so I could hang out with them. So they took it hard. They took it real hard.

"One night, Terry was messing around in the bedroom. I looked over and he had a brown grocery bag. He was sticking clothes in it. I said, 'Where you going?' He said, 'I'm leaving.' 'When you coming back?' He says, 'I'm not.' And he gave me this red velvet beret he used to wear all the time. He said, 'Here, take care of my hat. And . . . take care of the family.'"

Timothy laughed humorlessly at the recollection of it. His brother running away, repeating the parting admonition of their father. "He crawled out the window and I didn't see him again until I was a grown man. That just left me and Eddie there. At that time, Eddie was entering his senior year in high school. He was getting ready to graduate and he had already told me he was thinking about joining the air force. Dad was in the air force, so I guess he figured he'd go ahead and follow suit.

"By this time, I'm out of the fifth grade. And I know my dad's not coming back. It's really clear, because there are no letters, no contacts. And your friends start asking you, 'Where's your father?' That's when you know he's not coming back. Matter of fact, my teacher in the fifth grade was told by my mom that we were supposed to be leaving for Panama so we weren't going to be there for the whole school year. So they threw a going-away party for me. And I came back to school the next day.

"The teacher is like, 'What are you doing here?' [I said], 'I guess we're going to go a little later.' You start lying at first, but after a year or two, you realize . . . he's not coming back."

A year later, Timothy's brother Eddie joined the air force. "So there's no other guys in the house. I had five sisters, a mom and myself. And that's when the feeling of loneliness comes. That's when the impact finally started settling in."

He was a seventh grader. And he had just become the man of the house.

"I didn't get a chance to be a regular teenage guy," said Timothy. "There were too many things that needed to be done. All that fixing up, and guy stuff that needed to be done around the house, that became my responsibility. I took that on myself. There was no way for me to neglect it or refuse to do it. If something messed up with the plumbing or there was a problem with the door sticking or whatever, I was always raised that men are supposed to take care of women. I know it's old-fashioned, but that's just the way I was raised.

"I felt the pressure starting to mount up. I still had no father, the money's tight, and my mom's starting to feel the pressure herself. I can tell, because there's more than a few occasions around the first and the fifteenth of the month where she's at the kitchen table and there's a pile of bills in front of her and she's sweatin' it. She's really sweatin' it. You can tell in her face that it's not going easy."

Something inside him broke then. For a short time—for a very short time—he rebelled. Began dealing drugs, cutting class, getting into fights, hating the world. "That lasted from seventh grade until the middle of my eighth-grade year. That's all the time I've ever rebelled.

"It was me and a couple of friends of mine, Mike and Jeff. We were really close, really tight. Together, no one would mess with us. I don't consider us a gang; we were just three guys that were really tight, would help one another. Just so happened that we sold weed and did those kinds of things."

It all came to an end the day school officials found a stash of marijuana belonging to the three-man drug ring. That day, said Timothy, school officials appeared in his class and called him and Mike out. "They take me down to my locker, search it, nothing's there. Then I go out, down to the front of the school and Jeff was leaning on the sheriff's car in handcuffs, crying. They're trying to walk us to the office to call our parents. I see him out there crying, so I run there real quick. And he says, 'Don't say anything. I said it was all mine.' They came to get me, they put me in the office, they called my mom, they sent me home, they put Jeff into juvenile hall.

"That night," recalled Timothy, "Mom comes into my room. I'm thirteen years old and she comes into my room and says I can't hang around Jeff any more, I can't hang around Mike anymore. I told her, 'You can't tell me what to do! You can't tell me who to pick as my friends.' And then there was this side of her that I'd never seen before."

Timothy shook his head at the memory of what happened next. "She came at me as hard as she could with her right hand, with her fist, punched me square in the face. I flew back onto the floor. She came down on the floor with her knee in my chest, she grabbed me by the throat, she was choking me and she started crying. She said, 'Your father left, your brothers are gone, and I'll kill you before I lose you to the streets! Do you understand me, boy? I'll kill you. As God is my witness, I will *kill* you before I lose you to the streets!'

"I couldn't move," he recalled. "I couldn't say anything. I was choking, my lip was bleeding. She was just sitting there crying and her tears were dropping on me. That had a really good impact on me. It wasn't that I was afraid of her; it was that I knew how badly she wanted me to be good."

Timothy was suspended from school for "a week or two." His friend Jeff was expelled. "Last I heard, he was in jail for manslaughter. It's like our lives just went in two separate directions.

"I went back to school and I had pretty much failed all my classes that first quarter. I had straight F's, so I knew what I had to do if I was going to finish up and look halfway decent that third quarter. I had to get all A's to bring 'em up to C's. Then I had to get all A's again, bring 'em up to B's to get out of school at a decent GPA. So I just hit the books. I got real busy."

By the time the eighth-grade year was over, Timothy had brought his grades back up. That summer, he found a job working as a groundskeeper at Mather Air Force Base. Everything he earned, he brought home. "When my mom was at the table with the bills, I'd put my check on the pile."

One night, while his sisters were sleeping, Timothy asked his mother to explain that pile to him. "You don't want to know," she told him. But Timothy persisted and his mother gave in. "She showed me the whole layout: the mortgage note, the utility bill, the phone bill, the food. She showed me her whole budget and how she does it. That's when I stuck my nose in it. She and I became more like partners. When summer was over, I got another job that took me through my ninth-grade year. After ninth grade, I got another job.

"It was not pushed upon me by my mom," he said, "but she welcomed the assistance. We developed a different type of relationship. I would go to school in the daytime, I would get out of school around three, I would start work at four. Then I would work from four until about nine or nine-thirty. She would be there to pick me up after I got off work. We'd go home, then she'd fix dinner while I was looking at bills and stuff. That's how the rest of my teenage life went. There was no prom or ball . . . none of that. I didn't have time."

Timothy went to summer school two years in a row, got extra credit for his work experience, and graduated from high school when he was just sixteen. "My teenage years, they kept shrinking. Before I knew it, I was sixteen years old . . . already registered for college."

Did he resent the fact that adult concerns were stealing so much of his childhood away? "I didn't resent it then, but I realize how much I gave up in retrospect now. I think when you become a parent, it's really clear how well you lived as a child or how you did not live well as a child. I don't think it's ever, *ever* a child's position to be anything more than a child when they're growing up. They shouldn't have to be. I believe that when you're a child, regardless of the circumstances, you have every right to grow up, go through your grammar school years, go through puberty, be a teenager in high school, and then go to college and move on through life. I believe that's a right for any child, and any parent that wants to raise a child should make sure that that child has those rights."

Fourteen years after Timothy's father put on his dress uniform and walked away, he returned. Timothy's mother called to say he had been hospitalized at a nearby military base for surgery. "She asks if we want to come down with her to see him. I'm like, 'Why?' Finally, she says, 'Well, I'd like you to be there.'

"So I go over there and I meet up with him. Daddy was in a little room and they brought him out into another room where he could sit down at a table and there were some chairs there. My mom is saying, 'How are you doing?'—she called him Jake; that was his nickname, I guess. They're like all cordial with each other, right? They're hugging each other as if life was all good."

Timothy leveled no-nonsense eyes at me. "You've got to understand," he said. "I don't know this guy. *I don't know him.* I never got a chance to bond with him—he bailed on me when I was ten, so I really never had a chance to know his personality. Eddie's like, 'Pops, how's it going?' He's giving him a big hug and everything. And [my mother] goes, 'This is Timmy.' He's coming up to me like he wants a hug or something. I just shake his hand like, 'How you doing? I'm Tim.'

"Anything else is fake—for me. I'm not going to be a hypocrite: 'Daddy, I love you.' Come on! I *don't,* okay? I never had a chance to develop that. People are talking to him like, 'How have you been, what have you been doing?' Nobody's asking this guy, 'Hey, man, why did you leave?' Nobody's asking him that. And I'm wondering if somebody rehearsed this whole thing before I got there. My sisters were all talking, my mom was updating him on everything . . . 'Well, you've got a grandson, his name is William. . . .'

Meanwhile, Timothy sat off to himself at the far end of the table, staring his father down. At one point, his father glanced up and caught his eye. Whatever the older man saw there made him turn away very fast. "I'm thinking in my mind, 'You've got a bucket-load of kids here, you drop off the planet, fourteen years later you come back, and we're gonna like, just *rap?* Come on, man! What's up with that?'

"I didn't say anything, because I didn't have anything to say. We were getting ready to leave and he looks at me and he says, 'So, how you doing?' I said, 'Fine, thank you, sir.' And I shook his hand again. That was it."

On that note, father and son parted company again. Timothy said that afterward, his sister Marie approached him as an intermediary: "Daddy really wants to talk to you, Timmy." He spurned the offer.

"Got to be honest with you, Marie," he told her. "Kind of old now, can't be Timmy, son, little boy, carry the tackle box. I'm kind of out of bonding here, okay? I mean, if he wants to talk, I'll run into him, I'm sure at some kind of gathering and he can talk. But right now, I have nothing in me to make me want to reach out to him." I was tired.

"That's when the resentment started to well up again. Because when I was twenty-four, I saw my mom and dad hanging out with each other at the hospital like it was no big thing. But I had just gone through all of my teenage years, being Dad. And they're sitting at this table talking about old times. That didn't register too well with me. That wasn't cool at all. He wants to hang out and talk and everything and I'm like, *why?* Especially if you had an opportunity to do so all those fourteen years."

The father and son finally did meet again at a family gathering—a party at Eddie's house—ten years later. "Terry comes down from Portland and for the first time in, like, ever it seems, all the guys are in the same place at the same time. Eddie was there, Terry was there, I was there and my dad was there. My wife got a picture of all of us together.

"And then, I go outside to get a breather and he follows me out there and gives me this long story about how he didn't leave, but it was like a separation that him and my mom had agreed on because they weren't getting along. He gets into this long ol' story and I'm just listening to him, and all I come out of it with at the end of the story was that, number one, it wasn't as my mom said, because the original story was that he deserted us and she didn't know it was going to happen.

"Then I start feeling that resentment part. Because now you have to look at, Well, I *could've* played ball in high school, *could've* kept some of the money I made, bought a car. I don't like to be judgmental, but I gotta tell you: If I have a bucket-load of kids in a city, and I can't get along with my wife, I'll understand that and I'll move on. But I'm not going to just forget about them. You can't do that."

As a young man dating, he made himself a promise: "If I couldn't guarantee that any child I make could come onto the planet and be 100 percent child all the way through school *and* college and live their life the way I know they should, then I wasn't going to make a baby." He was exacting in relationships, he said, quick to end it if he had a hint that he and a given woman had no future. Where birth control was concerned, he was careful to the point of paranoia. There would be no accidental children.

Timothy finally got married when he was thirty-two to a woman he'd known since the second grade. She had two children already and that, he figured, was enough. "I made the decision that I would help her as best I could raise her two and I wasn't going to have any of my own. So I went and had the vasectomy and told 'em to clip 'em, burn 'em, *and* stitch 'em. I don't need anything coming undone."

I asked Timothy to what degree his selectivity in choosing a mate and his decision to have a vasectomy were a response to his father's behavior. "Seventy-five or eighty percent," he said. "Everything that happened in my childhood, almost everything, has had an impact on me as an adult. I appreciate my time more, I relish my space, and I'm intolerant of irresponsibility."

Nevertheless he is, in his own estimation, a good stepfather. "The children are in no doubt as to what I'm about and where I'm coming from. They know my expectations. They know that I'm not ever going to just trip for no reason at all.

"A structured environment is what they desire most as children. They need to know that they can come home and be kids. One hundred percent. Good or bad. They need to know they can do that. And to know that means they don't have to worry about any of the dumb stuff that's not their responsibility. Got a roof, got food, got clothes, got some allowance, got medical coverage, got dental coverage, got all that dumb stuff taken care of so they can just be kids."

He feels, he said, that both his parents failed their children in that regard. "Okay, fine. My mom and dad couldn't get along. There were five girls and three boys, and they couldn't get along. Well guess what, guys: If you had a problem, it didn't just happen in Sacramento. You had a problem a long time ago. First question is, why are you still making babies? Second question is, now that we're all here, what about us? As a child, I don't *care* that you can't get along. Somebody better be there in support of me. I better have two parents in this household in support of me."

I asked Timothy if he is still angry with his father. He shook his head. "No," he said. "It's graduated into a nice, comfortable indifference. I would lie if I said I loved him, but there's no emotion there to hate."

And there the situation sits. No happy ending, no bittersweet resolution of father and son, but no carrying the pain forward into the next generation, either. He has found a way to function despite it, found a way to become Dad. Which is, of course, precisely the point of all this. Everybody hurts. We all walk wounded through our days. But some of us—*many* of us—go forward regardless.

It can be done. We know this because it is done every day. It is, said Timothy, important that people understand that.

"There is a *large* number, growing ever so much, of conscientious black men in this country that own up to their responsibilities as head of households. Instead of all the stereotypical, goofy homeboys they show on TV, singing and dancing and playing ball.

"There's a large population of us and all we do is work and pay our taxes and head our households. We've all come from broken homes. And *ours* ain't broke."

FOURTEEN

The sun awoke to the sound of drums. Rhythmic and resonant African drums, brown hands slapping against taut skins, calling out an awakening. Holding out a change as fingers of first light stretched themselves over the great dome of the United States Capitol. From all over the country, men left homes and families, jobs and jails, campuses and street corners, and gathered in the shadow of that building, journeyed into the embrace of brethren, came together looking for the change the talking drums sang.

I'll always remember that day, October 16, 1995. It was clear and brisk as we bundled up and left the house, my sons Marlon and Bryan, and I. We waited on the platform in a morning crowd of black men, then boarded the subway into Washington. There were hardly any white people on the train and precious few to be seen on any of the stops along the way. White Washington—not unlike white America—was nervous. Had watched the day approach with trepidation. And now, was staying home to observe what unfolded on television.

We got off at the Smithsonian station, my sons and I walking behind a group of men who hit the escalators at a trot, moving in time to a deep and rhythmic chant, like a step team from a black fraternity. We followed them above ground into a Washington we had never seen before. A Washington of black men come seeking answers.

The boys and I wandered toward the Capitol building, but the crowds were so thick there we could hardly move. So we made our way west along the Mall instead, passing knots and clusters of laughing, hugging, back-slapping black

Marlon, Leonard, and Bryan at the Million Man March

men, face after face that looked like ours or somebody we knew. And for once, for this one blessed moment, those faces were not fortresses, the eyes did not warn you away as they do on unforgiving streets in uncaring neighborhoods. For once, masks and armor were laid aside. A brother met a brother with a smile and a handshake and said, "Pleased to meet you, how you doing?" Or simply, "Good morning, black man."

A Washington of black men come searching for answers had already found at least one, albeit implicitly. More than white people, more than government, more than the families that love, need, and miss us, *we* as black men carry the seeds of our own redemption.

The National Parks Service later said that 400,000 people were there that day. ABC Television engaged an independent agency, the Center for Remote Sensing at Boston University, to study crowd photos, and on that basis reported that there was a minimum of 837,000. Organizers in the Nation of Islam would place attendance at 1.5 million.

And none of the discrepancies mattered in the end. It was what it was, the imprimatur of bureaucrats and head counters notwithstanding. It was the Million Man March.

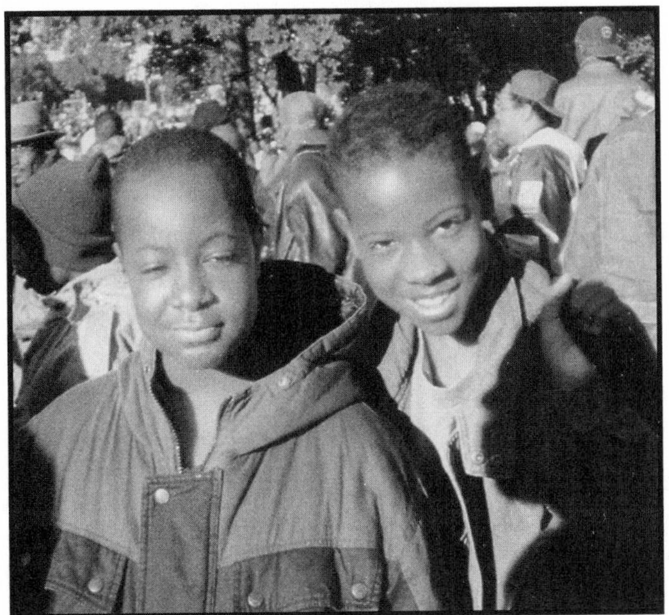

Bryan and Marlon

Much of the nation was simultaneously drawn to and repulsed by the idea that black men would gather in answer to the call of Louis Farrakhan, who is, after all, a firebrand with a history of ugly anti-Semitic remarks. Many white pundits and some black ones fixed upon and hammered home a single idea—that to support this thing was to support the mercurial leader of the Nation of Islam. Within black America itself, there was lively debate over the need for the march, its aims, and its planned exclusion of women.

Controversy billowed above that day, but for me, at least, it all dissipated that morning like a bank of fog under the dawn. I passed the drummers as they pounded rhythm from their instruments while other men stood around, arms linked high upon another's backs. And I knew that I could not, in good conscience, have been anywhere else that morning.

I lifted my face to the weak autumnal sun and listened as the Mall on Washington echoed with the thunder of drums.

It was not an easy time in the life of black America. The acquittal of O.J. Simpson was recent history and as a result, race was a raw wound. Blacks and whites who had invested a relatively routine murder trial with portent and emotion beyond what it deserved were feeling variously vindicated or outraged by the outcome, and never mind that both were out of all proportion to the actual dimensions of the case. We were beyond thinking then, glaring at one another from across chasms of recrimination and accusation.

Black and white people of whom you would ordinarily have expected better seemed to feel themselves at liberty to give vent to their basest passions and fears. Hateful code words sang through the air like shrapnel. "I have a dream" seemed a distant and tired phrase and indeed, all the idealism of Civil Rights years seemed to have reached its nadir, seemed to have curdled into this ugly, formless *thing* which coiled, serpent-like, in the collective soul of the nation.

It was not a good time for black men to sojourn in the nation's capital. Not a good time for anybody to do anything except breathe deeply and appeal for calm.

Sometimes, though, need moves by its own calendar.

But how to explain that?

All the people bemoaning Farrakhan and his unhappy history of Jew-baiting and separatism . . . how to explain to them why you felt the need to strike this bargain with your own conscience and join him on the Mall? Why you felt the need to look past antipathy for the man and show up for the march?

How to explain to them when it's hard enough to explain to yourself? After all, the stated purpose of the event was to allow men to take stock of their lives, account for themselves, atone for their sins, and decide what they could do to change. But many of us felt no such need, at least not as individuals. I was happy enough with my life, never felt that I'd done anything as a father, a husband, a friend, or even an employee that required public apology, never thought there was anything wrong with me that demanded a dramatic change.

And yet, I had to be there. Had to have what this day offered.

Because what it offered was not about the individual me, but the overarching *us.* Black people live by "us." The country does not, after all, know us as individuals—personhood is the first casualty of racism. So in some sense, it's never mattered much what I did or didn't do in my own life. I am linked to, share the fates and treatment of, a million black men I don't even know. We are reviled together, criticized together, belittled together, stereotyped together, and mistreated together, and I have felt every blow.

This day we would be *lifted* together. This day, we would lift one another. And if I couldn't explain what that meant, neither could I *reject* what it meant. This day was for healing the larger *us.*

And it was also for getting us beyond a place where we have been too long stranded. As the biggest victims in a nation besotted by same, African-American men spend too much time bemoaning the things that are done to us and too little advocating the things we can do for ourselves. This is no exoneration of white racism, no attempt to minimize its destructive force in the lives of African Americans.

But we are not powerless.

That's a stark truth that often gets lost in the fuzz and static of racial dialogue. A man may wake up every day, his life hemmed in by the realities of low income, substandard housing, poor education, and police harassment, but his defeat is still not preordained. Not so long as he remains in control of himself and his actions and still makes it his business to strive and seek and search out ways to push back the boundaries, shove them away bit by bit until one day, he gets up and he can see clear to the horizon. You're never beaten in life until you are beaten in mind.

Too many African-American men *are* beaten in mind, chained in internal servitude to limiting and demeaning notions of what it means to be black and male. That must change. More to the point, we must position ourselves to seize the opportunities of the future. And that means, at least in part, claiming the lessons of the past, embracing once again those things in our history that were empowering and ennobling. Among them the idea that we owe certain things to one another.

Listen to the old people talk and they'll put flesh on that African proverb Hillary Clinton loves so much, the one about a village raising a child. They'll tell you how it felt to be answerable not just to one's own parents, but to the entire block. The adults were interwoven, laced together like fingers, and they nestled the children safely between them. If Mama didn't get you for what you did, you could rest assured Miss Johnson would.

Now we fear the children. *And* Miss Johnson. But let the men come back home and reclaim the communities, and you've gone a long way toward weaving back together that which was broken. You've gone a long way toward banishing the fear.

Some of us already know that, have been hard about the work of strengthening families and communities. Some of us are committed and caring fathers, intimately involved in the upbringing of our children. Some of us get up early on Saturday morning and go to a ball field to coach young minds in the finer points of hitting and fielding and life. Some of us go to Big Brothers or some other mentoring group and sign up to be paired with a young man who has never known a father. Some of us organize in our cities or just reach out on our own, using personal money and personal time in the service of children who ache for the knowledge that a man is invested in them and cares what they do.

Some of us are there. But more of us are needed.

To walk that green field in downtown Washington, to stand in the shadow of the Capitol dome amid the echo of drums, was to be tempted by promise, seduced by the vision of what we could do if only we could agree that nothing came before our children, and then move on that sacred accord. On the podium, speakers were speaking and singers singing—Maya Angelou, Stevie Wonder, Jesse Jackson—and from time to time, I would stop to watch and listen. But most of what I heard that day bubbled up from within, a wondrously liberating sense of all the things black men might do—small things, big, world-changing things—for their own children and for the children of the larger *us*.

A father I met once recounted to me his failures, spoke to me of his shame at the way he had carried himself and then asked, "But, what should I do?" In other words, How can I seize a change, how can I make it different, how can I make it right?

Black men—four hundred thousand or a million or more, it doesn't matter—marched in the name of answers that day in October 1995. Their overarching solution, of course, was an embrace of accountability and atonement—a willingness to acknowledge our failings and repent them.

But after that is done, then what? How to take what we have learned and actually put it into action?

Actually, it doesn't take too much imagination to fashion from these grand themes of the march smaller pieces, more modest steps a man might take in the context of his own life.

What should I do? a man asks. And so many ideas suggest themselves that one hardly knows where to begin.

If a man has no children, he should:

- **Not make children he doesn't want**

It seems like a matter of common sense, an impression that lasts only as long as the first conversation with some man who found himself stuck with a child—or *children*—he didn't want. To talk to such a man, you'd believe birth control technology was still in its infancy.

So the basics bear reiteration: Anyone who doesn't want to become an accidental dad should avoid casual sexual relationships and shouldn't engage in *any* sexual relationship without a certain knowledge that his partner is faithfully and correctly employing birth control.

Besides which, birth control is a double-edged responsibility, meaning that a man has obligations here as well. "Pulling out" and hoping for the best is a surefire path to eventual paternity. Condoms offer much more reliable protection; virtually every major city has at least one all-night drug store.

And if all else fails, the zipper goes up just as easily as it goes down.

- **Consider borrowing someone else's children**

Big Brothers/Big Sisters, the national mentoring organization, has an especial need for African-American male volunteers. A black man who thinks it important that black boys have black male role models whenever possible can put his time where his mouth is by signing up. The screening process includes a questionnaire, police fingerprinting, and an in-home interview, after which the applicant will be matched with a boy who falls within a specified age range and has similar interests. You're asked to spend three to five hours a week with your "Little Brother." The organization sponsors group outings and offers occasional tickets to circuses, basketball games, and the like to facilitate that goal.

I mention this organization by name only because I was once a volunteer there and was impressed by the level of commitment I saw and the obvious difference it made in the lives of young people. But certainly, Big

Brothers/Big Sisters isn't the only mentoring program out there.

If for some reason what they offer doesn't appeal, a man might keep an eye out for other opportunities; churches and other social institutions sometimes run programs designed to match men with fatherless children who need them. Of course, mentoring can also be an informal affair. Maybe the single mother down the street has a teenage son who is drifting in the wrong direction. And maybe a man could help arrest that drift by taking the kid to a ballgame or movie now and then, or helping him with his math, or hiring him to cut the grass or just sitting him down to have a talk about his life and where it is going.

Nor is it necessary that the mentoring take place solely on a one-to-one basis. Is there a ball field in the neighborhood that needs a ball team? A lot that needs cleaning up? A wall that needs painting? Each circumstance presents an opening for a man to gather some children and spend a few hours making a difference, both for the community and for its young people.

The children are there, the opportunities are there. What we need, desperately, is for the *men* to be there.

On the other hand, if a man has children "out there somewhere," he should:

- **Find them**

Call friends and neighbors. Check the phone book. Access the Internet. Hire a detective. Do whatever it takes. But don't let a child hang "out there" like a shirttail, a loose end no one thought important enough to tie down. How devastating that must feel. How humiliating. A man owes his child better than that.

- **Establish a relationship**

Write a letter, make a call, or, if at all possible, visit in person. You'll never do anything more difficult in your life. Nor more worthwhile.

There may be anger, recrimination, and pain, and, worse, there is no guarantee of resolution. But at least a father will know that he did own up to his responsibility, did not leave the child to his or her own devices. More importantly, a *child* will know that "Father" is not an abstract concept, just a name with no face conjured by Mother in moments of anger and anguish.

A child will know that Father is real, that he is tangible and that he cared enough—albeit belatedly—to find him or her and let them know.

The bond—if there is to be one—won't form overnight. May take weeks and months of persistence and pain. A father has to know that he can't go in and be "Daddy" on the first day—maybe not even the fiftieth. He surrendered the prerogatives of "Daddy" when he abandoned the child. Now he'll have to earn them back.

He'll have to be honest to do so. Can't go in with excuses and justifications for his behavior. With rare exceptions, there *is* no justification; the man who willfully abandons his child perpetrates a singularly indefensible act. And he has to admit that, first to himself and then to his child. Acknowledge the failure and then commit to move on from there.

- **Establish paternity immediately if he has not already done so**

When our daughter had her son, we contacted the boy she said was the father. He lives in a city forty-five minutes north and promised that he would come soon to see the baby and resolve the issue of paternity. Two and one-half years later, he had not fulfilled that obligation. We've never heard from him again.

The baby will never want for material goods, but I suspect that as he comes of age, he will want to know something about the person who sired him and that the not knowing will be an empty space inside.

A child has a natural need to see where he came from. It is selfish and short-sighted to deprive him or her of that. A man whose name is not on the proper forms should see that it gets there. Should fight to do so if necessary. A man should make sure his child never has to look around wondering who and where he is.

- **Establish a working relationship with the mother**

Obviously, this is not always easy. In some instances, not even possible.

But to whatever degree it is possible, a man should work—swallow hard and meet her better than half way, if necessary—to ensure that he and the mother of his children are able to communicate on matters of a child's welfare. If apologies are necessary, make them, make them heartfelt, and make them stick. Nothing hurts worse or does more to create acrimony than buying into insincere contrition. So if a man says he's going to change, he'd better do it; else it'll be that much more difficult to get anyone to believe in him next time around.

Children do not ask to come here and they deserve to find, at a bare minimum, two adults working together in their best interests. The key word there being adults. Adults do not use children as spies. Adults do not use children as go-betweens. Adults do not use children, period.

A father and mother should agree that their disputes, whatever they may be, will be kept between them. And, excepting only truly life-threatening circumstances (Dad's addicted to crack, for example), a mother ought not use visitation rights as a means to force Father to do as she wishes him to. Indeed, if she thinks a father's house unsafe for any reason, both parents might agree to explore alternatives, such as confining visitation to some neutral site and/or having visits supervised by an agreed-upon third party.

Ideally, though, parents should have enough trust in one another to render such extreme measures unnecessary. It is important to a child that his parents are able to cooperate because non-cooperation produces levels of tension and acrimony that are toxic to his well-being. And because if parents work together as a team, it increases the chance that decisions made on the child's behalf will be in his or her best interest.

Fathers and mothers need to get beyond the notion that fathers are expendable. The optional parent, as it were. A pregnant young woman I know is considering moving across country with the father of the baby she's carrying, which would mean separating the child she already has from its father. She rationalizes this by saying that the child's father is not a good man. She fails to understand that the man and his child have the right to know each other and that one doesn't just glibly break that bond because you don't get along with the dad.

Fathers are not expendable parents.

- **Pay your child support**

"I don't get along with the mother" is not an excuse. The money is not a bargaining chip in your relationship with her, not a means to punish her or express disapproval of her. Indeed, it has nothing to do with her. Child support is not money a man gives, but an obligation he owes to his children. A good father doesn't need to be told this. He pays child support and he does so consistently and on time, even if this requires him to sacrifice personal luxuries and things he wants for himself. Sacrificing for their children is what parents do.

- **Resist the urge to buy forgiveness**

Often, the impulse is to use money as a shortcut into a child's affections. Buying bicycles, athletic shoes, and designer shirts as a way of saying, "I'm sorry I never came to see you before; I apologize for not being a part of your life." And because ours is a materialistic society, the ploy can seem to work. You watch a kid light up as you put some expensive bauble into his hands and you fool yourself into thinking a connection has been made. But as trite a sentiment as it is, the Beatles had it right: "Money can't buy me love."

Lawrence, the counselor, discovered that for himself the hard way. When he went down south to visit his daughter for the first time in ten years, he took her, at her request, on a birthday shopping spree. "What came out of that," he said, "is we actually grew further apart after I saw her than we were before I became reintroduced in her life. Think about it: When we do something wrong to someone, the first thing we want to do is go out and buy something to give to them. And that's all I did while I was down there. She wrote me back on an e-mail, saying, 'You think you can just buy your way back into my life. I hate you.'"

- **Make promises sparingly and keep the ones you make**

Before you can win the heart, you have to win the trust. You don't do that by making grandiose promises, then failing to deliver. If you're not sure you'll be able to do a thing, say something like, "I'll see if I can," or "I'll try my best." But don't promise something unless you know you can do it.

Children hold to promises. There is something uplifting about the purity of their faith. And they are resilient. If you break that faith, they might give you another chance. Even a chance after that. But sooner or later, the hurt gets to be too much. One too many times, they'll sit in the windowsill awaiting the promised visit that never comes. One too many times, they'll dance impatiently around, anticipating the bicycle you said you had for them.

And then faith is gone. You become someone they used to believe in.

Finally, if a man is active in his children's lives, he should . . .

- **Get help if necessary**

We do not, many of us, know how to do this father thing. Fortunately, there are many sources of help available to the man who is not too proud to seek them out. Some are informal, some are organized, and one, though close at hand, might be easily overlooked. Meaning the black church.

It was telling and appropriate that *Get on the Bus*—the drama about a group of men en route to the Million Man March—opens with a modest cross jutting heavenward from the roof of a church. The image served the same purpose as the faded flag with which Steven Spielberg opens *Saving Private Ryan*—a reminder of, and a visual lament for, how far we have traveled from that which once provided our lives with succor, purpose, and shape. In Ryan, it's patriotism. In *Get on the Bus*, it's the notion of the black church as a unifying moral force in the black community.

For most of the years of Jim Crow, the church not only ministered to the psychic wounds segregation inflicted, but also organized and even led the resistance to overthrow it. The men who piloted the Civil Rights Movement—not just Martin Luther King Jr., but also Jesse Jackson, Wyatt Tee Walker, Ralph Abernathy, C. T. Vivian, and many more—were ministers. And yet now, as black America faces a crisis of its fathers and families, the church's will seems spent, its moral authority eroded, its propensity toward social activism diminished. The church has been largely silent in a time when its voice needs to be heard.

Charles Brooks, the pastor and father from Los Angeles, says the church experienced a "lull . . . a dry period" after the Civil Rights Movement. As he sees it, the black middle class "dropped the ball" in terms of reaching back to the communities from which it sprung. That class, he said, drifted away from the values that have always tethered African Americans. "[They removed] God from their lives and when you do that, you're always headed for disaster."

In Pastor Brooks's view, that tendency is beginning to reverse itself and people are again turning to the black church even as it works to again become responsive to the earthly needs of its parishioners. Black men in particular. Brooks, for example, leads a men's group that is, he said, devoted to

Pastor Charles Brooks

helping men "grow in every area of their lives. In their relationships, in their finances, in their careers, in their ministry, in their relationship with God, in their relationship with the women in their lives. What we do is, give them an opportunity to talk about who they are and what their experience has been in life. Who their heroes are, what's broken their hearts, what turns them on, what turns them off."

Black men, said Brooks, have been conditioned to distrust one another, to shun emotional intimacy as a sign of homosexuality or even simple weakness. In the more-macho-than-thou ethos of black manhood, these are often perceived as unforgivable sins. Black men pride themselves on being tough, on needing no help and having no vulnerabilities. "But in the context of the church and discipleship," said Brooks, "we create an environment that's safe enough for men to say, This is my experience and here is where I'm weak. This is who I have a desire to be, but I really don't have a clue how to get there."

Not that the church is the only route to reaching that place. There are numerous men's groups and counseling centers whose work is aimed at helping fathers to hone their fathering skills. Prominent among them is the Washington-based Institute for Responsible Fatherhood and Family Revitalization, founded by Charles Ballard in 1982. The Institute has offices in six cities (San Diego, Yonkers, Milwaukee, Nashville, Washington, and Cleveland), each staffed by a husband-wife team of counselors whose job it is to live in the affected community and model successful family life.

On a less formal level, a man who needs help with fathering might simply seek to model himself after successful fathers he has seen. If there's someone in the neighborhood who has done well with his children, ask him about it with an eye toward finding in his example lessons with broad applicability. Watch the way he interacts with his children and seek to emulate that within the confines of your individual situation. Or if a man was raised by a single mother, he might explore whether there are things to be learned from her example as well. The same goes for the man who was helped along the way by a father surrogate. Perhaps the surrogate can impart things a father can use.

Though African-American men tend toward a macho self-reliance, the fact is that there is no sin in admitting to what one doesn't know. Indeed, you can't know what you've never seen, and many of us have never seen successful fathering.

So asking questions is the first step on the road to wisdom. A man who wants to be a good dad has to be willing to seek guidance and role models wherever they may be found.

- **Set boundaries**

It is an old-fashioned truth, but still a truth: Children like to know how far they can go. They like to have boundaries and rules, even though they don't always know that they like them. Meaning that the child who doesn't get his way will always compare his situation to that of the child down the street whose parents let him do as he wishes. "Rasheed's parents don't care if he does it! Why can't I?" The implication being, of course, that Rasheed's parents are forward-thinking and liberal-minded while you're running a Soviet-styled gulag.

But there are two things to keep in mind. One is that there's a good chance your child is lying about Rasheed's parents. The other is that the child who can brag truthfully that his parents "don't care what I do" must soon come to realize that they also don't care about him. Or, at a minimum, that they aren't mature enough to function as parents ought.

As a father, you have to master the difficult balancing act of allowing a child enough freedom to explore and learn about the world, but not so much freedom that he experiences things he is not ready for or that would be detrimental to his emotional well-being. In our house, for example, children are generally not allowed to date or see movies with mature subject matter until they reach their middle teens.

Granted, there are many parents who impose no such restrictions on the grounds that kids, being kids, will find a way to do the forbidden thing anyway. But that, emphatically, is not the point. Of course kids will do what they've been told not to. But in the very act of telling them not to, a father tells them that they must learn to live with limits, restrictions, boundaries, imposed from within and without. When they grow up, the law will tell them they cannot do certain things, but conscience will tell them they should not do others.

Without conscience, a person cannot be moral. He comes of age lacking an understanding of limits, believing that his wanting to do a thing supersedes all other concerns, including concepts of right and wrong, and regard for the feelings of others. For him, no interests are important except his own. Such a person often finds himself brought up short by a lesson he should have learned in childhood.

So it is important, sometimes, for a father to just say no.

- **Explore alternatives to corporal punishment**

As not every legal offense mandates capital punishment, not every family offense calls for physical discipline. Indeed, physical discipline is the court of last recourse, to be used sparingly if used at all. Like most black men, I got my whippings—but not every day for every single thing I did wrong. There were gradations. Corporal punishment wasn't usually imposed simply by reflex but, rather, after other methods had failed.

The distinction is important. A father should master a range of disciplinary techniques. He should be able, for example, to effectively express displeasure by talking to a child; the angry lecture can be quite effective in modifying behavior. Similarly, grounding a child or forbidding access to a favorite toy or pastime can also work wonders.

- **Praise them**

Children flower when parents praise. They begin to seek ways to earn approval more often. They gain confidence in their own abilities.

We've all heard of the technique of motivating by the carrot and the stick. Some parents, though, seem to use a different method: the stick and the bigger stick. With them, all is disapproval and fault-finding and the best a child can hope for is to moderate the amount.

But children deserve—need, I think—to feel good about themselves. So a father should never let pass an opportunity to cheer creativity, good work, or even a good hard try. Make a fuss. Learn to say, "I am proud of you."

- **Create structure and stability**

It's hard to win a race when the finish line is constantly being moved. In the same sense, children do better when they know what is expected of them, when there is some consistency in parental standards and when misbehavior brings predictable punishments.

So a good father should embrace routine and seek, within reason, to minimize jarring upheavals. The aim is to give a child a sense that there are certain things upon which he or she can always depend and to avoid the difficulties insecurity can bring.

- **Talk about sex**

Yes, it ranks at the bottom of the list of topics one can comfortably discuss with a child. Unfortunately, it ranks near the top of the list of things a child has to know about in order to navigate safely through this world.

Things have changed. A father I know asked his fifteen-year-old son if he was still a virgin; the boy applied in the affirmative, but the tone of his voice gave the impression that he was deeply shamed by the admission. The impression was confirmed when he added, imploringly, "Please don't tell anybody."

This is the world in which our children come of age. The virginity of a fifteen-year-old is a source of embarrassment to him. But what else can we expect? A child today is exposed to more explicit sexual material at an earlier age than his parents ever were. From music video vixens to JonBenét Ramsey, the little beauty queen who went about tarted up like a woman, to the infamous Calvin Klein ads that appeared to many to skirt the edge of child pornography, popular culture allows and even encourages the sexualization of little children. It strip-mines their innocence and sells them in return a tawdry vision of human coupling that concentrates on the mechanics of the thing and says little or nothing about the emotions. And children are left jaded beyond their tender years.

It used to be that there were two primary dangers associated with promiscuous sex. One was that you might contract a venereal disease; indeed, there was a time when syphilis struck terror in people's hearts and herpes made headlines. The other fear, of course, was unwanted pregnancy. We saw what an awful problem that was in the '80s, as the nation endured a deluge of underaged black mothers that strained social services, often past the breaking point.

But here's the thing about this new day. While early and promiscuous sex still carries those other two dangers, nowadays it can also simply kill you.

So it is important for a father to exercise leadership in this area. Emphasize to his daughters that sex is not a way of getting someone to like you, and a baby is not a toy you create so you'll have something of your own. Emphasize to his boys that sex is not a game of conquest where he who bags the most women wins, and a baby is not something a real man—a good man—can just walk away from.

A child should know that there is no shame in not being ready for sex. And he or she should also know how to prepare and protect themselves when the time finally comes.

- **Make the children understand that nothing comes before education**

Not Nintendo, not music videos, not girlfriends or boyfriends. And certainly not the pernicious anti-intellectualism that touts the notion that authentic blackness precludes academic excellence.

It's not difficult to understand why some in the African-American community may have soured on the promises of education. Integration failed, rendered unworkable by white flight, the unwillingness of white communities to sit still long enough to be integrated. And the notion of finishing high school in order to get a good job seems quaint and antique in a day when the economy has moved away from unskilled labor, when even the assembly line at the auto plant incorporates high-tech machinery, and when the student who doesn't have a computer on his desk or lap is considered disadvantaged. Worse, the early indications are that affirmative action rollbacks of the middle and late '90s will have a deleterious effect on black college enrollment.

Still, the truth is we need greater commitment to education, not less. If the ability to provide is one of the indicators by which a man judges himself as father, then higher education becomes an indispensable tool. For all the apocryphal tales one hears about college grads flipping burgers and waiting tables, experts say the truth is otherwise: graduates earn more and are unemployed less. Additionally, the educated man—like the man with money—will always enjoy more options in life than those who are without.

- **Love and honor Mother**

We teach by what we are. We teach more by what we do.

Where the interests of women are concerned, African-American popular culture has been downright poisonous in recent years. It has become routine for rappers, sports heroes, and comics to refer to them using scabrous, demeaning language. They are depicted as calculating, money-grasping whores good for but one use and disposable after that. The ultimate insult one man can level against another is that he is "a woman." Or "a bitch." In the thinking of today's hard men, there is nothing more contemptible than that.

The strange thing is that, absent the ministrations and strength of black women these last decades, there is a very good chance that the African-American family would not even be as healthy as it is. A disinterested observer could only conclude that it is an awfully strange brand of gratitude that black women have reaped for their efforts.

So a good father deals gently and lovingly with Mother and allows his children to see him doing so. He does this as a gift to his daughter, so that she will understand that she doesn't have to settle for mistreatment at the hands of some unfit man under the mistaken impression that this is the way it's supposed to be. He does this as a gift to his son, so that he will understand that popular culture has taught him lies and that a real man honors his woman and thereby honors his children and himself.

- **Be available to your children**

A sitcom character once said that nobody ever lay on their deathbed regretting that they didn't spend just a little more time at the office.

This is true. We become so absorbed sometimes in our own lives and concerns that we forget to leave doors open for our children to reach us. Everyone gets overwhelmed sometimes; the demands of the day can be unforgiving.

On the other hand, what is more important than this? What can come before being there for the children who represent, after all, both a man's legacy and his best bid for immortality? The man who is a distant stranger to his children shortchanges them and shortchanges himself.

A good father spends time with his children. He encourages them to talk with him, and when they are reticent he asks questions that draw them out. He connects them to their extended family by way of stories and traditions and teaches them to honor elders.

A good father is not afraid to play with his children, doesn't think it a compromise of paternal dignity to wrestle on the floor, plays basketball in the driveway or Monopoly on the dining room table. He has a store of bad jokes ready at hand and is not above being the butt of the joke himself from time to time. He knows that his shoulders are the best seat in the house for small ones and he is as generous in offering that seat as an aging back allows.

A good father makes it to open houses, dance recitals, karate lessons, and school plays. He takes children to the zoo or the amusement park, the mosque or the church. He knows the names of teachers, best friends, and movie idols. He can tell you what a son or daughter wants to be when they grow up.

A good father fixes meals and changes diapers. He tends scrapes and dries tears. He mediates disputes and dispenses allowances. He pumps air in bike tires and repairs decapitated baby dolls.

And a good father knows that there comes a day, a hated day, when it is time to let go. He understands that children are born moving away. That the baby who gurgles and coos learns soon to roll over and then to crawl and then to walk and then to run and then to fly. He understands that he is their standard, that they will test their progress against him and, one day, surpass him. He understands that the pain that comes is necessary. As is the pride.

A good father loves and is there.

FIFTEEN

If the onus is upon black men—and it is—to make themselves better fathers, let the record show that there is also work here for white men and women. That by their actions and inactions, by their misperceptions, well-meant and otherwise, they often make the work of fathering more difficult for a black man to do.

For me, at least, the well-meant misperceptions are especially frustrating. I'm in agreement with something Martin Luther King, Jr. once said: "Shallow understanding from people of good will is more frustrating than absolute misunderstanding from people of ill will."

A story by way of illustration: On the first night of the 1992 L.A. riots, I walked into the bedroom where my youngest daughter was sleeping in her crib. We were living in Florida then and I had just spent hours before the television watching the city of her birth and my childhood going up in flames. Finally I had to get away, so my feet took me into this dark and quiet room where she lay sleeping, a baby girl with curly hair ringing her face. It occurred to me that she was the only one of my children who had never been called "nigger." And it occurred to me, too, that that would change one day, too horribly soon.

What would I tell that pretty little face? How do you explain to innocent eyes that there will be those who hate just because?

It is one of the hardest damn things a black father ever has to do. Because with the explanation comes a confession you'd rather not make to a baby who still believes in Santa Claus. The confession that the world is not fair, that things don't always make sense, that being a good person is sometimes not enough.

And the confession that hurt will come . . . and there will be nothing Daddy can do about it.

She was five when I started explaining it to her. She hadn't yet had that first bad experience that comes to black children, but I wanted her to be ready. It was difficult. In the first place, she had no idea what I meant when I described her as a black girl. After all, she knew her colors, and she knew her skin wasn't black. "But, Daddy, I'm *tan*," she insisted, as if wondering how I could make such an obvious mistake. She even held up her arm so that I could see her golden skin.

You're right, I told her. You're tan. But you're also black.

I put my arm, with its deeper brown hues, next to hers. And I explained that "black" is what people like us are called, people with dark skin. There is nothing wrong with being black, I told her. Your skin is beautiful and besides, skin has nothing to do with whether you're a nice person or not.

But not everyone understands this, I said. And one day, someone is going to call you names because you're black. Or they're going to treat you badly and act as if you're not as good as they are.

When that happens, it's going to hurt, but I want you to remember what I told you. They're stupid people and they just don't understand. Don't let anyone make you feel like you're bad or like you can't do anything you want to do. Do you understand?

She gave a solemn nod. I extracted a hug and sent her off to play.

As it happens, I wrote about that episode in my newspaper column some weeks later. I received a letter from a white lady who was absolutely scandalized that I would say such things to my daughter, put race on her mind at such a tender age. Reading that, the only thing I could think of was how criminal it would be for me *not* to prepare her as early as I could. It would have been like watching someone run full-tilt toward a brick wall they couldn't see and not even trying to cushion the blow.

I'm sure that woman meant well, but her lack of understanding was frustrating. I had to remind myself that I live in an America she doesn't know.

So many things are different in that America, but one thing is exactly the same: *We* love our children too. Wish for them and want for them and break our backs to provide for them. Worry for them and pray for them and sometimes lose our way with them. And race just makes it that much harder.

It is mud in clear water. It takes the everyday occurrence and layers it with level upon level of suspicion, acrimony, and doubt, spinning your perceptions around till you no longer know if you're coming or going—that which was simple is not simple anymore, and that which was already difficult enough becomes damn near impossible.

Race gives me a headache.

Yet race can't be ignored. Not by anyone whose wish it is to see more black boys become better black fathers. Nor by anyone who thinks it valuable that all our children come of age in a nation where America's citizens have become, finally, a single people. Because as things now stand, and absent the unifying effects of war, political scandal, or some other trauma, Americans often seem less a people than a collection of interconnected fiefdoms, each looking out for its own.

Some white people are fond of saying that this is the inevitable result of living in a time when our citizenship and, presumably, our loyalties are pulled in two directions at once: Asian Americans, Native Americans, and, of course, African Americans, to name but a few. It seems, though, that those who make that argument are looking at the right picture and drawing the wrong conclusion.

The tendency toward dual identities is not a *cause* of division, but an effect of it. It was not, after all, America's racial minorities who put into effect a caste system, a de facto apartheid under which the color of your skin and the nation of your ancestry determine quality of life and access to opportunity. They have simply sought strategies to help them overcome it. So the fact that a black man feels the need to identify himself by a term that expresses dual loyalties and a double heritage is simply evidence that disunion lingers, and not the origin thereof.

If you want to know the origin thereof, it's not difficult. Indeed, it's a formula as elegant in its simplicity as kindergarten math. As two plus two equals four, so too does ignorance breed fear which, in turn, breeds bigotry.

In other words, it starts with ignorance. And if it is to end, it will do so in the same place. And white people must shoulder their share of that burden.

You got a sense of the distance yet to be traveled that day in Washington when the Million Man March came to town. Though most of white Washington had found other places to be, there were a few white people scattered about the Mall. Many were members of the media, running around with notepads out and cameras recording, trying to get The Story, but others were simply tourists who either hadn't heard or hadn't cared that this was supposed to be a bad day to be white in Washington.

They went about their way unremarked and unmolested, skirting the edge of the demonstration or venturing across it as the need arose. And all the while, watching it with a curiosity that was a little more than just idle.

Watching them watch us, I had the sensation—and not for the first time—that the lives and concerns of blacks were, to my white sisters and brothers, some tempting and inscrutable mystery. It left me with a certain sad sense that after all these years together, all these years of fighting for the same country, eating at the same fast-food counters, working on the same assembly lines, we are still strangers, one to the other. I read the questions right off their faces: the what? and the why? It struck me that the lingering existence of these questions, as much or more than any bigot's outright hatred, are the stuff of division between black and white America. And I struggled in my own mind to frame ways of response.

I know white men who would scorn the effort, so concretized in patterns of accusation and acrimony that they look at a person and see a group. "Those people" are hopeless, they say, so the hell with them.

And I know black men who would scorn the effort, too, who would say white people are a monolithic, irredeemable lot, and let them find their own answers. To hell with them all.

Ignorance is a hardy beast. But I can't buy into the notion that a man can be a group and the group hopeless, beyond the reach of reason. Not just because it's a logical dead-end, nor just because it denies the capacity of people to grow, nor even just because it's a slap in the face to every notion of individuality I hold dear. I also can't buy it because I am a father, and I owe it to my children to teach them how to operate in the world that *is* while doing whatever little thing I can to make for them the world that *ought to be.*

Change is rushing toward us. The old paradigms tremble and fall. Hispanics will soon be America's largest minority. What has for decades been a bilateral discussion between blacks and whites now becomes something else, something larger. Yet blacks and whites are still locked in the same old two-step, still debating issues older than the Civil War.

But what can we do? We keep dancing till we get it right. And we teach our children the same steps, hoping even as we do that they'll never have to use them.

It's foolish to underestimate the strength of the ignorance we seek to slay. Oh, I once had faith in objective truth. I believed that if I could show someone by numbers—not opinion, but irrefutable *fact*—that his beliefs were wrong and his antipathy toward blacks was based on insupportable evidence, he would have to give up that antipathy. A few dozen bruising verbal exchanges later, I have come to comprehend my own naiveté, come to understand that for some people, ignorance is impervious to fact. It is a darkness no light can penetrate. Some men cling to their stupidity as to a life raft in choppy seas.

Yet I can see no other avenue of attack. From ignorance to fear to bigotry . . . that was the progression, wasn't it? So to kill the weed, you have to pull it out from the root. You have to eliminate the ignorance. You have to educate. Seek this ultimate success, but at the same time, at all costs, guard your children against the things they will endure before success arrives. Racism hurts most when you didn't see it coming, when you weren't braced and ready.

Where racism is concerned, so much of a black father's duty involves simply being there in the aftermath of the bruising encounter. That's when you hear yourself saying words that, though perfectly true, are difficult to speak and, as much or more so, to hear. You try to shore your children up, give them the strength to deal with something they will face time and again. "This has nothing to do with you," I tell them, knowing even as I do that the very impersonal nature of it is what makes it difficult for a human mind to grasp. But it's still the truth.

It affects you, but it's not about you. Nothing you did caused it. And nothing you can do will, in all likelihood, make it go away. All you can do is get through it.

You get through it by knowing that people who look just like you have always gotten through it; that's our entire history here. You get through it by laughing, shaking your head at the foibles of bigots and—redundant, I know—fools. Most of all, you get through it by knowing with a certainty who you are and what you are and clinging hard to that knowledge when people who don't know try to convince you that you are something else entirely.

I wonder if those things would be understood by the woman who chastised me for talking race to a five-year-old. I wonder if she can see that it would constitute negligence of unimaginable proportions for a black father to know what the future has to offer and yet not prepare his child for the world she will encounter.

And I wonder what she tells her own children. The answer, I suspect, can be encapsulated in two words: Not enough.

White Americans often seem to think of race as the social equivalent of polio. Something that was crippling and awful in the dusty long ago, but which has been largely eradicated by the advancements of an enlightened age. Whenever whites are polled on issues of race, their appraisals tend to be significantly more optimistic than those of racial minorities. Of course, much of that can doubtless be attributed to the fact that whites are not the ones facing the brunt of racial animus. But I think it also comes of a sincere, if mistaken, belief that, in the language of the Civil Rights Movement, we have overcome. The success and visibility of accomplished African Americans such as Oprah Winfrey and Michael Jordan seem to bear this out for them, make them secure in their conviction that racism has been overcome, that blacks have as good a shot as anyone else of making it in this country (a *better* shot, according to some), and that any words to the contrary constitute a plea for "special treatment" or just simple "whining."

Then you read the news stories detailing ongoing discrimination in jobs and housing, you see where the Department of Agriculture admits to a long policy of institutional bias against black farmers, you read the heart-sickening tale of some violent racial atrocity being visited upon a black man, and you wonder just what planet these folks are residing on. But it's not just ongoing systemic oppression and occasional bursts of violence that ought to concern us. Rather, it's the endurance of something called white privilege.

And the first thing to acknowledge is that many white people would argue that no such thing exists. Whatever they have achieved in life, they will tell you earnestly, is owed strictly to the sweat of their brows, the solidity of their plans, the blessings of God. There was no head start granted them on the basis of skin color.

I can't blame them for saying this. If I were in their shoes—meaning that if I viewed myself as, in the words of one observer, the unracialized center of a racialized world—I might share that outlook. To be a non-Hispanic white person in a rich nation where the vast majority of the population is the same is to enjoy the luxury of seeing oneself as the norm, the average, an everyday Joe or Jane who lives beyond race and is therefore frequently vexed and perplexed by the minorities who seem obsessed by it. Never quite comprehending that, by the simple fact of belonging to the majority, one enjoys the benefit of certain assumptions blacks and other racial minorities never receive.

Understand: This is not about practicing white racism, but rather, about enjoying its benefits, willingly or not.

The best analogy I can offer has to do with gender politics: As a man, one need not practice sexism to enjoy its benefits. One need only be male. It's like a magic key, an entrée into a world where one is presumed to be a person of substance and sense until proven otherwise—where, on the other hand, a woman will be presumed to be insubstantial and flighty until she demonstrates that she is not.

My wife and I tried an experiment once. We went together to buy auto insurance and to open a bank account. At both places, I kept silent and let Marilyn do all the talking, ask all the questions, handle all the negotiations. At both places, when it was time to seal the deal, the person behind the desk addressed *me,* put *my* name topmost on the papers, handed them to *me* to sign, shook *my* hand, and thanked *me* for my business.

This is male privilege—they assumed I was the one in charge, even though I had gone out of my way to indicate to them that Marilyn was the one they should deal with.

White privilege works much the same way. And if it rewards a white person with an automatic assumption of worth, it degrades a black one by constantly requiring him to prove that he has even such basic components of productive personhood as honesty and a functioning brain.

I'm reminded of the time I went to see my doctor, a black woman, and found her seething at what she said was a too-frequent occurrence. It seems she had examined a white high school athlete and found him unfit for competition due to some potentially dangerous congenital condition. The parents, instead of being worried about their son's health, instead angrily attacked her credentials, strongly implying that because she was black, she was an inferior physician who had misdiagnosed the boy somehow. Maybe she had gotten through medical school on some special program or something.

As it happens, my doctor has been a physician since 1981. Nationwide, she is one of only a handful of women—say nothing of *black* women—in her particular specialty. If anything, she argued, those facts should have told the angry parents that she is a *better* doctor than average, not worse. Instead, they stormed away, having dismissed a conscientious and effective physician on the basis of assumptions they'd never have dared make had she been white or, yes, male.

That's what white privilege looks like. And it must be addressed in any honest discussion of the ways in which race constrains black life in general and the lives of black fathers in particular. It is difficult to hold a job if every day is like the first day—if, in other words, you are continually called upon to prove that you know what you're doing and that you belong in that position.

Acknowledging that, however, is not the same as offering an excuse for the failure to hold a job. As already noted, to the degree that they have failed to seize and exploit opportunities to better their own condition, blacks must bear responsibility for their own plight. The reflexive tendency to single out white racism—or, worse, some mammoth white "conspiracy"—for every ill suffered by black people reflects the worst sort of blame-shifting. Indeed, it's rather a self-inflicted insult, portraying blacks as helpless, impotent victims who cannot be asked to bear responsibility for their own lives.

By the same token, though, it's a fallacy, a delusion, and a denial of self-evident truth for whites to claim that race, racism, and simple white privilege are no longer factors and indeed, *compelling* factors that delimit, denigrate and demean the lives of black Americans. To assume that the isolated success of a black talk show host or an athlete, an actor or a writer makes some broad statement that doors of opportunity are being suddenly flung open to blacks everywhere is to do violence to logic and to belittle black strivings.

But then again, such silly suppositions are possible and, indeed, frequent, because the level of communication between white and black in America is so low as to sometimes seem nonexistent. Lacking personal knowledge, we subsist instead on inferred knowledge, like the astronomer who deduces the existence of a planet he cannot see by observing its effect on nearby heavenly bodies. The simile is telling: Sometimes, we seem as distant from one another as the stars.

Yet while inferred knowledge might work in an astronomer's lab, it is a disaster in the social arena. One often hears whites attributing to blacks motivations that wouldn't survive even the faintest scrutiny of logic, drawing with an expert's certainty conclusions they never would in cases where the principles were white. More to the point, conclusions that betray a conspicuous lack of knowledge about the subject in question.

I remember a conversation with an older white man who was sure—convinced beyond my ability to unconvince him—that not only is there a plague of blacks committing violent crime against whites, but that they do this as a means of racial retribution. The capper came when he blithely assured me that while he wouldn't dare walk the streets of some blighted inner-city black neighborhood, I, as a black man, could do so with impunity, apparently enjoying some sort of racial pass that would allow me to travel through unscathed. Never mind the mountain of statistics that says that when it comes to black crime, people like me suffer first, worst, and most frequently.

So if a black father could ask a white father any favor, it would be to teach his children well on the subject of race. Teach them with honesty and compassion so that they might react with the same qualities when they cross paths with my children. And so that they will not become part of the problem my children must overcome, but part of the solution we all hope our children will one day embrace. A white father should teach his children to take people one at a time. It's ridiculous to try to understand a population of over 30 million based on uninformed supposition and a couple of chance encounters. If a good black parent must teach his children that they will be the focus of generalizations, then a good white one should teach *his* children to be skeptical of generalizations and of people who lean upon them to excess.

White children—and, for that matter, black ones—must be raised to understand that whatever affects one group directly affects all indirectly. There is no impermeable barrier keeping the challenges and dysfunctions that plague the poor black inner city from creeping out to deluge the wealthy white suburbs. If a thing troubles one, it will soon, some way or another, trouble all. That was the point of one of my favorite Richard Pryor jokes: White couple driving through the inner city, seeing black kids strung out on drugs goes, "Tsk, tsk, isn't that a shame?" Same couple gets home, finds their son on drugs and screams, "Oh my God, it's an epidemic!"

We need to take the point. Need to grasp the interrelatedness of our lives. White Americans, I think, are often too quick to compartmentalize such enduring ills as job and housing discrimination, inner-city crime and, yes, fatherless black children, as awful things that affect "them" who live "over there." But truth is, "them" is all of us. And "over there" is our country. We ought to educate ourselves such that a white man who benefits from, say, job discrimination, is just as interested in ending it as a black man who does not. Because in the end, a workplace that does not draw on the talents and experiences of the widest possible pool of employees, that shuts one group out and forces it to earn a living by extralegal means . . . such a workplace doesn't benefit anyone.

These are the lessons white parents ought to learn if they don't know them already, the lessons they ought to pass on to their children.

It's a funny thing about kids. As many people have observed, very young people do not know how to be bigots. They judge the kid next door by the things that truly matter. Is he friendly? Can he do any tricks? And, after you've pushed him in the swing for a while, will he let you get in and then push you? The ability to prejudge isn't gained until later. So in effect, a child has to learn ignorance.

It should be a parent's task to keep that learning from them. It's easier said than done, of course, if only because as parents, we often have to overcome our own ignorance first. What is required is a daring and a caring and a willingness to venture beyond comfort zones and well-worn byways.

So many of us go to the same places, read the same things, and talk to the same people all the time. We don't try that which might challenge ingrained patterns of thought, we avoid that which we're not used to. We live in vibrant cities throbbing with a variety of peoples and cultures, yet we don't take advantage.

Granted, "multicultural" has become a catchphrase and cliché, robbed through earnest overuse of any blood and meaning it once had. It has become just one more thing to which we are supposed to aspire if we consider ourselves enlightened. It's social broccoli—good for us, so we swallow it.

But the fact is, the nation is changing, becoming more culturally diverse, and the child who has grown up with a healthy respect for and knowledge of other cultures will be much better equipped to navigate the new realities than the one who has not. She will be at home in more places.

There are, of course, those who say that rainbow-colored America is by definition a more fractured America, one so busy being multicultural that it lacks a single overarching culture to which all of us feel bound. They fret over the news that we no longer all listen to the same music nor watch the same television nor speak the same language.

But thing is, unlike other countries wherein the people are bound by shared blood and ancestry, Americans are bound by shared ideals. And foremost among those ideals—valued enough that it is enshrined in the very first line of the Declaration of Independence—is human equality. We've spent the better part of our history—from slave ships to Indian wars to internment camps to civil rights marches—getting it right. And we're still working on it.

But we cannot afford to stop because those shared ideals are bedrock, and making them real, learning to live them, is the fundamental stepping stone to truly becoming a people. When that's done, the rest will take care of itself and questions of culture will no longer affright us so. We will understand that as a mosaic is made up of a thousand tiny pieces, so is American culture no more and no less than the sum of all its attendant cultures.

Look at it from up close and you see the individuality of the fragments; gaze on it from afar and you see the beauty of the whole.

SIXTEEN

And finally, there remains for me personally but one more piece of business. I have to write a letter.

It's a technique Lawrence, the counselor, put on my mind. One he has used with men hardened by the absence of a father. One he has even employed to explain himself to his estranged daughters.

Write a letter. Seal your emotions in words and paper.

This is how you turn the page, burn the bridge, put the thing behind you. This is how you move on.

Write a letter. Address the father whose love you never felt. Address the children you may have wronged. Get the unsaid said finally and for good.

I am skeptical. Yes, maybe even a little bit afraid.

Not to mention that, in the case of my father, there's the little fact that he has been dead for nearly twenty-five years now. The Postal Service does not, to my knowledge, reach the afterlife.

But that's a cop-out, isn't it? The fact is you write a letter as much for yourself as for the person you address. It is a way of working things out in your own mind, resolving loose ends that have tickled at the edge of your contentment for too long. It's a way of finding peace.

Besides, in a very real sense, my father is not dead, never died. He's with me when I struggle to tie the tie, with me when I kid my children, with me when some stranger abuses his wife. With me. I only ever pretended otherwise.

And so I have to ask myself: Have I finally faced him, finally disinterred him and called him forward only to go mute at the moment of reckoning, only to leave needed things unsaid yet again?

No. Makes no sense.

Write the letter.

I gather myself and I begin to write. . . .

* * *

Dear Dad,

I keep trying to figure out if I love you. I do, I guess. And that annoys the hell out of me.

I met a man named Timothy who told me emphatically that he had no love for the father who abandoned him when he was just a boy. It's quite possible that Timothy was lying to me, maybe even lying to himself, but still, I couldn't help admiring the hard clarity of the declaration. No mushiness there, no hemming and hawing, no mooning over shades of meaning. Here was a man who knew his own mind.

"I'm not going to be a hypocrite," he told me, and say, "'Daddy, I love you.' I don't, *okay?"*

I found myself envying him that.

Maybe I'm the hypocrite, maybe just a fool, but I think I love you still, love you after everything you did and didn't do, and that troubles me because it smacks of the irresolution of a boy, not the clear-eyed decisiveness of a man. Feels like something I should have been over a long time ago. After all, there's no logic to loving you. You did nothing to earn it. I don't even know if you cared.

But I love you and it feels foolish because if pressed, I could give no reason more profound than this: You are my father. It was you that sired me, you that made me. Yes, I know men do it all the time. A moment of passion, a squirt of semen, and a life is created. But the act bound us still. You are of me and I am of you.

And I love you.

But oh God, I wish I could say more to justify that feeling. Wish it wasn't just this impulse that has no real connection with fond memories and warm thoughts. Wish it was more than biological imperative and emotional necessity.

Remember the time I blurted out that you didn't love me? Mama made you tell me that you did. You weren't particularly convincing, Pop. Yet now that I think of it, that is, as best I can recall, the only time I ever heard you speak affection to me.

Maybe you loved me, Dad, but you weren't good at showing it.

Men of your time seldom were, I suppose. They were taciturn as sphinxes, ill at ease with the language of affection. They defined themselves by doing. But Dad, you didn't "do," either. You didn't take a lunch bucket off to work every day to make money to support the family. Didn't sit at the table helping me with my homework after the dinner dishes were cleared away. Didn't take me outside and show me how to catch a baseball or throw a football.

And yeah, maybe I wouldn't have learned regardless. I know I was a difficult child for you to understand. Difficult for myself, sometimes. But still . . . you could have tried, Dad. Or else, just met me where I was. You could have let me know you were there, even if you didn't understand.

I heard someone yelling the other day and it reminded me of you. The person was harsh and cruel, heaping abuse upon an innocent, and it chilled me so that I had to get up and leave the room because it felt like you were in it. I ought to be able to remember you for finer things.

Sometimes, I find myself studying that picture of the two of us together, the one where I'm a baby and you're a new dad and you're shining with a palpable glee. I never knew the man in that picture; the image is at odds with my memories. And I remember your eyes upon me at the end, sadness and regret welling there so tangibly it made me turn away. Makes me grieve for everything that came between. Makes me wonder about the words you never said.

Would hearing them have made a difference? I don't know. I like to think it would.

Sometimes I wonder what it would be like if you were still alive. What would you think of me, I wonder? Would you be proud?

Maybe you would, but it's difficult for me to see you proud. In my deepest heart, I suspect we would not be very close, even now. For one thing, you wouldn't like my wife. You would wonder why I married a woman who already had kids; you would've been against it. Worse, Marilyn is a strong-willed woman, given to speaking her mind. You and she would probably have clashed from time to time. You would not, I suspect, have much of a relationship with my youngest son. Bryan is a gentle and dreamy kid, something like I used to be. You'd be drawn to Marlon, though. He's a swift, athletic, and engaging young man; he's the child you wanted when you got me instead.

If you were here, though, we would have talked by now. I know that for a fact. I would have asked you the question I never thought to frame as a child, the one that has troubled me ever after:

Why?

What did we do to you to make you treat us as you did? Why did you have such contempt for us? We were your family. Why couldn't you just love us?

Everything else in your life came before us. Do you realize that? Your sisters and brothers came before us, your friends came before us, and alcohol certainly came before us. You treated us as afterthoughts and inconveniences.

Aunt Annie says you told her you started drinking because the war left you "shell-shocked," traumatized by the things you had seen. I don't believe you. I'm sure you saw awful things in combat; maybe that's even where the drinking started. But I don't believe that's what sustained it. I believe you were a spoiled, middle child in a large family, most of them girls. I believe your sense of entitlement outstripped your ability to bring you to where you thought you deserved to be. I believe you were unable to conform to what a black man was expected to be in your time. And I believe you were cruel.

Shell shock, after all, does not explain why you beat my mother, why you held us at gunpoint, why you said those awful things, why you never made me feel the love to which I was entitled. Drinking doesn't explain it either. Not fully. There was a meanness in you.

And yet there was a love, too. We saw glimpses of it from time to time, like peeking through a knot-hole in a fence. I remember Christmas mornings when you were down on the floor playing with new toys with us like a big kid. I remember walking with you and you trying to teach me—I was hopeless, never had any rhythm—to march, military style. I remember you telling your tales, making up ribald stories so funny that even the person the joke was on had no choice but to laugh.

In the end, though, you gave us only glimpses, occasional glances at a man we never truly knew. In the end, you are defined by other memories, harsh as the light from an unshaded bulb.

Because of you, it is hard for me to be the man I want to be. I try my best, do everything I think a father should, but even in the midst of apparent success, sometimes I stop and ask Marilyn if I'm doing okay.

And even when I am and know I am, I'm still jealous of children with their fathers. Jealous of my children with me.

Whatever we could have been, whatever could have bonded us, alcohol took it away. I'm left with "might haves" and "ifs."

But I love you anyway. What kind of foolishness is that?

I went by the old house on Seventy-ninth and San Pedro Street the other day, the place we were living when you died. An old neighbor and I stood outside and caught up on each other's lives. And on the life of the neighborhood.

Remember Toot Sweet? I don't recall his real name. Just that he was one of your buddies who used to join you on our porch to drink cheap wine. I'm told that Toot Sweet is still drinking. Same liquor store, same corner, after all these years.

I think I saw him as I was leaving—a familiar figure sitting on a crate on the curb, legs crossed, hat cocked rakishly to one side, the way they used to wear them in 1975. Parking across the street for a moment, I sat there watching him and thinking of you. I was struck by the fact that everything in the world, everything in our neighborhood, has changed. Become better, become worse, but changed. And there he is, still sitting by the side of the road watching cars—and life—go by.

Would that have been you? Or would you have moved on by now?

I don't know why the old places hold me so, why I look behind instead of ahead. Maybe it's just that time in my life. Maybe it's my nature. Or maybe it's the unfinished business, the things left unsaid between you and me.

It annoys me that I love you, but I have to accept it, I think. Accept that you were my father and that you were the best father you were able to be. Accept and forgive, as best I'm able.

It's a funny thing about forgiving somebody. People think you do it as a boon to the person who wronged you. But I think it's a favor you do to yourself. A way of letting your own heart off the hook.

Let me tell you a story, Dad. There was this guy—he'd been a very close friend of mine—who cheated me blind in a business deal. All told, it probably cost me somewhere in the neighborhood of a quarter million dollars. Almost ruined me. And I hated him so after that. God, I loathed him. We had been like brothers, had shared hard times and confidences together . . . how could he do that to me? My mind couldn't rest. It seethed with outrage, boiled with the need for vengeance. When someone happened to mention him to me—maybe he'd enjoyed some small bit of good fortune—I would burn. When I drove past the freeway exit nearest his house, my stomach would contract in a painful knot.

Hating him was hurting me. And after a while, I couldn't take it anymore,

Dad. I let it go. I forgave him, though he had never asked and probably would have scorned the gesture. I forgave him as a means of letting my own soul rest, finding peace, moving on.

Do you understand what I'm trying to say here, Daddy? The same principle applies with us. I can go through the rest of my days angry with you for all the things you did and did not do. I can bear it like a heavy weight. Or I can choose to give you—give myself—this gift. And when you think about it that way, the decision is not difficult at all.

I forgive you, Daddy.

I must, because otherwise you hold me forever. You keep me from being all that I want and wish to be. I'll never quite understand why you were what you were, but I have to let go. Have to forgive and move on.

Maybe that's the process that began with your illness. Maybe that was the purpose in your lingering for two years until death. It strikes me now that those days of tragedy were in some sense the very best days you and I ever had.

You softened in those days and, paradoxically, came into focus for me. I was older and you were stripped by cancer of all meanness, pretension, and size. Finally, you were just my father and I was just your son, helping Mom take care of you.

So here we are almost twenty-five years later, and if you've taught me anything, it's that a man shouldn't wait until life strips away his facades to introduce himself to his children. The way you looked at me when you were sick is the way a man should look at his offspring every chance he gets. He should memorize them every day.

I've always been struck by the way we left it between us. All the words that were not said, all the anger that was not vented, all the sorrow not expressed and yet in the end, it was my lips against your brow. Me murmuring farewell at your ear without even knowing it.

It used to strike me as singularly out of place, an inappropriate capstone to the lives we had lived until then. Now I think of it as a kindness, God allowing me to acknowledge the rough passage we had made, to acknowledge without hearing them the words that had seemed to tremble, unspoken, on your lips all during your dying months.

Shall I, because of that failure, spend the rest of my life hating you, berating you, feeling sorry for myself and for you? No.

I know what you meant to say. I understand what was in your eyes.

And it's enough. If only because it has to be. Maybe I am a hypocrite, maybe a fool, or maybe I've simply been seeking explanations that don't exist and aren't really necessary.

I love you because you're my dad.

That's all the reason I have. It's all the reason I need.

SEVENTEEN

It is the moment where hopes and fears converge, where yesterday and forever collide. It is the moment that shapes everything that comes after, the moment you become somebody's father.

Charles still remembers when his wife told him that moment was coming—that she was pregnant. "I started running through our house," he said. "I was jumping and screaming and I was just extremely excited. I remember standing in the shower and crying. Just grateful to God . . . the thought of a child on the way was just amazing to me."

David still remembers when his wife told him that moment was imminent—that she was in labor. "I'm driving along and Tracey said, 'My water just broke.'" Down went the pedal, hard against the metal. "I was beeping through red lights and I got to the hospital," he said.

And when the moment finally arrived, well . . . poor Phil *doesn't* remember that at all. "I was there up until the point where I passed out," he said.

But David remembers. "I was convinced that I was going to have a boy," he said. "I was just *convinced.* And when they pulled her out, it just seemed like everybody in the whole room could feel the love I had for this child. I was like, 'That is my child.' I saw between her legs, the umbilical cord, and I thought she was a boy. They were like, 'She's a girl.' It didn't make any difference at all. I just fell in love with her."

It was the same for Charles. "She's mine," he whispered. "She's mine. This is my little girl. This is Daddy's girl.'"

And the same, too, for Phil—once they woke him up. "You see just

Photo by J. Albert Diaz

The Pitts Family (clockwise from top): Marilyn, Leonard, Markise, Onjél, Marlon, Bryan, and Monique

how . . . incredible what you've done really is," he said. "In fact, after childbirth, you watch the kids grow up and all, but everything else is kind of . . . it's not anticlimactic, but it's just, after you see that you've created something like that, it's just incredible. I don't see how any man who's been there at childbirth can ever not stay in a child's life."

Nor do I.

The births of all three of my biological children are pressed firmly in memory's scrapbook. With Marlon, I remember my wife's distress—her twenty-three and a half hours of labor. I can still see myself sitting there in the room about ten hours in, trying not to be scared. Still see nurses and physicians trading worried whispers. Marlon had the umbilical cord wrapped around his neck; it choked him every time they tried to induce labor. I still remember Marilyn being wheeled in for an emergency cesarean. Nate was there. My mother was there. We wore pathways in the carpet. Markise, five years old, was agitated because he was missing his favorite cartoons at home.

Then they brought me my son and the world fell away. Nothing else mattered. He was so tiny, so pale, so helpless. And he was mine, God had entrusted him to *me.* Something happens to you in that moment, something as powerful as it is indefinable. As mysterious as it is shattering. Something life-changing. I knew he belonged to me but, perhaps more to the point, I knew that I now belonged to *him.*

Felt the same when Bryan was born three years later, a planned cesarean. I remember, right after he was born, I went to a nearby restaurant and had this *huge* breakfast. Which doesn't seem like much, but our money was exceedingly tight in those days; we didn't do restaurants, ever. But I indulged myself that morning. I was filled with joy, so I went and fed myself well. Spent money I didn't have in celebration of the son I did.

Onjél came five years after that, the only one of my three biological children I got to see come into the world. I was giddy at the sight of it. Awed to see her come thrusting impatiently from her mother's womb. They cleaned her up and laid her under the warming lights and I went and stood over her and felt my heart leave my chest. "This is your world," I told her. "I'm going to spoil you rotten." I'd always wanted a girl and here she was, my beautiful little baby.

We took her home a day or so later. I walked her across the threshold, took her straight to my office and put the needle on my favorite record, which seemed appropriate to the moment. Danced with my daughter in my arms as the Temptations sang "My Girl."

This is the moment of hope and fear. The moment of becoming a father, of having this new life delivered into your care and considering all the things you want for her, all the possibilities that lie open to her, all the things that she might be, the barriers she might conquer, the greatness she might achieve. Yet, you balance that against darker considerations. The pain she might suffer, the wounds she might sustain, the losses she might incur, the failure she might grapple.

And you realize that her mother and you are in large part the fulcrum, the thing that balances her between the two extremes, the difference between her living the one life and the other.

Small wonder that hope is so often attended by fear.

Thinking of hope and fear makes me think of Jermaine and Mark, the two young men who, when I met them, were eighteen-year-old expectant fathers. Several months later, both babies had been delivered, and I wanted to see how the new fathers were handling their new responsibilities. I called Jermaine's house first. His father, Jerry, answered the phone.

It was, he told me, a difficult labor. The baby—a little girl—had to be delivered by cesarean section. But his son, he said, "did not panic at all. He was very calm and collected and thoughtful. He was compassionate toward the situation and really comfortable to the mother."

I asked Jerry to assess what kind of father his son had been so far. "He's been an excellent father," said Jerry with pardonable pride. "From Thursday to Sundays, that's when he gets the child. Prior to him having the child, we always told him if he ever got into that situation, he would have to take some days out of the week and help in raising that child. He has to get up with her at night, change her diaper, feed her, bathe her, all that."

It is not, said Jerry, just an object lesson, not just a way of teaching his son responsibility. It is also a matter of allowing him to bond with his daughter, something that can't happen if the little girl spends the entire week with her mother and Jermaine is just a drop-in visitor for a few hours each week. "And he gets to enjoy some of the time of being with her," said Jerry. "We wanted him to [have] the three-in-the-morning experience. It also gives the mother some free time."

In addition to helping to raise his daughter, Jermaine was going to school and working full time. I asked Jerry if there was ever a time when he sat down and explained to his son the things a father ought to do. He said no.

"What Jermaine really learned," he said, "[was] probably by example and observation—the way I was able to handle the family responsibility. It was no one time he ever came to me. We periodically have talked about situations like [premarital pregnancy] and some of his friends have gone through those situations. We looked at those things. So when it did come, he knew some of the answers and he knew some of his parents' expectations. So it was not just one time; it was an ongoing conversation."

Still, said Jerry, he recognizes that it would be a completely different situation if he were not in the picture, if he had not been available to Jermaine. His son would not be the father he is had Jerry not been the father he was. "It probably would have been a little more difficult for him, if not a lot. But he has the kind of personality and the character that he doesn't run from responsibility."

Jerry told me he's adjusted well to being a grandfather. "I'm proud that he's a good father," he said, just before he put his son on the phone.

Jermaine was still as low-key and matter-of-fact as he'd been the day we met. He struck me as a very solid person, a well-rooted young man unlikely to be spun this way and that by life's prevailing winds.

"When she was born," he said of his daughter, "it turned out to be a sort of emergency. There were a few complications with the labor."

Worse, he said, when the doctor announced that the baby would have to be delivered by cesarean, his girlfriend became very emotional. Jermaine took it as his obligation to be very cool and deliberate. "Mainly to keep her calm," he explained. "She really wanted to have a natural birth. When she found out they were going to have a C-section, she kind of broke down. I figured I had to stay calm, stay strong to help her get through it."

But the experience itself, he said, the fact of walking into the hospital a man and coming out a father "was something I'll never forget. It was real interesting to see the procedures and be able to see the different technology that they have to take care of any problem they may find. I was in a daze, sorta kinda. It was a lot going on around me."

And when it was over? When the emergency had passed and he was holding his baby in his arms? "It was kind of a relief, finally, after the nine months. To finally get to see who and what all that was for. It was a sense of relief. And happiness."

Caring for his little girl half a week is no problem, he told me. "It's a time I look forward to, just to spend time with her and play, change diapers, and go places. All that stuff. I look forward to it every week."

I asked Jermaine how things might have been different for him if he hadn't had his own father to study and to learn from. "I wouldn't have all the knowledge I have as far as responsibility and what's expected of a father," he said. "Just the things that come along with being a father as far as making sure her needs are met. I know it's a responsibility I have to take care of. I know I have to do whatever it takes."

I tried to call Mark after I spoke to Jermaine. Couldn't reach him. Indeed, this went on over a period of about three weeks. Twice, I made appointments with his girlfriend, with whom he lived, to talk to her in his stead. She didn't show up for either one. I gave her my number and asked her to have Mark call me. He never did.

When we met, Mark had been in counseling with the Institute for Responsible Fatherhood and Family Revitalization to help him prepare for the obligations of fatherhood. Someone who knows him told me Mark had dropped out of the program. Said he was going through a very difficult period. His girlfriend told me they had been fighting.

So there it sits. I don't know where he is. I don't know how he's doing. All I know is that his baby—a daughter—was born. He's a father. And I'm haunted by the last thing he told me, the words he whispered to me in that soft, sad voice of his. He was, he said, scared of fatherhood.

"But I can't get scared now," he said. "I know with my baby coming, I got to be a different person. I can't be gettin' high, drinkin', cussin', all like that. Lettin' my baby see my mood swings. If the baby see something like that, he gon' think it's all right. I've got to change my ways."

But he didn't seem at all certain that he would—or could. And he finally confessed it: "I don't know what kind of father I'm going to be," he said.

I don't know what kind of father he became. I suppose I never will.

But I'll always remember how hope and fear stalked him that day. And how fear seemed to have the upper hand.

I guess hope and fear stalk all fathers, but it's different with black men, isn't it? Different when money is tight and the world unforgiving and you lack a guiding hand. Then someone puts this new life into your arms and tells you to be a father.

Hope and fear. What do you do now?

The question is difficult, but not impossible. Too many men have had too much success for us to believe otherwise.

Our problems are great, but our potential greater, if only we can find in us the courage to believe in us. If only we choose to rise and do. If only we move by the spirit we found that singular day on the Mall when drums serenaded our highest hopes and men embraced as brothers long lost and fear seemed a distant cry, dimly heard, as, with everything in us, we strained firmly toward hope.

And I'm reminded of the black man who asked me once, What can I do? How shall I turn this thing around?

Stop being helpless, brother. That's a start.

"When we take control of our own lives," said the psychologist Cones, "and when we look at ways that we can influence society and influence the images that are out there, then we can build healthy ways of being."

Sitting on the Mall as morning turned to afternoon, I had felt the same thing in different words. The ground was hard-packed beneath us and my boys and I sat cross-legged to unpack our lunch from the backpacks we carried. Large screens and speakers brought the action on the podium to us, but the thing we had come to experience had little to do with what was going on out there.

All around us, black manhood swirled. Hip-hoppers and be-boppers, dreads and fades and cornrow braids, old school cools meeting new school brass. Men with their babies and homeboys. And some walking with arms around women they obviously, brazenly, loved. Keepers of the castle coming back home, returning to themselves and the embrace of community, claiming their lives once again. Hope was so bright it burned.

We had found the answers we came for. Finally understood the truth that had been dangling before us all along.

We were never just the problem. We were also, always, the solution.